PEACE ANONYMOUS

PEACE ANONYMOUS

The **12 STEPS**
To **PEACE**

Johnny F

To order additional copies of this book, contact:
Xlibris Corporation
1-888-795-4274
www.Xlibris.com
Orders@Xlibris.com
109615

CONTENTS

·

This book is dedicated to my Mom, the most patient person in the world; my Father, who, without knowing it, lived his entire life according to the principles expressed in these pages; my children, Sherry and Craig, for having faith in me; and Delicia, for being my angel.

MEDIA STATEMENT REGARDING ANONYMITY

In these pages, I discuss my involvement with Alcoholics Anonymous (AA). I am, therefore, obligated to maintain my anonymity, and I am publishing this material under the name of Johnny F.

Tradition Eleven and Twelve of the fellowship of AA reads as follows:

11. Our public relations policy is based on attraction rather than promotion; we need always maintain personal anonymity at the level of press, radio and films.
12. Anonymity is the spiritual foundation of all our traditions, ever reminding us to place principles before personalities.

Since the beginning of AA in 1935, the media, which today also includes the internet and all other electronic media, has been respectful of the traditions of AA. For that reason, the media does not post pictures or publish the last names of people regarding their membership in AA.

The process of recovery in AA stems from individual members telling their stories. By sharing our experience, strength, and hope with each other, we learn to identify with the similarities. Had I not heard the stories of others, I would have never been able to grasp the true nature of my problem. And had I not heard the stories of success and witnessed the love and compassion the members of AA have for each other, I would have been either institutionalized or dead today.

Imagine having nowhere left to turn and, in a final act of desperation, you arrive at a meeting of AA only to find the intimate details of your life disclosed on the front page of the newspaper the next morning. People *must* be able to come to AA and feel safe without the threat of having their identities, and the intimate details of their lives, disclosed. It is obvious that the good work done by AA would be seriously threatened if it were not for the tradition of anonymity.

There are many famous people who have found their way to the rooms of AA, and one would think that in a world filled with multimillion-dollar endorsements, AA would canvas these people to adorn their billboards in an effort to promote their cause. However, it is the principles, not the personalities, which are the focus of our fellowship. It is therefore, the AA message, exemplified by the changes in the lives of our membership that have materialized as a result of these steps, which is given center stage. In a world filled with glamour and glitz, alcoholics have learned to be cautious of the spotlight and its temporary gratifications. And we have found peace and serenity not in wealth, fame, and fortune, but in setting aside our egos and embracing the principles of humility, honesty, love, and tolerance of others.

In writing this book, I use my personal story to provide an example of the kind of change possible as I have followed the footsteps of millions of others. Regardless of your thoughts and opinions on the contents of this book, I ask those, especially in the media, who may wish to offer their thoughts and opinions, to continue to respect the Tradition of Anonymity as they have for decades. Your thoughtfulness is gratefully appreciated.

THE TWELVE STEPS—A BIT OF HISTORY

In 1935, Bill Wilson paced a hotel lobby. He had been sober for six months, but he was anxious, and the business trip he was on wasn't going well. He looked at the hotel bar and seriously considered going through the door and having a drink—an action that on countless occasions in the past had resulted in devastating consequences. Instead, he picked up the phone and called a local clergyman who directed him to Dr. Bob Smith, who, like Bill, suffered from the disease of alcoholism. What they discovered was, as individuals, they struggled with the insanity of alcoholism, but together, by helping each other and sharing their victories and defeats, they could stay sober. On June 10, 1935, Bill W. watched Dr. Bob have his last drink in an effort to steady his hand for surgery. Neither man ever drank again, and they became dedicated to helping others find a solution to the insanity of alcoholism, creating the organization of Alcoholics Anonymous in the process. AA has helped nearly three million people change their lives and recover from the disease of alcoholism. Seventy-five years later, the manner of living offered by the Twelve Steps has been instrumental in helping millions more overcome a variety of life's problems within such programs as Al-Anon for friends and families of alcoholics, Narcotics Anonymous for drug addicts, Gamblers Anonymous for gambling addicts, Sexaholics Anonymous for compulsive sex addicts, and Overeaters Anonymous for compulsive eaters. In 1999, *Time* magazine listed Bill Wilson in the top 20 of the *Time 100: Heroes and Icons of the 20th century*.

THE TWELVE STEPS AND TWELVE TRADITIONS

Peace Anonymous has been granted permission to adapt the Twelve Steps and Twelve Traditions of Alcoholics Anonymous from AA World Services, Inc. It has been requested that we provide the reader with the original version of the steps and traditions, as per AA, in order for the reader to note any changes made by Peace Anonymous, accompanied by the following disclaimer. In an effort to comply with the wishes of AA, the steps, traditions, and disclaimer are printed here followed by the adaptation for Peace Anonymous. We wish to extend our thanks and gratitude to AA, especially those at World Services and the General Service Office in New York.

Disclaimer

The Twelve Steps and the Twelve Traditions of Alcoholics Anonymous are reprinted and adapted with permission of Alcoholics Anonymous World Services, Inc. ("AAWS") Permission to adapt the Twelve Steps does not mean that AAWS has reviewed or approved the contents of this publication, or that AAWS necessarily agrees with the views expressed herein. AA is a program of recovery from alcoholism only—use of the Twelve Steps in connection with programs and activities which are patterned after AA, but which address other problems, or in any other non-AA context, does not imply otherwise.

The Twelve Steps of Alcoholics Anonymous

1. We admitted we were powerless over alcohol—that our lives had become unmanageable.
2. Came to believe that a Power greater than ourselves could restore us to sanity.
3. Made a decision to turn our will and our lives over to the care of God *as we understood Him.*
4. Made a searching and fearless moral inventory of ourselves.
5. Admitted to God, to ourselves, and to another human being the exact nature of our wrongs.
6. Were entirely ready to have God remove all these defects of character.
7. Humbly asked Him to remove our shortcomings.
8. Made a list of all persons we had harmed and became willing to make amends to them all.
9. Made direct amends to such people wherever possible, except when to do so would injure them or others.
10. Continued to take personal inventory and when we were wrong promptly admitted it.
11. Sought through prayer and meditation to improve our conscious contact with God, *as we understood Him,* praying only for knowledge of His will for us and the power to carry that out.
12. Having had a spiritual awakening as the result of these steps, we tried to carry this message to alcoholics, and to practice these principles in all our affairs.

The 12 Traditions of Alcoholics Anonymous

1. Our common welfare should come first; personal recovery depends upon AA unity.
2. For our group purpose, there is but one ultimate authority—a loving God as He may express Himself in our group conscience. Our leaders are but trusted servants; they do not govern.
3. The only requirement for AA membership is a desire to stop drinking.
4. Each group should be autonomous except in matters affecting other groups or AA as a whole.

5. Each group has but one primary purpose-to carry its message to the alcoholic who still suffers.
6. An AA group ought never endorse, finance, or lend the AA name to any related facility or outside enterprise, lest problems of money, property, and prestige divert us from our primary purpose.
7. Every AA group ought to be fully self-supporting, declining outside contributions.
8. Alcoholics Anonymous should remain forever nonprofessional, but our service centers may employ special workers.
9. AA, as such, ought never be organized; but we may create service boards or committees directly responsible to those they serve.
10. Alcoholics Anonymous has no opinion on outside issues; hence, the AA name ought never be drawn into public controversy.
11. Our public relations policy is based on attraction rather than promotion; we need always maintain personal anonymity at the level of press, radio, and films.
12. Anonymity is the spiritual foundation of all our traditions, ever reminding us to place principles before personalities.

The Twelve Steps of Peace Anonymous

1. We admitted we were powerless over war and violence and that our world had become unmanageable.
2. Came to believe that a Power greater than ourselves could restore us to sanity.
3. Made a decision to turn our will and our lives over to the care of God *as we understand Him.*
4. Made a searching and fearless moral inventory of ourselves, our communities, and our nations.
5. Admitted to God, to ourselves, and to another human being the exact nature of our wrongs.
6. Were entirely ready to have God remove all these defects of character.
7. Humbly asked Him to remove our shortcomings.
8. Made a list of all persons we had harmed, and became willing to make amends to them all.
9. Made direct amends to such people wherever possible, except when to do so would injure them or others.

10. Continued to take personal inventory and when we were wrong promptly admitted it.

11. Sought through prayer and meditation to improve our conscious contact with *God as we understood Him,* praying only for knowledge of His will for us and for the power to carry that out.

12. Having had a spiritual awakening as the result of these steps, we tried to carry this message to those seeking peace, and to practice these principles in all of our affairs.

The 12 Traditions of Peace Anonymous

1. Our common welfare should come first; personal recovery depends upon PA unity.

2. For our group purpose, there is but one ultimate authority—a loving God as He may express Himself in our group conscience. Our leaders are but trusted servants; they do not govern.

3. The only requirement for PA membership is a desire to live in a peaceful world.

4. Each group should be autonomous except in matters affecting other groups or PA as a whole.

5. Each group has but one primary purpose—to carry its message to those who seek peace.

6. A PA group ought never endorse, finance or lend the PA name to any related facility or outside enterprise, lest problems of money, property, and prestige divert us from our primary purpose.

7. Every PA group ought to be fully self-supporting, declining outside contributions.

8. Peace Anonymous should remain forever nonprofessional.

9. PA, as such, ought never be organized; but we may create service boards or committees directly responsible to those they serve.

10. Peace Anonymous has no opinion on outside issues, unless they pertain directly to the issue of peace; hence the PA name ought never be drawn into public controversy.

11. Our public relations policy is based on attraction rather than promotion; we need always maintain personal anonymity at the level of press, radio, and films.

12. Anonymity is the spiritual foundation of all our traditions, ever reminding us to place principles before personalities.

The 12 Principles of Peace Anonymous

The following principles as they relate to their corresponding step:

1. Truth—We became acutely aware of the impact of war in our society. We became committed to looking past our denial and the false messages created by those who profit from violence, to clearly see the truth of who and what we have become.
2. Faith—We strive to develop a sense of faith that the Power of the Universe will guide us in our search for peace.
3. Surrender—We realized our future, due to the nature of mankind, would see violence continue to escalate. Man's way clearly did not work and we asked God *as we understand Him, to* guide us. This guidance may be reflected in the collective conscience of the group as a whole.
4. Honesty—We searched our souls and looked at the impact our behavior had in creating or allowing violence to exist in our lives and in our communities.
5. Integrity— We strive to develop and maintain a moral set of values upon which we build our lives and our communities.
6. Acceptance—We accepted our imperfections as being part of who we are, and at the same time, we became entirely ready to let go of the defects that stood in the way of our progress in our search for peace.
7. Humility—We grew in our capacity to see the truth of who we are as individuals, communities, and nations. We realized our limitations as human beings and discovered that a reliance on a Power greater than ourselves was necessary to guide us into the future.
8. Willingness—Developed a sincere willingness to do whatever was necessary, in a non-violent manner, to bring peace into our world.
9. Forgiveness—Came to believe that it is only through forgiveness of others and ourselves for the wrongs we have committed in the past could we achieve peace.
10. Maintenance—We monitored our behavior and the actions of our nations in an effort to maintain our spiritual well-being. We realized that we are all imperfect human beings and when we made

mistakes we promptly accepted responsibility for our actions and made amends to those harmed.

11. Gratitude—To be thankful and to embrace my relationship with God *as I understand Him* in an effort to live in peace.

12. Service—To carry the message of peace to those who wish to have it.

Getting Some Facts Straight

> There is a principle which is a bar against all information, which is proof against all arguments and which cannot fail to keep a man in everlasting ignorance—that principle is contempt prior to investigation.
>
> —Herbert Spencer

I do not believe I will encounter many arguments if I state that in order for the world to become a better place for all of us, some things need to change. We may have different opinions on what those things are, but we can begin by agreeing some kind of change is necessary. Throughout these pages, I discuss in detail the changes I have experienced and the changes I have witnessed in others, due to my relationship with the lifesaving, spiritual program of AA.

Prior to your reading any further, I feel obligated to stress none of the opinions, thoughts, or observations contained in these pages have been endorsed, sanctioned, or supported in any way by the organization of AA. In fact, members of the fellowship of AA may, or may not, agree with the contents of these pages. That is their prerogative. They may take what they wish and leave the rest. That being said, I most certainly wish to offer my sincere thanks for the blessings they have bestowed upon me, and millions of others, through their unselfish sharing of the amazing gift of the 12 Steps.

All that is required for involvement with Peace Anonymous is a desire to live your life with a greater sense of peace. In fact, there are no rules in Peace Anonymous. Our only goal is to live life on a spiritual basis by which we maintain a peaceful existence with each and every human being on this planet. Peace Anonymous is about accepting and embracing our differences and our imperfections through our individual stories. By coming together to share our stories, we come to understand the problems that violence has caused in our homes, communities, and nations. By sharing our experience, strength, and hope, we develop a sense of community and come to know ourselves, and each other, at a deeper level. We develop a clearer understanding of the nature of the problem and realize we are not alone in our fear and our feelings of helplessness. We are then able to find ways of overcoming the problems created by violence.

Coming to AA is part of my story and what I have discovered is that there exists something deeply spiritual, magical, and fun about the AA way of living. Throughout the course of the last nineteen years, I have witnessed huge changes in my life and in the lives of others, as we struggled to overcome our addictions and become productive members of society. I have sat in AA meetings with Judges, lawyers, police officers, and murderers where no individual, regardless of their position, held the moral high ground. The gift of anonymity makes us all equal and allows us to focus on the principles, rather than the personalities, as we help each other in our desire to resolve our common problem.

In 2005, I was working in Yemen where war and poverty had gone hand in hand for decades. I was scheduled to leave at the end of June, which provided me with the opportunity to attend the International Convention of AA in Toronto. At that time I was twelve years sober and had never been to an International Convention. What I witnessed there changed my life. There were fifty thousand smiling, happy, joyous people under one roof, and the sense of peace was overwhelming. These people, who had known more tragedy, pain, and suffering as a result of their drinking, had had their lives transformed by simply adopting a way of life, which created a joyful existence with their fellow man.

The change was not only obvious in the lives of the people in attendance. The bartenders in downtown Toronto lamented, with huge grins, "We aren't making any money, but we're sure meeting a lot of nice people." The police, to my knowledge, didn't make a single arrest. Their roles for the weekend were relegated to that of tour guides as they provided directions for convention attendees and advice on where to garner the best doughnuts. I tried to imagine the tears, bloodshed, and anguish that would have resulted from having fifty thousand alcoholics under one roof had they all still been drinking! I tried to imagine how the roles of paramedics and police would change by simply adding a few truckloads of alcohol.

Despite the fact I had been sober for years, I left Toronto with absolutely no doubt in my mind; change of significant magnitude was possible, and the program of AA worked miracles. And then I began to wonder if the 12 Steps of AA could be adapted to bring peace into our world.

My life was hopeless when I came to AA, but the people there told me that I had a choice. I could choose to pick up a bottle and continue to live in the insanity, or I could choose to embrace the manner of living they suggested. Trust me, I didn't like my choices. But up until that point in my life, I never knew I even had a choice. And nineteen years later, I still have that choice. My old life is right there waiting. I can go back to it anytime I wish. And perhaps I would go back drinking if I could see that my life would be better as a result, but I am pretty content with the fact that I woke up this morning and chose to be sober again today. Being human is a very imperfect process, and perhaps we all can learn to make better choices? Perhaps, rather than reacting with violence or supporting a political system that encourages war, we can see that there is a better way and we can actually choose peace? Perhaps by working together, by building a community dedicated to promoting peace, we can move in that direction.

In addition to my experience with AA, I have also been blessed with the opportunity to travel extensively throughout much of the world, including Yemen, Libya, Iraq, and Afghanistan, where violence seems to rule. But contrary to the beliefs commonly held in the west, or certainly portrayed by the western media, my experience tells me the majority of Middle Eastern citizens would gladly welcome peace. This then begs the obvious question: If the majority of the people there want peace, and the majority here wants peace, why do we not have peace? That is a very interesting question indeed, and perhaps the answers to that question, and many more like it, will be revealed as we continue to discuss our common problems.

Peace! Is it really achievable? I believe it is, but I can't do it alone. The President of the United States can't do it alone. The United Nations can't do it. But perhaps *we* can do it, together. By working together, I have witnessed thousands of people change their lives. Impossible you say. I am sure that is what the founders of AA were told on numerous occasions when they began to help the thousands of men and women who were dying from the disease of alcoholism. What I believe today is that together we, the citizens of this planet, and with the help of God, *as you understand Him*, have the power to do anything. It is my goal to invite you to join us, and perhaps together we can find the answers. As difficult as you may perceive it to be, I think we are all well aware of what will result if we do nothing, and your voice, albeit a single voice, when added to the millions of others who seek peace, may make a noticeable difference in the future of your home, our home; this place we call Earth.

In the past, numerous people and organizations have confronted the problem of war and violence on the world stage. Rock stars have had concerts, and actors have made movies. Politicians have had summits. Greenpeace and Amnesty International have done their best. While they all deserve great applause, the truth is we have slipped further and further away. To simply say, "Stop killing," has proven to be as effective as simply telling the alcoholic to, "Stop drinking!" We needed more. We needed a design for living that was flexible and could be agreed upon by anyone, anywhere, who wanted to live in peace. It had to transcend the archetypical view of religions and politics, not to discredit any, but to include all. It had to include Arab and Jew, black and white, rich and poor; and it had to do so equally. The ability to agree on our common problems, and work together towards a solution, is something the Twelve Steps have proven themselves to be capable of achieving. It has not done so flawlessly, because people are involved, but the spiritual way of life has met with a much greater degree of success than anything else known to man. The proof, they say, is in the pudding.

In his book "The Tipping Point", Malcolm Gladwell discusses how our world adopts change regarding fads, fashion, and technology. One of Gladwell's examples regards cell phones. I remember seeing my first cell phone. It was large and awkward, and yet I could see the effectiveness of being able to take the office with you. Then there was the second phone and then the third, and suddenly, almost overnight, cell phones were everywhere. Today I wonder if peace can be adopted in that same manner. Can the seed be planted and embraced by enough people that the idea of peace becomes viable and sustainable; perhaps even fashionable? In the past, we have been sold guns and we have been sold wars. Can we not sell the idea of peace? Isn't it possible for the idea of peace to become cool and sexy in an effort to prevent us from blowing our sorry asses off the face of this planet?

Throughout the following pages, you will encounter numerous questions, which are designed to provoke your thoughts, and I encourage each of you to search your soul for your own answer. Some of the questions I ultimately asked myself about my drinking were, "Is this working? Is it making me happy? What direction is my life going in?" When I honestly looked at the answers, I was not impressed; something had to change. You may find a similar path in your search for peace.

As human beings we are all blessed with an abundance of imperfections. Alcoholism appeared to be a significant one of mine. I didn't want to be an alcoholic, but living according to the 12 Steps has transformed my "problem" into the greatest gift I have ever been given. The fear and the shame that came with accepting the fact that I am an alcoholic has morphed into a deep sense of gratitude, and my life has changed dramatically as a result. I discovered I had a choice and instead of having the past repeat itself, I can learn from my mistakes and use that knowledge to build a better life?

No doubt some of you are rolling your eyes and thinking that my goal is to get you to quit drinking, move to a commune, and join a cult. I will relieve your anxiety now by stressing that unless you have a problem with alcohol, there is no need for you to quit drinking to be involved with Peace Anonymous. However, I would suggest that in an effort to maximize your efforts as an individual, and your contribution to the group, you be clean, sober, and peaceful during meetings or functions of Peace Anonymous. Nothing would damage our credibility and our future success more than seeing our effectiveness diminished by a media frenzy regarding the party animals at the Peace Anonymous meeting. We wish to encourage fun and want you all to enjoy the experience, but we must respect our goals and the process if we are to be successful.

As we trudge along the path to peace, there will be discussions of God and other spiritual aspects of life. We realize that some of you may be either offended by the fact God is involved at all, or perhaps it isn't the "right" God. A glimpse at history would render Peace Anonymous useless if we were to embrace any specific concept regarding either the existence of or the form that God may take. Any concept you may have on a personal level is perfectly acceptable and people are completely free to believe whatever they wish. Therefore, any reference to God refers strictly to *your* personal understanding of what God means to you. You are welcome if you are an atheist, Hindu, Buddhist, Christian, Muslim, Moonie, Gravitational Existentialist, or a combination of any, or all of the above. Our goal is to be inclusive for the benefit of all people of all faiths and all beliefs. For many of us, our Higher Power is a simple faith and belief in the collective conscience of the membership of Peace Anonymous, or the collective conscience of human race. Surely the power that exists in the congregation of the earth's people exceeds your power as an individual? But, as stated, you are free to believe whatever you desire.

In living our lives, we have found that the principles of honesty, open-mindedness, and willingness are indispensable. Honesty allows us to accurately see the truth regarding where we as individuals, communities, and nations have gone wrong. It is only in honestly seeing and accepting our own shortcomings that we can begin to change. Open-mindedness provides us with the opportunity to consider options that we may have not considered in the past, which may include answers of a spiritual nature. Willingness is a sincere desire to change and to not repeat the errors of the past as we strive to live according to sound principles and do the next right thing.

Our work will never end. Violence will not cease to exist because of the presence of Peace Anonymous. I have personally worked through these steps on numerous occasions, and there are always new and valuable lessons to be learned. There is no end to the spiritual path. In fact, during the course of writing this book, the self-discoveries I have experienced regarding my own life have been overwhelming, and I have come to know and understand myself at a deeper level and my life has changed, again. As a result of these steps, I have developed a deeper and clearer understanding of myself, the world, and God, *as I understand Him.*

These steps have not rendered me or my friends in AA, lily-white, and there remains more than sufficient insanity to make my life extremely entertaining. Laughter makes up a substantial part of our lives. However, there are days, in fact too many days, when I still react harshly and in a negative manner. Awareness, I am reminded, is the first step, but there are many steps that follow, and as a result, there remains a great deal of room for improvement. I am not a saint, but I am happy to say I am slowly making progress. I most certainly am not the same heathen I was twenty years ago. Today, I have the hope and the opportunity to forgive myself for my shortcomings and to try, once again, to be the best person I can be, while reminding myself that the goal is progress, not perfection.

And most days, with the help of my God and my friends, I am at peace.

INTRODUCTION

If you want to awaken all of humanity, then awaken all of yourself, if you want to eliminate all of the suffering in the world, then eliminate all that is dark and negative within yourself. Truly the greatest gift you have to give is that of your own self-transformation.

—Lao Tzu

January 2011

I landed in Iraq a few days ago and perhaps it is fitting, or perhaps it is due to some strange alignment of the planets, that these pages find their genesis in this war-torn desert. As we journey out from the Basra airport, the ditches are littered with burned-out tanks and vehicles, the remnants of a decade of war.

The security force responsible for our safety is headed up by Ahmed (not his real name), a thirty-year-old Lebanese Christian and veteran of Middle Eastern strife. He is congenial but moves like a cat and, although smaller in stature, I have no doubt that behind the warm handshake and the boyish grin he is more than capable of handling the Ak-47 resting by his side in the front seat of the Land Cruiser we ride in.

Majid (not his real name either) is behind the wheel as Ahmed explains the "game" to me. I hear bits and pieces of how Majid's family has been in Basra for generations and is very well connected. He tells me they work the system from inside and out and that Majid's network would find out almost instantly if anyone messed with us. "People in Basra know to leave us alone," explains Ahmed. "They would not last long if they didn't."

We arrive at our camp, which is surrounded by concrete "T" walls. We pass through several security gates where the undercarriage of our vehicle is checked for explosives by more security personnel. Ahmed goes to the

unloading pit to ensure there are no rounds left in the chamber of his
weapon and then we enter the compound. As I exit the vehicle, he helps
me out of my body armor, shakes my hand and, with a grin, tells me he
will pick me up at 7:00 a.m.

As I walk away, I realize that despite being a committed peacenik, I have
already developed a deep respect for Ahmed. I think we will be friends.

We throw our bags in the room and head to the mess for a long overdue
dinner. The place is a mishmash of humanity from all over the world, and
I somehow feel at home in this cultural blender. People are friendly and
helpful as we are seen immediately as being new, which, for this place, is
nothing new.

After dinner, we retire to our room, and I begin to fill my journal
with the details of the trip thus far. My roomie, Abdul, turns on the
television, and the first news regarding the shooting of Gabrielle Giffords,
the Arizona Congresswoman, captures our attention. In critical condition,
she lays in a hospital bed after being shot in the head at a local political
event. Six others, including a nine-year-old girl, have died at the hands of
twenty-two-year-old Jared Loughner. Even by Iraq standards, it seems a
senseless tragedy.

The words of the local Sherriff hit home as he talks of intolerance and
the polarization in society. In the days to come, gun sales in Arizona will
increase by 60 percent which seems to make little sense in the light of what
has happened.

But then again, perhaps to some it makes perfect sense. Perhaps in a
world where the media constantly tells us we live in a divided world, I must
protect myself from "them". We hear the media telling us over and over
the stories of Muslim against Jew, White versus Black, Capitalist versus
Communist, and rich versus poor. Sadly, the actual bloodshed may be
factual. But I wonder if perhaps somewhere along the way I have missed
a piece of the puzzle because the majority of the people I have met in
my numerous travels around the world, whether they be Black, Hispanic,
Jewish, Arab, Buddhist, Irish, Communist, or American, have all been pretty
damn decent people with no intention of harming anyone. My experience
tells me that mothers in Afghanistan, Columbia, and Cambodia share the
same concerns as mothers in England, Canada, and the United States.
Educating and feeding their children are most mothers' great priorities.
But when we watch the evening news, many of us are led to believe that
people's priorities in Yemen are somehow different from those people in the
local coffee shop in Missouri. Given the level of violence depicted on the

evening news, my observations support the conclusion that the discussions around the news desks, board room tables, and in government back room offices must differ dramatically when compared to conversations that take place around kitchen tables all over the world.

If you can accept, even for a moment, that we are all similar, with similar priorities, why the violence? What drives a twenty-two-year-old boy to senselessly kill and maim a group of people at a small political gathering? What is it that makes a couple of young men go on a killing rampage in a Colorado high school? And why do the citizens of the world actively support and participate in the wars orchestrated by politicians, even when the information supporting such action is flawed, unsubstantiated, and inconsistent? Why would we send our children to fight these battles under such circumstances?

Perhaps we will never be able to adequately answer the question, why? And perhaps that is the wrong question to be asking. Perhaps the questions we should be asking are: Is this working? Is a gun the answer? Are we healing? Are we moving closer to peace? In a world full of violence why do people keep inflicting pain on others? Did a violent response work yesterday, last week, last year? Why do we keep doing the same things over and over again expecting different results?

Something else we must ask addresses the question of responsibility. Who, after all, is responsible for finding an end to war? For decades, if not centuries, we have looked to our political leaders and organizations such as the United Nations to find answers to these issues. Perhaps asking who is responsible for finding an end to war can be better understood if we ask ourselves who benefits from war? There must be something in it for someone, somewhere, or the entire exercise would be pointless. There is obviously no profit in peace. If there was, you can be sure we would be living in a hippie's paradise. Forgetting for a moment what our trusted leaders might say, is it realistic to expect governments to be fanatical about finding an end to war, when there may be much more profit in creating enemies so we have someone to buy our bombs?

Therefore, if government is not interested in resolving the problem, whose job is it? Who has the power? Who has the ability to choose peace over violence? Who is ultimately responsible for the safety of our children and the future of our planet?

I believe *you* are. Each and every one of you holds the key. We must arrive at the "Tipping Point" because it is only when enough of you decide things must change, will things change. It is only when enough of you believe that peace is a choice each of us can make, and enough of us do make that choice, will peace become possible in our homes, communities, and our world.

Am I insane to believe that after centuries of killing each other, mankind can actually find a way to live in peace? Perhaps I am, but I challenge you by asking is it not insane to keep doing the same things over and over again, expecting different results. Isn't killing anyone insane? Isn't killing for peace like fucking for chastity? Is it not possible to change how we deal with the issue of violence in our world?

For decades we, in western society, have been instructed in our schools and by our leaders, how incredibly fortunate we are to be living in a democracy and I concur. We are extremely fortunate. We not only have the legal right to voice our opinion and to peaceful protest, but I believe we are obligated, for the benefit of future generations, to hold our governments in check and to question their motives. Yes, we have rights in a democracy, but we also have responsibilities. We have forgotten that the politicians actually work for us.

To be part of a democracy means we submit to an acceptable level of control by government institutions, which we inherently all agree are necessary for our common good. We accept the fact we need educational services, police, and military. But what happens when this level of control very gradually morphs into oppression? And doesn't almost every violent situation stem from someone's need to control others? Think about the control issues in domestic violence? Think about control issues in military actions? Think about violence in every single country around the world and how violence is attached to the control of wealth? Violence is directly connected to control, and in a democracy, the people are supposed to have the control. What has happened in our world? Is the shoe not on the other foot?

How many of you know the truth? We all hear the violent tales of misguided foreign dictators and terrorists. While there may be some merit to those statements, how many of you know the truth regarding the actions of your own government? How many of you have ever listened to people from Afghanistan, Cambodia, Columbia, or Angola? How many of you have listened to people from Cuba, Chile, Honduras, or Guatemala? Where are you getting your information? Do you exchange information with people from other countries or do you simply turn on the television and rely on their version of the truth?

Of course, not everything you see on television is spun or outright propaganda. But it is only through extensive reading and substantial traveling that I have been fortunate enough to discover that most people in this world are decent and want to live in peace. The version of the news I get from the mainstream media in North America is never complete. You see my problem is what I have witnessed around the world doesn't match with what I've been told by the media, and, as a result, I have developed a sincere willingness to question everything the media and politicians tell me. Today, in conjunction with the mainstream media, I turn to several of the hundreds of online news services in an effort to get a more balanced perspective. While I am convinced that none of us have anything more than an educated guess at what the truth is on a daily basis, history teaches us some interesting lessons. And what I have learned isn't pretty.

The truth does hurt. I will not lie to you as you have been lied to enough. There is nothing simple or easy about looking at the truth; however, the only way to get to peace is to see exactly how we have arrived at where we are today and then be willing to do what we can to change it. You are not alone. There are millions who feel frustrated, lost, and confused by the daily events. I think when we first get a glimmer of what lies ahead we are overcome by a sense of helplessness, which is why so many of us look the other way. It is painful. Again, you are not alone.

Can we continue in our current direction? If we see that to continue on the path we are on is only prolonging the inevitable, would it not be prudent to work toward a peaceful transition that would restore some kind of sanity to our world now? History clearly shows us that nothing goes in a straight line forever. Every political system ever known to man has at some point changed. The one issue that history can't teach us, but one we must learn is how do we live in peace in a nuclear world? That problem is ours to resolve.

Is there is a way out of this? I believe we can resolve anything, if we really want to? It is not easy. To continue down the road we are on has consequences none of us want to think about, but perhaps the silver lining is that we can make choices today and change our world. History, I have learned, does not have to repeat itself. What if you discovered there is a group of people who have already laid the groundwork for you? What if you discovered this group has a proven plan for change that has already brought peace into the lives of millions of people? What if I told you that I have sat in a room with fifty thousand people who had once been mired in tragedy, violence, and pain? What if I told you that these fifty thousand people have gone on to change their lives and become prosperous, functioning, positive members of society who today know peace like no other group on the planet? Perhaps if you heard how they changed their lives, you would come to believe that the possibility for peace at least exists. And if you can believe that peace is possible perhaps you might choose peace instead of buying that gun you think will protect you.

The beauty of what AA brings to the world, and what I wish to share with you, is the simple and peaceful manner with which recovering alcoholics have learned to live in an increasingly chaotic world. In order to live happy and peaceful lives, the program of AA has a design for living that, if followed, provides its fellowship with such contentment that they no longer wish to drink. The problem, it appears, has been removed.

In my case, I arrived at a place in my life where I didn't want to quit drinking, but I knew, deep down inside that if I continued to drink, it was going to kill me. AA not only taught me how to escape the insanity of drinking, but also that I can live very happily without wanting to drink and that change, one day at a time, is possible. And a few years later, I am surrounded by thousands of people who really wanted to change as well, and, in addition to being sober, we have been given the additional benefit of a peace and serenity we never dreamed possible. I went to AA to get sober and was given so much more.

So here is the deal: if a bunch of drunks can overcome a life-threatening addiction, and in the process discover a life of peace and serenity, this change should be easy for those of you who do not have to overcome the addiction issue—right? The truth here, however, is that the disease of alcoholism had driven us alcoholics to the brink of death, and it was only when we faced the reality of death were we willing to change. But problems do not solve themselves, and I ask you how much further down the road of war and insanity must we travel to discover that to continue will be the end for us all? How much closer to the brink do we wish to travel?

If you're not an alcoholic, I don't suggest you quit drinking. If alcohol isn't creating a problem in your life, why would you? However, if you are seeking peace as a way of life (you're reading this so I am assuming), there is a recipe here that, based on my observations, works. It changes people's lives, and you can't argue with the results.

As a drinker, I ultimately had to ask myself if I was an alcoholic. Finally, after years of denial, I could no longer avoid the devastating effect alcohol was playing in my life, and I had to answer "Yes, I am an alcoholic." It was only then that I could ask myself the next question: What am I going to do about it?

As a member of society, my question to you is: Are we addicted to violence? Our homes, schools, and place of work are inundated with violence. Based on our perceptions, imagined or real, we choose sides in the playgrounds of our schools, our countries, and our world. Religious differences, political standpoints, and economics all fuel these perceptions. Violence has become a way of life for many of the people in this world just like alcohol had become a way of life for me. Ask the women walking down the street on a warm Houston evening if they have a gun in their purse or if they're just glad to see you. I know what the overwhelming response will be. "Hey kids, as soon as mommy loads her gun, we can go for ice cream!" Is that really the world you want to live in?

When I honestly faced and accepted that my alcoholism was going to kill me, the people at AA told me that not only could I live without alcohol, but also I could have a life much better than anything I ever dreamed of. I couldn't choose sobriety for you, my neighbor, or my brother, but I could help them if they wanted help. So I ask—is it possible to change the world one person at a time by choosing peace?

Perhaps we can learn a lesson from corporations which have sought, through globalization, to harvest the world's resources for their personal profit. Perhaps we can bypass the traditional roles of government and media and we can communicate directly with others who seek peace in Afghanistan, Iraq, and Syria. I can attend a meeting of AA in almost any country in the world today. Why can't those of us seeking peace grow and globalize as well? If you believe there is a market for weapons, I can assure you those seeking peace outnumber those seeking guns by 100 to 1 in every country in the world, and it is a sad story that those doing the killing are getting all the headlines, and most of the government support, including financial support.

By myself I was hopeless, and I am sure that I would have died as a result of my disease. But together we can achieve great things. I have sat with fifty thousand people from seventy-seven countries representing every religion known to man and from every walk of life. And the feeling of love and peace was palpable. I know that nearly three million people have learned to live in a manner that creates a peaceful existence despite color, religion, or economic status. The 12 Steps of AA consistently creates peace in people's lives, while the governments and the UN just don't seem to get there. I don't have all the answers, but I do have a recipe and, perhaps, together we can do this. Perhaps this thing will work—if we want it bad enough.

I do believe together we can find a way out of the darkness. Only because I have seen others do so. If you want peace, we can only suggest you look at these steps and ask yourself if perhaps herein lies a solution. It may not be for you, but, ultimately, peace is up to you. It is your responsibility. Nobody can do it for you.

If you find some hope in these pages read on. Take what you wish and leave the rest.

May God, *as you understand Him,* bless you.

OUR STORIES

The only tyrant I accept is the still, small voice inside me
—Mahatma Gandhi

I find the great thing in this world is not so much where we stand, as in what direction we are moving.
—Goethe

We all have a story, a history. It was when I heard others in AA speak honestly of the events in their lives, was I able to see the truth in mine. It was suggested that I set aside my arrogance and my ego and focus on being open-minded. It was suggested that I carefully consider what others had to say and that I didn't have to agree with everything I heard, but I may find it beneficial to look for the grain of truth in what others offered. When others spoke of their loneliness, fear, and pain, I could identify with those things in my life. When they spoke of denial and how they had lied and deceived others throughout their lives, they spoke to me. By listening to the truths of others, I came to see the truth about myself. I came to see where I had been in denial and lying to myself about my life. I came to see where I had been at fault and how my misguided thoughts and actions had led me to the place where I could now begin to change.

I also came to see the power of our stories. As I travelled throughout the world, and, in particular, the Middle East, I began to see how the stories I heard firsthand from those I met differed from the rhetoric of CNN and FOX. The news always focused on the power brokers who comprise much less than 1 percent of the population. What about the people? In my travels, I began to listen to stories from Afghans, Iraqis, Yemenis, Indians, Libyans, and Lebanese, as well as Americans, British, and Canadians. The message I seemed to get from the media was that those who are not like us and who do not believe as we do, are somehow less than we are, and therefore, bad. The message I heard seemed to suggest there are two kinds of people in this world, us and them. And our fears and hatred are rooted in these differences. But what I discovered has changed my life. Most people everywhere valued family, education, and being treated with respect. Most people had no desire to harm anyone and were much too busy trying to survive to trouble themselves with being a threat to those on the other side of the world.

What I have learned is that nobody owns the moral high ground. Nobody is all right or all wrong. There is a bit of bad in the best of us, and a bit of good in the worst of us. The one observation that seems consistent, regardless of culture, was the poor always pay a much higher price than those with wealth when it comes to war. This perspective is clearly revealed in *Every Man in This Village Is a Liar* where Megan Stack provides an accurate and realistic account of the plight of the common man throughout several countries in the Middle East by simply telling us the stories of the people.

Our stories reveal how incredibly imperfect we all are. How human we are. It doesn't matter if you are a CEO or a BUM, none of us have this thing called life completely figured out, and we can all learn from each other if we are willing to do so. We all have a story, and I will tell you mine. If you can grasp who I was, what happened, and what I am like now, you may be able to understand the change, which is possible as a result of these steps.

My story is not special, different, or unique. As strange as my life seems as I document the events of my past, my ordeal seems like a walk in the park compared to many others who have been blessed by the steps. And regardless of our personal tragedies it seems, when we are willing to honestly put our cards on the table and reveal to others who and what we really are, we discover just how much alike we really are. When I can see past the fear that I have been taught and discover that I am just like you, I am no longer afraid. And in the wake of my disappearing fear, a void is created. I can choose to fill that void with whatever I wish, and so can you.

I hope you choose peace.

*

My Story

(Note: Most of the names have been changed.)

What It Was Like

I grew up in a very small farming community nestled into the vast prairie exactly thirty-seven miles south of the middle of nowhere. My father was a grain buyer and my mother, a brilliant woman who could have done anything she wanted, dedicated her life to raising five children while perfecting the art of rhubarb pie. If I had to pick parents all over again, I would be more than grateful to be blessed with the two loving people who did the very best they could in providing for their family. Of course, it is only as I grow older do I recognize exactly how fortunate I truly was.

As far back as I can remember, I was a square peg. I felt lost a great deal of the time and had no idea where I fit in. Years later, when I arrived at the doorstep of AA, I discovered many alcoholics felt the same way.

I was a reasonably good student and managed to pass my grades without doing much work. As a young student there was always the comment on my report cards, "Johnny could do better." I had a restless nature, which would be diagnosed years later in adulthood as ADHD. The overabundance of energy that I carried in my youth was burned up in sports, which I loved and where I excelled.

In June 1969, I was thirteen years old. The school year was winding down as my older brother, a friend, and I stole some lumber from the railroad and built a large raft. We hauled it out to the local reservoir and left it a good distance from the water's edge so it could not be easily pushed in. Our plan was to return a few days later with a chain and an anchor with the ultimate goal of using it as a diving platform.

However, within a couple of days, a large group of smaller kids made their way to the reservoir for a swim on a hot afternoon. They managed to push the raft into the water and climbed aboard. As they drifted away from shore, they abandoned ship and swam back. A short time later, the phone rang and we were informed of an emergency at the reservoir. My parents, my older brother, and I climbed into the family car and arrived at the reservoir a few minutes later where we discovered that my youngest sister had not made it back to shore.

Minutes later, I was sitting in the backseat of the car with my mother. My father sat alone in the front and was naturally in a great deal of pain when he turned, looked at me, and asked, "Why did you build that raft?" I know it was not his intent, but it felt like an accusation, and it became the weight I would struggle to carry for many years to come.

It is only in hindsight that I can see what my relationship with alcohol was really like. The first time I drank, I became thoroughly intoxicated. I spent a substantial part of the evening hanging onto the ground as the world spun rapidly around me. I was violently ill and vomited everywhere. I don't remember much. What I do remember is that I couldn't wait to do it again. In short order, and with committed practice, I learned to drink without getting sick. My ability to consume alcohol increased, and I began to drink every chance I could. I failed to pass my grades my first year in high school, and today I know it was because of my drinking. However, at the time, I thought I was just having fun, and I justified my actions by blaming my teachers, who were obviously incompetent. It most certainly wasn't my fault. Nothing was my fault, and I was incapable of seeing that I had already crossed the line.

The truth is the death of my sister devastated our family. My mother was never the same, and I, who had never felt like I belonged anywhere to begin with, felt even more distanced. I couldn't comprehend myself being the little boy who was in so much pain and who felt so responsible for orchestrating the death of his sister. I was also incapable of seeing the effects of alcohol and that I drank to numb the pain I felt. I couldn't see that it was alcohol and my ego which changed me into the fun-loving guy I thought I wanted to be, instead of the guy who built the raft that had taken his sister's life.

I remember the little voice from deep inside me rising up, and I wondered if I was doing the right thing. I knew something was wrong, that I was somehow making a mistake. But drinking worked. It changed how I felt. It allowed me to escape and avoid facing the pain. Alcohol would drown out the little voice inside me, and, without my knowing it and without my permission, alcohol would influence every decision I would make for the next twenty years.

I began to miss a great deal of school. I was the quarterback on the football team, so I would go when we had a game, but if there was no sporting event scheduled for that day, the chances are pretty good that the bus left without me. I began to drop out of life, and the only interests I had seemed to have were those that involved drinking. So when the school guidance counselor stopped me in the hall one day and asked why I bothered to come to school at all, I embraced the fact that I had finally encountered a teacher who understood me and I could clearly see his point of view. I quit school and got a job.

A paycheck is exactly what every aspiring alcoholic needs; a job?—not so much. Bosses had these crazy notions about employees actually coming to work . . . every day. As the money trickled in, the alcohol consumption went up, and it made getting to work a little troublesome. But like my teachers, these guys, my bosses, didn't really get it and so I changed jobs, regularly.

Somehow I knew at a very deep level that I was heading down the wrong path. In order to rationalize and justify my ever increasing insane behavior, I developed an ego, which would insure that I was right especially when anyone would question my drinking. Where others would question, and correct, their behavior, my ego would step forward and justify even the most bizarre actions. To look inside was painful, and deep down, this alcoholic hated the person I perceived myself to be. I was incapable of seeing my entire view of the world was skewed by alcohol. The pain I carried and the fact that I felt so responsible for the pain of others made for very low self-esteem. I couldn't see the truth, and so I developed this persona that was much more acceptable. I locked the guilt-ridden, lost, frightened little boy in a closet. The "me" I showed the world was intelligent, charming, and a damn good dancer. Occasionally, in a moment of stillness, the small voice would rise up from within me and point out how frightened and lost I felt. A few drinks would usually silence it, and the more improved manufactured me, would then step back into the spotlight. It was good to be king.

By the time I had traveled this far down the road, I was a well-seasoned eighteen-year-old, and I went to work for a company that repaired grain elevators. I hated the job, but we drank hard every night. Our crew was working in a small town when I met Linda. She was beautiful, and she loved to party. I fell in love with her. She was attending college in a nearby city, and I would go and see her almost every night. I was once again in trouble at work because there were a lot of mornings when I just couldn't leave her in order to go to work. A few months later, I did the only thing that could possibly make matters worse; I asked her to marry me. Unfortunately for Linda, she said yes.

Once again the little voice spoke to me suggesting that perhaps marriage may not be a good idea, and once again I ignored it. The deep-rooted sense that I was somehow doing the wrong thing, combined with our drinking, didn't make for marital bliss. I loved Linda, but the fact is I was no more prepared for a marriage commitment than I was for a high school commitment. Within weeks of being married, we discovered we were to become parents. I was overjoyed. Linda was due exactly nine months from our wedding day, and my mother-in-law was grateful for the fact that Linda had the decency to be two weeks late in delivering.

I fell in love with our daughter, Sherry. I lived to get through a day of work and then race home to have that little girl spend her evening on my knee. I had never known so much happiness, and my drinking declined as my life was filled with the simple joy of being with her.

My work, and subsequently the cash flow, was sporadic. I accepted a job that took me out of town from Monday to Thursday, and while it paid more money, it put an additional strain on the marriage. I really missed Sherry, and being on the road simply meant that I had an opportunity to drink more, which didn't help the financial picture or the marriage. At one point, Linda and I parted ways. I was hurt and angry, and there was no way I was going to be without Sherry. I quit my job to look after our daughter.

The separation didn't last long, and I convinced Linda to come back. But things never were very good. The pain of our failing marriage increased, and, of course, pain was the catalyst for my alcohol consumption. The more I drank, the more I struggled to control both our lives and our marriage. My ego, the part of me that knew everything and what was best for everybody, did its utmost to get Linda to see things my way. The need to control the situation stemmed from my insecurities, selfishness, and my ego. There was no doubt I was right, and I was incapable of listening as I closed my mind off to anything she might have to say. I blamed Linda for everything that went wrong and the harder I tried to get her to see how "right" I was, the more things spiraled out of control. Years later, when I arrived in AA, some wiseass muttered that, "Alcoholics didn't get into relationships, they took hostages." In hindsight, I agree.

When it became obvious that this marriage was never going to work, I was faced with a real problem. I loved my daughter, and I did not want to be away from her, ever. So how was I going to end the marriage and keep my daughter with me? And then Linda became pregnant again, and I remember thinking that if we had a son, I could drive her out of the house and I would never have to have anything to do with a woman again. In my mind love, or what I thought was love, was simply too painful. And into that insanity Craig, our son, was born.

I was delighted to be a father, again, but being a husband sucked. By this time, we were doing things to each other that were simply designed to hurt. To the best of my knowledge, I never physically abused Linda, but I most certainly verbally and emotionally abused her. While I considered myself to be a good father, I was not a good husband. It became harder and harder to be under the same roof, and yet I did not want to be away from my kids.

One day in February 1981, I went to my construction job and was laid off. I didn't go home that night. In fact, I didn't go home for weeks. I couldn't. Something inside me wouldn't let me. Instead, I drank. I was in so much pain and couldn't see a solution. All I remember from that time period was drinking heavily and feeling this huge emptiness where all that existed was the thought of my children and self-pity. And, while I drank, I focused on the pain and the pain grew. What I didn't know then was that the alcohol was blinding me from seeing the solution.

I would occasionally call and talk to the kids, who were only two and four years old. Then one night I called and told Linda I was coming home. When I arrived the kids were there with a babysitter and it was obvious Linda wanted to avoid me. I was so happy to see them. I hugged them until they turned blue, and then I put them to bed. I then packed a suitcase for Linda, put it on the doorstep, locked the door, and went to bed. The egomaniac, control freak was now home.

The children lived with me for the next several months. It was an adjustment for me, and I am so grateful to my mother for all her help at that time. Things seemed to be getting a little better for me. I was happier being out of the marriage. I was drinking a lot less. I had met Sarah, who was a great woman, and I had an interim custody order granting me custody of the children. Then one afternoon, several months after I had assumed custody of the children, Linda stopped me on the street and informed me that we were going to court regarding custody. "Mom says I am out of the will if I don't fight for the kids," she said. My heart sunk.

As the relationship with Sarah blossomed, she agreed to move in with me and the kids. They loved her, and I know she loved them. I began going to University, and I finally felt like I was doing the right thing. I had a full schedule of classes, was getting great marks, and loved the challenge. I had a great life and my drinking all but stopped. It was the happiest time of my life.

Overshadowing all this was the impending court case. I hired a lawyer and simply assumed that my best interests were being taken care of. When court date came around, it was scheduled to cover two days. I remember looking at Sarah thirty minutes into the first day and saying, "We're screwed." My lawyer was bombing. Later, when I discussed the proceedings with character witnesses who knew us both and who were speaking on my behalf, they all said that my lawyer didn't ask them any of the questions she said she was going to. None of it made sense and I was very afraid.

When the judgment came down, we had lost. My lawyer never billed me, stating that she felt responsible. I retained a new lawyer and immediately appealed. I lost the appeal. But the three judges, who wrote the decision, all said they could not understand what had happened and that none of it made any sense. However, they added, there was not sufficient evidence to overturn the decision. The lawyer I had retained to handle the appeal told me that if the Court of Appeal overturned one custody case, they would be flooded with Family Court cases. He also told me the Appeal Court judges in their decision went as close as they possibly could to overturning the decision, without overturning it, and in that way they were sending a message regarding future cases. He added that it was obvious to the judges at the Court of Appeal there was something not quite right about this case, but they couldn't see what is was. I was not alone.

Upon hearing the news, Sarah was devastated. I managed to keep a lid on my emotions for three entire days until I finished my last exam. It was the end of April, and the kids were supposed to go and live with their mother the end of June when school was over. Sarah and I discussed the situation and considered several factors. I hadn't worked for several months due to school, and we needed a paycheck. If the kids had to move to the other side of the city, we thought it might be best for them to go sooner, that way they could meet some of the neighborhood kids in school, and have somebody to play with through the summer. In addition, we were both exhausted and thought if this had to happen, let's get it over with.

Sherry and Craig went to live with Linda in short order. Our house seemed very empty. My soul seemed empty. A week later, I sat on a plane heading to a bush camp for work. The little voice screamed at me to get off that plane! I didn't listen. A few nights later, I was in a drunken stupor when a young woman invited her way into my room. I didn't resist. Anything to stop the pain, but it didn't work. Moments later, in an effort to exorcise my guilt, I made a phone call. That was the beginning of the end of my relationship with one of the finest human beings I have ever known. Over the next few months, Sarah tried to hang on, but I had slipped into the abyss, and there was no coming back. She had done everything possible to stand by me, love me, and be a good partner. And I simply did what selfish, self-centered alcoholics do: I hurt a beautiful woman and destroyed our relationship in the process.

I ended up with a job in sales, and I did very well. I had some clients in the oil business, who drank a lot, and I just happened to have an expense account. I broke sales records and received all kinds of accolades from my employer. At one point, my manager called me into his office and I was informed that it was only halfway through the year, and I had already spent the expense budget for the entire branch. Then with a smile he handed me a significant bonus check. Life was good.

Most of my time was spent either working or drinking, and I began to see less and less of Sherry and Craig. I did not want them to see me drunk so I would not go and pick them up if I was drinking, which was most of the time. If I was sober, the anger and bitterness I carried made any exchanges between Linda and I extremely ugly. I blamed her and her family, for all my trouble.

Around that time Linda, with the help of her parents, purchased a house. She had no desire to conceal from me the fact that it had been my original lawyer in the custody case, who had handled the legal work on her behalf. And she had done it for free. I took this shred of information to the lawyer, who had conducted the appeal. I will never forget the look on his face when I told him. The pieces fell into place as I began to understand how the system really works. "You, my friend, have been screwed," he said. I would later discover that my lawyer's husband, a group of politicians, and a group of businessmen, including Linda's father, were all close friends. I understood the uneasy feeling I had in the courtroom that first morning and my lawyer's doing "free" legal work for my ex-wife. The pieces did fit, and I became even more resentful. And so I drank.

Somewhere in that haze, I convinced myself that Sarah and I still had a chance. I was drunk and melancholy. I felt empty and hollow inside, and I was convinced that if I could just get Sarah to listen to me I could get her to understand. I went to her apartment one night prepared to resolve all the issues. Of course, I was drunk. Sarah let me in, and as we talked, the conversation didn't go the way I wanted. My recollection, which is far from reliable, recalls her reaching for the phone to call the police and my trying to stop her. The neighbors must have heard the commotion and called the police, and I woke up the next morning in jail with a gash in my head and an assault charge pending. I was drowning in a sea of shame and guilt. As with my problems with Linda, my ego tried to convince me that somehow this was all Sarah's fault. I simply could not see or accept, the truth regarding my actions.

A couple of months passed, and I went to Mexico for two weeks with my brother, Mac. He was eight years younger, and I didn't really know him all that well. We had a lot of fun if you call getting completely intoxicated for two weeks fun. It was the first holiday I had taken in almost two years, and a couple of things happened on that trip that had an impact on my life. First, I met Marcia. She was beautiful, and there was a chemistry there that was evident from the first time we met. Her boyfriend was also kind enough to play golf every day, and despite the fact I had taken my clubs, I didn't play golf once. I liked Marcia a lot. The second thing of note to occur, while I was busy spending my latest bonus check with wild abandon, was the bottom fell out of the oil market and I knew, unless it miraculously rebounded overnight, my job was going to be nothing like it had been. My bonus money would be gone, and I knew the company that was actively supporting my drinking via my expense account would be putting a stop to my party. They would tolerate the expenses when the business was there, but there was no way they were going to be paying those kinds of expenses without the revenue to support it.

Marcia and her boyfriend left after the first week. I missed her, and many of the people staying at the same resort suggested that we made a great couple. We partied hard the last week in Mexico, and Marcia was at the airport to meet me when I staggered off the plane upon our return.

The oil market did not rebound, and a short time later, I quit my job and moved three hundred miles to live with Marcia, who had ended her relationship with her boyfriend. The floundering oil industry had resulted in thousands of lost jobs, and it was difficult to find work. In addition, I am not sure Marcia's old boyfriend received the memo regarding their relationship ending. This may explain why he was waiting outside the door one night and hit me with God knows what. It was obvious that things were not quite finished between them, and it appeared he was not at all happy how this was working out for him. That memo I understood implicitly.

Again the little voice spoke up, and I occasionally listened. Marcia began to spend more time away from home, and the pieces of her story never fit together quite right. After a couple of months, and a good whack upside my head, it was obvious that things between her and I were not going to work out. I packed my bags and headed home for a quick visit with the kids and my favorite bar stool, before heading east to work in the steel mills.

The job, like all jobs requiring manual labor, wasn't my cup of tea. I had done well in the sales game, and anything that didn't have an expense account and a company car fell short of my expectations. I was, however, committed to making the best of it, and I began looking for a watering hole that fit my requirements. When I walked into Charlie's on a Monday night and met Dyan, I knew this was my place. She was beautiful. I had given her the name of the hotel I was staying at before I found out that she was living with her boyfriend. My heart sunk as I did not want a repeat performance of the Marcia scenario. I left that night and didn't go back to Charlie's until the night my phone rang. I explained the boyfriend issue (my head still hurt from the last boyfriend), but she suggested I come down so she could explain. An hour later, I knew I was in over my head—again! Dyan had convinced me that her situation at home was in the process of changing. My fears were calmed by a few drinks and a woman, who would break my heart into a thousand pieces.

Dyan had a daughter who was a sweet kid with a gift for telling stories. I also learned that Dyan's father had passed away at a young age and that alcohol had been a contributing factor. (At the time, this seemed to speak to my soul and today I know why.) The thing with the boyfriend was a little more difficult than I had hoped, but it was a small issue compared to the fun Dyan and I had. Our lives revolved around music, dancing, and drinking. She moved out, and I moved in with her. There was something there that I had never known before. We were madly in love and totally inseparable.

Dyan loved to party, and she could hold her booze better than anyone, man or woman, I had ever met. We went out all the time, which wasn't cheap and our occasional differences of opinion usually regarded finances. My work wasn't like the party my sales job had been. Construction was demanding, with long hours, and so was the partying. It was hard to do both, so I opted, as usual, for the party and subsequently, I missed a lot of work. I was laid off, rehired elsewhere, and laid off again.

I took Dyan and her daughter on a holiday home to meet my kids, and we talked about moving back west where my kids were. I was so much in love with Dyan that the thought of being without her never crossed my mind. But the insanity wasn't over as once again the little voice came through, loud and clear.

Dyan never worked Saturday night, and we almost always went out drinking and dancing. Early one Sunday morning, I was catapulted from a deep, sound sleep. I remember suddenly sitting straight up in bed and clearly hearing the words, "If you don't get out of here now, you never will." I was bewildered. It was so much more than a passing thought, and I didn't understand what was going on. I sat there trying to sort out this overwhelming feeling. I couldn't go back to sleep. I got dressed, poured a coffee, and went for a long drive in an attempt to understand where this sudden shift had come from. But that didn't help.

I loved Dyan. I knew I drank too much, but I had never considered for a second not having her in my life. From that exact moment forward things began to fall apart between Dyan and me. I knew I couldn't blame her. Not this time. I was a mess and didn't understand why. I couldn't figure it out, and the more I struggled to understand it, the worse things got. I had no idea where I was supposed to go or what I was supposed to do. Staying seemed like the wrong thing, but I couldn't bring myself to leave. The confusion and pain would cause most people to seek counseling or at least find a quiet place to make some decisions about what was best for them, and the other people in their lives. Me? I drank.

I never did try to explain this to Dyan. How could I? I thought she might not understand, and to this day, I am not so sure I do. For the next three or four months, I became more irrational on a daily basis. I remember a bartender suggesting I get some help as I sat nursing a beer and muttering to myself one afternoon while the rest of the world was at work. Ultimately, it was Dyan who made the decision regarding whether I should stay or go. I was driving both of us crazy. I was so in love with her, and yet I was acting like an irresponsible fool, and I knew it. Nothing in my world made any sense to me at all.

Looking back twenty-five years later, I believe what I was experiencing was the struggle between my soul—my spiritual center and my brain—where my ego resides. I understand the scenario better today, but, at the time, I was bewildered. I thought all I had to do was make my mind up about what I wanted in life and have the conviction to go for it. But at that time I didn't have a relationship with the spiritual side of my life, so I was incapable of understanding the inner turmoil caused when my ego pulled me in one direction and my soul tried to go in another. It was a difficult thing to explain to those who have trouble grasping things of a spiritual nature, which is why open-mindedness is so critical. Believe me, I was a skeptic regarding the spiritual aspects of life, despite the fact my life seemed inundated with spiritual events. How we "feel" is often quite different than how we "think", and I was consuming large amounts of alcohol so I wouldn't have to feel. In my head, I wanted it all to make sense.

I wanted it to be logical. But why would faith and trust be necessary if everything in our world made perfect sense? Today I know I have a choice. But ultimately, when it comes to doing the "right" thing, I must listen to my soul. If I want to be happy, I must let go of what my ego, (my brain), wants and search deeper for the answers I seek. Learning to listen and to trust the voice of my soul took a lot of work and a lot of time. My ego was massive and did not want to give up control. Some people fascinate me as they seem to have lived from their soul their entire life, while the next person has no idea they even have a soul. But most of us, I believe, are like me and were simply never still enough, sober enough, or perhaps, willing enough, to listen to their own heart. And, as a result, I made a lot of bad decisions, which hurt a lot of people.

I left Dyan on January 08, 1988. The road heading out of town went over a mountain, which provided a spectacular view of the city. But I refused to look back as something deep inside me broke.

I was on the road home because I could think of nowhere else to go. I had only driven a few hours, when I stopped to see Victor, my father's youngest brother, and his girlfriend, Betty. I have never met anyone better at reading people than Betty, and it took her all three seconds to see that something was terribly wrong with me. We talked and had something to eat, and they convinced me to stay the night. I stayed three years.

Vic and I became involved in a couple of businesses together. We did some construction work but would often go for lunch and spend the afternoon, playing darts and drinking beer. There was never a complaint from me. I began to party with the cousins, whom I had never met before, and the new friends I acquired, many of whom are still great friends today. Otto, who was married to my cousin, became a great friend, and I would go on to abuse his hospitality, and his friendship, as my drinking escalated. We did, however, share some great moments, and we still laugh our asses off whenever we get together today.

Regardless of how I dressed it up, the emotional pain of leaving Dyan haunted me. I missed her terribly and was overjoyed the day she called and told me she was coming to see me. We spent the weekend together. She told me she loved me and wanted to spend her life with me. I was optimistic that things would work out. I had to go to Chicago for a few days, and we made plans for me to come and see her in a couple of weeks. But things did not work out. She wouldn't return calls, and I needed to find out why. I drove three hours to her place to discover she wasn't home. I went for a beer and occasionally would leave the bar and drive by her house. By the time, her car was home I was half-smashed, and when she answered the door, she was with another guy. I was not pleased. There was a discussion, and he left. At some point, during my conversation with Dyan, I said something she did not like, and she slapped me. In a blink of an eye, she was on her back. Almost as fast I was on my knees, apologizing for hitting her and trying to help her up. I spent that night in jail. I am not sure if Dyan asked the police not to charge me, but I was released in the morning. I remember the night watchman in jail asking me what I had done to land up in jail. "I'm in love" was my response. And I was in love, with alcohol.

The truth is I didn't know anything about love. While alcohol prevented me from feeling the pain in my life, it wasn't selective; it numbed all my feelings, good and bad. My capacity to feel anything was being smothered by the booze, and what I thought was love was simply my ego's need to control another human being. Everything was on my terms, according to my demands. Dyan's well-being never entered into my mind and all that mattered was my getting what I wanted. After all, isn't that what happens in a hostage situation?

The business ventures Vic and I were involved in failed, largely due to my drinking. We had been working on a project with Chrysler that would be a financial windfall for us if we got our way. After three years of testing, I remember having a meeting at World Headquarters with several of their engineers. The meeting was scheduled for 7:00 in the morning, and I was still drinking at 4:00 a.m. I arrived drunk. Needless to say things didn't go well. I walked out of that meeting knowing that three years of work had gone down the toilet, a fact that today I am grateful for. The last thing a drunk really needs is a pocketful of cash. Had the Chrysler deal worked out, the revenue generated would have provided sufficient revenue for me to drink myself into a grave. But rather than look at myself and see where I had failed, I blamed them. In the process I became angrier, more resentful, and acquired one more reason to drink. The little voice whispered, and I knew I was in bad shape, but I refused to listen.

The truth is my drinking was, and always had been, a reaction to pain. I had never dealt with my pain. Instead, I used alcohol, sex, and occasionally drugs as a way of medicating myself in order to not feel, to numb myself to the events of life, while my pain piled up in the basement of my mind. I had never dealt with the pain of my sister's death, and I discovered alcohol numbed the feelings I didn't want to feel. The pain of divorce, of losing custody of my children, of loss and betrayal in relationships, of job loss, of business failures, and the pain of simply knowing that I, as a human being didn't measure up, that I was no good, and did not deserve to breathe the same air as the rest of you, that I was worthless, were all prevalent feelings. Who would want to feel that? And those feelings went away when I drank. But it was taking more and more alcohol to change how I felt and I no longer felt like the life of the party. I became more solitary, more alone, and was well-past feeling anything, other than numb.

*

I don't remember all the details regarding how I arrived in the chair on the other side of Robyn's desk, but I do remember that she was pretty, and she spoke to me with a kindness that I was not familiar with.

It was 1991, and I had made my way to the west coast courtesy of an invitation issued by my younger brother, Mac. The last few times I had talked to him he had asked if I was ever coming out to visit him and his family, and once again I put the wreckage of my past in the rearview mirror as I headed west. I had pretty much worn out my welcome in the east, although, at the time, I had simply rationalized it as a run of bad luck. The truth, however, is I had drank away my business and had no real reason for staying, and so I threw my meager belongings into the car and hit the road.

I thought the world of Mac and had hardly seen him since our trip to Mexico, several years earlier. He had married, had two small children, and had learned to assume some responsibility in his life. I couldn't relate, and I believe today, had he known the person I had become, the invitation to travel west would have been given much more consideration.

Mac and his wife put me up in their spare room, and I immediately went out and found gainful employment. It had been a long time since I had worked for anyone else. I showed up on time, and I did know my business, as I had been well-trained. The boss was good man, and through our discussions, I learned he was very happy with my work. But with me being an alcoholic, the positive aspects of my arrival would be short-lived. I worked hard at controlling my drinking, especially around Mac's wife and kids, but the simple fact is things had reached the level where my thought process swam in a sea of negativity, and I was no longer the fun-loving guy, Mac had remembered going to Mexico with. Work, it seems, I could handle, but I was no longer capable of handling the intricacies' of personal relationships.

It wasn't long until the night came where I had gone out, gotten drunk, and was pulled over by the police while driving Mac's car. Mac had wanted to use my car to move some things because it was bigger, so we had traded vehicles for the day. I had gone to a music festival, where I managed to get mildly intoxicated. I slipped behind the wheel, as I had for years, without a second thought, but I didn't get very far before I was pulled over by the police. In the ensuing discussion the officer discovered he could never make the charges stick if he took me in for a breath analysis. There was a legal technicality I was very much aware of which would get me off, and in the interest of public safety, I will not explain how it works, but it was a scam I had been aware of and used for years. Rather than wasting his time going through the legal process simply to see me walk away, the officer suspended my license for twenty-four hours and was then kind enough to call me a taxi while my brother's car was left on the side of the road overnight.

The next morning, I had to explain to Mac where his car was, and then he and his wife had to go and get it. They were not pleased, and I was consumed with guilt as the little voice inside me whispered, somewhere around hundred decibels, "Man you have got to stop this shit." In fact I was so overwhelmed with shame that I called a government agency that worked in the field of drug and alcohol abuse, and a few days later, I showed up for the scheduled appointment.

I arrived at Robyn's office sober. (With this alcoholic, it always seemed necessary to designate the degree of earnestness by my blood alcohol content.) I explained how much I had loved my kids, and Robyn listened. I explained how I had left my hometown nine years before, after losing custody of my children, and Robyn listened. I went into all the angry and sordid details of how the world had done me wrong, and Robyn listened. I bitched and moaned and blamed every single human being I had ever crossed paths with for all the problems in my life, and Robyn listened. It was a painful exchange, and Robyn sat quietly and thoughtfully listened to every word. When I had exhausted the litany of my life's perils, Robyn reached across the desk, touched my hand, and in the softest voice I had ever heard, she said, "Why don't you go home?"

My mind reeled, and I was dumfounded. It was an option I simply did not want to consider, and yet I immediately knew it was the right thing to do. As I digested that concept Robyn stood signaling the end of our meeting. She walked around the desk, gave me a hug, and said something that would puzzle me for months to come, "When you leave here go and do something nice for someone." It didn't make sense. I was the victim here

I thought, and you want me to go and do something nice for someone else? I didn't understand, but at that point in my life I was incapable of grasping what Robyn knew I needed. I walked out the door, and a few days later, I was heading home.

It was now November 1991, and winter had assumed a firm grip in the mountains. The trip had been relatively uneventful, but at one point, on a particularly icy stretch of highway, at a very high altitude, and with large trucks barreling past me, I had an anxiety attack. I thought my heart was going to leap out of my chest as I clutched the wheel and fought to maintain control of the car. As my desperation mounted I searched for, and finally found, a place to pull over. I had promised myself I wasn't going to drink on the road; however, my desire to be sober dwindled in comparison to the simple Neanderthal reaction to save myself and get my ass off this mountain in one piece. I reached into the backseat and grabbed the safety provisions I had brought along, and I don't remember ever drinking three beers that fast in my life. It wasn't much, but it was all I had, and a few minutes later, I pulled away still shaking, but with enough calm restored to move on. To this day, I am not sure if it was the knowledge that I could not stay on this mountaintop for the rest of my life, or the need to find more to drink, that was the chief motivator in getting me to move.

I arrived in my hometown the next day, and I got a job which was scheduled to last seven to eight months, at which I would make more money than I ever had in my life. I stayed with my older brother, Rick, and slept on the floor underneath the kitchen table on an old mattress. I went to work every day, and when work was over, I drank as much as I could possibly drink. I was only 140 miles from my kids, and occasionally, I went to see them, but there were weekends when I packed my bag and headed in their direction and woke up Sunday morning sick and broke, never having left town. On workdays, my brother suggested I ride to work with him. I avoided this by telling him I parked in the other parking lot, and the second he closed the door to leave, I would pull the rum bottle out and take several long pulls in order to stop my mind from racing and my body from shaking. I honestly believed I couldn't make it out that door and into work without that drink to start my day.

Christmas of 1991 landed in the middle of that job. When that job had started, I owed $2400.00 on my car, and I owed $2100.00 when it was over. The $300 difference was a payment I made a couple of days before Christmas, and so you can imagine my surprise (sarcasm here folks) when, on Christmas Eve, I looked out the window of my sister's house to see a tow truck backing up to my car. I ran outside to confront the driver, and I explained to him, in all my self-righteous glory, that if he put my car on the hook, I was taking him to court. I explained that I had the paperwork to prove I had made the payments, and if he wanted to wait, I would show him. He finally agreed to leave, but by then my entire family and some of the neighbors had gathered to observe the confrontation. My father didn't say a word, but I will never forget the look on his face as I climbed out of the snow bank I was standing in. It was a bitterly cold night, and I had come out of the house in a panic. I had not put on a jacket or shoes. But I didn't forget to bring my drink, which I grasped firmly in my hand.

The job would last four or five more months, and two weeks after it was over, I was broke. I don't believe I made another car payment. The little voice inside me was becoming relentless. I needed a miracle.

What Happened

I believe today, had my sister known the extent of my problem, she would never have asked, but she needed some help with her kids. And coincidentally, I needed a place to stay. My nephew had started school but came home for lunch. He would then return to school with my niece who went to kindergarten in the afternoons. The arrangement gave me a place to sleep and the afternoons and evenings to work out in the bar of my choice. What more could a guy want?

One extremely cold morning, I was nursing a particularly bad hangover. My nephew dressed for school, and as he headed out the door, I put my niece into her snowsuit. Moments later, we were in the car heading to the liquor store so I could buy breakfast and put a stop to the pounding between my ears. (Today there is nothing that really defines alcoholism for me as the thought of hanging out in front of the liquor store desperately waiting for it to open with a five-year-old in tow.)

When we returned home, I immediately cracked open a beer and poured it down my throat. The physical relief was almost instant and the twinge of guilt that accompanied the thought that most people don't live this way evaporated even faster than my physical discomfort. I settled down in front of the tube and began a review of the morning's various talk shows when I stumbled onto the *Phil Donohue Show*. That particular day as I sat drinking breakfast, Phil's guests included three women who were all roughly of my age. (I was thirty-seven at the time.) They were all very attractive and well-spoken. As they revealed more and more about themselves, I was impressed with their honesty. But more important was the emotional level at which I could identify as they discussed the major issues that had impacted their lives. Drugs, alcohol, gambling, eating disorders, an inability to maintain relationships, financial problems, and the feeling that they somehow never really felt that they fit into the society they lived in seemed commonplace in all their stories. When one of the women described the "hollow and empty" feeling she'd had for much of her life and how she had been driven to find a way to fill up that emptiness with drugs and alcohol, I knew exactly what she meant.

As I listened, the lights began to come on. I had spent years fighting with the world and had tried everything imaginable to fill the empty void that had become my life. Motivated by fear and pain, I had done everything I could to control people, places, and things, believing if I could just get the world to do things my way, everything would be wonderful. Obviously, my ex-wife hadn't wanted to do it my way and neither did any of my previous employers. The courts and banks didn't rush to fall in line either. Failing in my attempts to control the events of my life, I blamed everyone else. I then eased my pain by turning to drinking, drugs, and sex, which all worked temporarily, but in reality, they only added to the illusion that I was in control, while my life was spinning out of control. My ego, aided by denial, prevented me from acquiring sufficient humility to see the truth about who and what I had become.

And so there I sat beer in hand at 10:00 a.m., watching The Phil Donahue Show, and for the first time in my life, I was able to really identify with another human being about how I thought and how, deep down inside, I felt. I was no longer alone; there were others who felt and thought as I did. The still, small voice inside me told me this was the path, and by the end of that show, something inside me had changed. (Later I would learn that the sharing of our individual experiences with other alcoholics is a cornerstone of the program of AA.)

I would love to tell you that I ran right out, joined AA, and lived happily ever after, but that is not the case. Change doesn't come that easy for me, and I find that I will continually reach for an even bigger hammer before I realize there is no way I am going to get that marshmallow in the piggybank. The truth is that over the next six months, my drinking escalated as my ego worked hard at trying to convince me that the still, small voice could be ignored. But the more I drank, the more I began to sense that something had to change. And true to alcoholic form, the more uncomfortable I felt, the more I needed to drink in order to suppress the uncomfortable feelings that were caused by my drinking. I was on the alcoholic merry-go-round and knew that something in my world was very, very wrong. The Donahue experience had planted a seed and from that moment on my drinking career would never be the same.

For those who have never had any experience with addictions, this may all seem ludicrous, but an alcoholic may often be the last person to see the truth about his drinking problem. He may be quite capable in other facets of his life, but when it comes to drinking his thought process goes right off the deep end. Denial runs deep, and we are incapable of accurately assessing our own situation. We may be jobless, homeless, and broke, but will firmly believe we are okay and the rest of the world is somehow at fault. To counter the obvious feelings of inadequacy, we develop major egos, which we present to the public while we convince ourselves that we are in complete control and know exactly what we are doing. We do our best to convince the world, and ourselves, that we have it all together, that we are all right, but oh boy, the rest of the world is most certainly in one hell of a mess.

And so it was with me.

However, the miracle was only beginning to unfold. About this time, I walked into one of my favorite bars, and there sat my ex-wife with her new boss, Pam. It only took a minute to discover that Pam had been married to a man that had mentored me in my line of work several years back. Ironically when I had begun working with Sam, it had been his first day back on the job after a thirty-day stint at a treatment center for alcoholism, and I soon discovered that Pam had been sober for eight years.

Pam and I became good friends. I was attracted to her candid and honest perspective. She didn't know I was struggling with my drinking, but our conversations over the next few months always seemed to be centered on recovery. We would go for coffee three or four evenings a week and talk for hours, and I was beginning to like the sound of sobriety. The nights I didn't go for coffee with Pam, I would go out and get completely trashed. It took a while before I told Pam about my problems with booze, and she informed me that she had suspected because of all the questions I had asked her about recovery. I am very grateful to Pam today, and I am not sure if I would even be here had she not been such a tremendous example of sobriety as she watered the seeds that had been planted by Phil Donahue.

Through the summer of 1992, I struggled. While many alcoholics suffer from blackouts (I had my share), I was also fortunate to have been plagued by some ugly memories, which pushed me toward sobriety, and there was one night, in particular, that I would have liked to have forgotten because I knew it put me way over the line. And because I was alone, there was nobody I could blame it on.

In the middle of the night, I maneuvered down the road heading toward my parent's place at the lake, coming back from who knows where. I was drunk, and my limited focus was largely taken up by one of those big, oversized plastic bottles of beer that I had acquired throughout the course of the evening. My parents had gone to the city to visit my sister, and I was alone for a few days. I remember being very disgusted with myself because I was drunk again and, in an act of resolve, I threw the beer out of the window as I made the turn off the main road into the lake subdivision, all while vowing to never drink again.

The next morning arrived in all its painful glory, and I stumbled about the place, looking for something to ease the pain. I was sweating, my head pounded, and I was in the grip of overwhelming anxiety as I searched for anything to take the edge off. I couldn't find a drop, and desperation was setting in.

And then I remembered the beer I had tossed out of the window.

Minutes later, I was combing the ditch searching for the bottle that only a few hours earlier had marked the end of my drinking career. I remember the feeling of victory as I tripped over it in among the weeds. And I remember the demoralizing feeling when I discovered the bottle contained only a couple of ounces. I tipped it up to discover that the contents had been spoiled from the sun. Regardless, I drank it down, and in hindsight, I realize that I no longer had a choice about whether I drank or not; the booze was now calling the shots in my life.

I couldn't take it anymore. I had managed to work a bit but stayed at my parents much of the time, which made my drinking even more difficult to hide. Despite that problem, I still managed to get away almost every night to get smashed and would return late so I wouldn't have to answer any of their questions. In the mornings, I would wake up with terrible hangovers and suffer through at least a portion of the day until I could get away to start all over again. Initially my goal was to just drink enough to stop the pain, which could be achieved with a few beers. But the truth is once I started, there was no stopping, and I would end up getting completely obliterated. It seemed the only way I could tolerate myself.

These events were what led up to the late night phone call to the detox center in October 1992. The high-school quarterback who had thought so incredibly well of himself was beaten. There had never been anybody I was able to tell about how I thought, or felt, or what I had done to arrive at this point in my life. But Michelle, Ken, and Bill at the detox seemed to know exactly what my problem was. In fact, they, like Robyn, spoke to me in a language that I had never really heard before but could understand implicitly. They explained the symptoms of alcoholism, and I identified with practically all of them. I answered the list of twenty questions, which were to dictate if you were an alcoholic. I was told if I answered yes to three or more, I was probably an alcoholic. I said yes to seventeen and lied about two more. I had become unteachable. I couldn't keep a job (I didn't even want one) and had done nothing to accept responsibility for my life. It seems that all I wanted to do was drink, because not drinking hurt like hell. Then came the day in a group session where I cracked and choked out the words that little voice had been whispering to me for years, and the words I had been avoiding all my life, "My name is John, and I am an alcoholic." That moment my life changed. A weight had been lifted, and for the first time in my life, I felt like I could breathe.

We also studied the "Big Book" of AA, and I was only there a few days when I read these words:

> Selfishness—self-centeredness! That, we think, is the route of our troubles. Driven by a hundred forms of fear, self-delusion, self-seeking and self-pity we step on the toes of our fellows and they retaliate. Sometimes they hurt us, seemingly without provocation, but we invariably find that at some time in the past we have made decisions based on self that placed us in a position to be hurt.

> So our troubles, we think, are basically of our own making. They arise out of ourselves and the alcoholic is an extreme example of self-will run riot, though he usually doesn't think so. Above everything, we alcoholics must be rid of this selfishness. We must, or it kills us! God makes that possible. And there often seems no way of entirely getting rid of self without His aid. Many of us had moral and philosophical convictions galore, but we could not live up to them even though we would have liked to. Neither could we reduce our self-centeredness much by wishing or trying on our own power. We had to have God's help.

Suddenly Robyn's words made sense to me. "Doing something nice for someone else" stemmed from Robyn's knowledge that, as an alcoholic, my basic nature was to be selfish, and it is only through the desire to help others that I could find a path out of my disease. And when it came to making a fearless and thorough moral inventory of who and what I had become, I could clearly see that selfishness and self-centeredness was a huge piece of the puzzle. In fact, my reaction to Robyn's suggestion a year earlier was a perfect example of my selfish alcoholic thinking—"What about me? Am I not the victim here?"

I had always wanted to be a good father, son, brother, husband, and employee. But the fact was that once I put a drink in me, I had no idea what was going to happen. However, if I didn't drink, things weren't much better. I was a very angry man, with a very negative thought process. Without the numbing effects of alcohol, my mind would drift toward some ugly memory, usually the custody case, where I believed I had been victimized. I knew I had to get past the selfishness and the anger if I were to experience any peace in my life.

After leaving detox, my friend, Pam, took me to a couple of AA meetings, and I hated it. She introduced me to Dave, who had been sober for four years when he was released from prison and was now twenty years without a drink. He was a soft-spoken guy with a big grin, and the first time I met him, he said something that I really needed to hear and have never forgotten. "Kid," he said, "whatever you're thinking you're wrong."

I went to one or two AA meetings, but I failed to make the decision to do everything I could to maintain my sobriety. I had been sober a month, and I hated it. All those feelings I had drank to avoid were right at the surface, and the anger surrounding the custody case dominated my thought process. I wasn't as angry at Linda as I had been at her parents' involvement in the case. I believed that had they not become involved, the kids would have stayed living with me, and the world would have been as it should be. I had so much to learn and still believed that everything would be perfect if the world just learned to do everything my way.

My anger and resentment built up much quicker than any degree of real sobriety. I was a ticking time bomb, and finally one night the volcano erupted in an ugly and bitter argument with Linda. After that argument, I drank "at" her. The anger, resentment, and fear all slowly dissipated as the alcohol entered my system. I was at the end of my rope. I sat on my bar stool, knowing I couldn't continue to live like this, and yet I did not have the courage or the strength to deal with it. It was the uncertainty of life that seemed to baffle me the most. Drunk I understood, and I knew what my life would be like, but sober? What in the hell was going to happen to me if I was sober? Fear held me in its grip, and I ordered another shot.

The people in AA had told me that every relapse is planned, and, in hindsight, I agree. My drinking, I rationalized, would, therefore, be my ex-wife's fault. She was to blame, and I, once again, was the victim. I couldn't see how messed up my thought process was. I couldn't see that I was afraid of change and the life sobriety offered. I couldn't see how I had created the argument with Linda, which I used as an excuse to drink. There was so much I couldn't see, and alcohol seemed to have had a negative impact on my eyesight. Sobriety was foreign territory, and despite the fact that I knew drinking was going to kill me, it seemed much less painful than trying to live sober. The people in AA had told me I would arrive at the "jumping off place" where I couldn't imagine life either with, or without, alcohol, and I was now caught in that revolving door where I knew it was killing me, but I didn't think I could live without it.

I stayed pretty much drunk for the next six months. I rarely saw my kids and hid from those that loved me as it was common knowledge within the family that I had gone to detox and wasn't supposed to be drinking. I am not sure if I didn't want them to see me or if I didn't want to see them, but the result was the same. Every day I would wake up shaking and jittery, with the little voice inside me whispering relentlessly. I didn't care about anything other than finding enough to drink in an effort to calm the storm raging inside me. I couldn't see that I was drinking in an effort to change the way drinking made me feel. I couldn't see the insanity, but inside, deep inside, I knew that I couldn't go on for much longer.

Somewhere around mid-April 1993, Sherry, my sixteen-year-old daughter, told me she was pregnant, proving to me that the only thing that can provoke change, real positive change, is love. I drank for eight more days after I found out I was going to be a grandfather. For eight days, I twisted the facts of my existence round and round as I searched for an easier, softer way to deal with the mess my life had become. For eight days, I did everything to find a solution that would allow me to keep my best friend, alcohol, in my life.

As hard as my ego tried to defend my drinking, and my denial tried to make me look the other way, I knew the voice deep inside me spoke the truth. I knew I could no longer continue on the path I was on. I knew I was dying, and I knew I had so much to live for. I decided that if I was going to be a grandfather, I was going to be the best grandfather I could be. I had missed so much of my children's lives, and my sixteen-year-old daughter was handing me the key to unlock my insanity and put me on the path to recovery. I really did love my kids, and I had been such a selfish ass.

On April 25, 1993, I went back to the detox to inform the staff that they were right about everything they had attempted to teach me regarding the disease of alcoholism during my first visit. I told them that living my way did not work. Dave had been right when he told me, "Whatever you're thinking you're wrong." I needed somebody else to do my thinking for me because my way of thinking got me drunk, and I finally accepted the help I had been graciously offered. Weighed down by the pain of the years of drinking, I surrendered and I made a decision to do whatever the folks at the detox and the good people at AA suggested. Millions of others had changed their lives with the help of AA, why couldn't I? If they could find a way to live sober perhaps there was hope for me. I had nothing left to lose.

That was nineteen years ago, and my granddaughter, Delicia, has just started university. She is my angel. I know John Lennon was right—all we need is love!

What It's Like Now

When I first came to AA, I was told the only thing that has to change is everything. It seemed like a tall order, and I was overwhelmed. I was given all kinds of wonderful advice. "Don't worry about tomorrow, kid, because you only have to stay sober one day at a time, and any asshole can stay sober for one day," and then would come the grin. There was always the grin. They offered such supportive suggestions as "Stay away from the first drink, kid 'cause if you get hit by a train it isn't the caboose that kills you." They were all rocket scientists. "Asshole" was a term of endearment, and due to the frequent usage of the term, it was obvious these guys loved me a lot. Nobody shoved this thing down my throat. The men and women I met never pretended to be anything other than imperfect human beings. I had at one point thought that I was somehow mentally deficient to have found myself in a meeting of AA and was greatly relieved when Jack was kind enough to inform me that, "I have never met a stupid alcoholic. We may be a lot of things but stupid isn't one of them."

And one of the greatest gifts I received in those first few days in AA was the ability to laugh like I had never laughed before. And the laughter gave me something else that was new in my life: it gave me hope.

Today, as I survey the past, I realize the only thing that has changed is everything. Nineteen years later, they still love me; either that or they have a new term of endearment and didn't inform me. There are moments when I find it almost impossible to believe that I am still the same person, who stumbled around a ditch desperately searching for a mouthful of warm, skunky beer. I have been given a second life. The hole, the emptiness, which was revealed to me so clearly that morning as I watched Phil Donahue, has been filled by living a spiritual life as suggested by the fellowship of the AA. I love my life.

To live according to the Twelve Steps means I have recognized that my way of living did not work and, as a result, I became willing to change. It means striving on a daily basis to do the next right thing. It means living with gratitude. It means becoming open-minded enough to honestly look at myself and finding enough humility to see, and admit where I make mistakes. It means listening to, and honoring, that little voice inside me. It means being of service to my fellow man. It means stopping my selfish attempts at manipulating and controlling everything in my world in an attempt to indulge my ego, which could never be satisfied as it has never known the meaning of enough. When I drank, there was never enough booze, or money, or sex, or (fill in the blank), and the harder I tried to control my world, the more out of control it became.

Our stories continually speak of our imperfection and the mistakes we made. When we share our stories, we allow others to identify, not only with our pain, but also with our solutions. There are many stories of hope and courage. A few nights ago, a frightened young lady sat in our meeting and told us she had just finished a month long stay in a drug and alcohol rehab facility. She told us she felt like she was standing on the edge of a cliff and couldn't go back to where she had come from, but was afraid to move forward. I spoke to her afterward as I could clearly relate to her predicament. You see, early in my sobriety, I had told an old timer in AA the exact same story. He suggested I step off the cliff and that the people in AA would catch me. I was terrified of drinking, and I knew things had to change. I needed to trust, and I didn't know how. But I stepped off that cliff. And, as a result, the only thing that's changed in my life is everything.

I have travelled a great deal in the process of writing this book and have met hundreds of people. Many do not wish to discuss the issue of peace. Some blame others and angrily defend our military actions. Like an alcoholic recklessly spending the rent money, I listen to people rationalize and justify our government's actions in the world. Most people, regardless of their opinion, have no idea or are unwillingly to acknowledge the truth in who we are and what we have become. Others admit to feeling helpless, because it is too painful to look at the truth. They live in denial and often admit to looking the other way while burying their heads in the sand. I understand because writing my story, seeing my truth, is the most difficult aspect of my work here. It hurts to look. It is a painful exercise. It is much easier for me to point out where others have been at fault as my ego steps in to defend my actions. It is much more convenient for me to rationalize and justify my behavior than it is to see the truth. But the truth is I abandoned my children. I hit women. I didn't pay bills. I stole from my friends and my family. I would not accept the responsibility for many of the things I did, and for the things I failed to do. I lied, cheated, and conned people all in an effort to get my way. I was selfish, self-centered, greedy, and full of fear.

By shining a light on my painful past, I also see the great gift I have been given. I have been given the gift of choice. I can acknowledge my shortcomings and learn from them. I do not have to repeat them. I do not have to drink. I do not have to lie, cheat, or steal. I do not have to kill. I do not have to keep repeating the same mistakes over and over. I can be responsible. I can be of service to my fellow man regardless of his religion, ethnicity, or economic background. I can change as millions have changed already. I can choose to gratefully follow in their footsteps. My story is painful, but I can change. And if I can change, you can change.

Together, we can change our communities, our countries, and our world. And we can live in peace.

Step One

Admitted we were powerless over war and violence and our lives had become unmanageable.

Focus on the Principle of Truth

Here is the truth: It matters, what you do at war. It matters more than you ever want to know. Because countries, like people, have collective consciences and memories and souls, and the violence we deliver in the name of our nation is pooled like sickly tar at the bottom of who we are. The soldiers who don't die for us come home again. They bring with them the killers they became on our national behalf, and sit with their polluted memories and broken emotions in our homes and schools and temples. We may wish it were not so, but action amounts to identity. We become what we do. You can tell yourself all the stories you want, but you can't leave your actions over there. You can't build a wall and expect to live on the other side of memory. All of that poison seeps back into our soil.
Every Man In This Village is a Liar, p. 51

—Megan K. Stack

I have read these words from Megan Stack a hundred times, and I have come to see the parallels between my alcoholism, and the war and violence, which have become prevalent in our society. You see as an alcoholic I lived with my "polluted memories". I know, deep down in my soul that "we become what we do." I understand completely that, "you can't build a wall and expect to live on the other side of memory." Looking the other way, or trying to justify the actions that we take, as an individual, or as a nation, has little effect. You cannot erase your past. You must live with yourself.

In order to change, we must find a way to accept and forgive ourselves for the reality of who we are, and what we have done, to prevent the "poison from seeping back into our souls." Of course, before we can resolve anything, we must determine what the problem is, and we embark on a voyage of discovery in an effort to learn the truth about who we are.

Many alcoholics struggle with the guilt they carry regarding what they have done or failed to do, throughout the course of their lives. As alcoholics, we lied and offered rationalizations in an effort to justify our insane behavior, just as the perpetrators of war work at lying and rationalizing in their efforts to conceal their true motives and to justify their actions. As a society, we rationalize and justify our need for war. Most of us, knowing what we know today, would not have supported the Vietnam War. Most of us, knowing what we know today, would not have supported the Gulf War of 1990-91, the invasion of Afghanistan in 2001, or the Iraq Invasion in 2003. It seems only in hindsight do we draw the conclusion that war is a bad idea. In the moment, like an alcoholic in the middle of a spree, we charge into battle, despite being armed with the knowledge, deep down inside, that our behavior is severely flawed. No alcoholic in the middle of a drunk ever swears to never drink again. Remorse, we learn, comes later, after the damage is done; but for now we pursue our insane behavior with no regard for the outcome.

The gift of my alcoholism is that I ultimately had to face the fact that my drinking was going to kill me. I arrived at a place where I could no longer hide behind my ego and had to face the truth: my world was being destroyed by my own actions. I could no longer blame anyone or everyone else. My biggest problem was the guy staring back at me in the mirror. Had I somehow continued to avoid facing this fact, there is a good chance I would be sitting God knows where, reasonably incoherent, with today's favorite bartender, and you would be spared this rant. I hope you are half as joyful at seeing these words as I am in writing them.

For years, the still, small voice from deep within my soul spoke to me, and I knew it spoke the truth. "You have to stop drinking," it would whisper, "This is killing you." It was like a small dog scratching at the door. At first I could hardly hear it, and if I busied myself doing something else, it went away entirely. That "something else" was usually more drinking. Over the course of many years, my drinking increased in magnitude, and so did the dog. I arrived at the point where it took more and more alcohol to silence the dog who had grown to the point where he was about to tear the door off its hinges if I didn't let him in. Things needed to change.

Nothing in this world terrified me more than quitting drinking. My life was reasonably predictable when I was drinking. I had no idea what a sober life would look like. The uncertainty overwhelmed me. But I knew it couldn't go on the way it had. I knew I was going to die and sobriety appeared to be only marginally more attractive choice than dying drunk.

One of the first lessons in sobriety was learning to be responsible for myself. I had either avoided, or shirked, responsibility for my thoughts and actions for most of my life. I had blamed others or had simply walked away when things became too difficult. I carried a great deal of fear and trusted no one. Today I look at things much differently. Today I recognize *we are what we do* and if I am going to be happy, joyous, and free, my thoughts and my actions must be free of selfishness, dishonesty, and resentments. To prevent a return to the insane behavior guaranteed by my drinking, I had to become aware of what made me tick; I had to know the truth about me, and I had to develop a sincere willingness to change those things in me that did not serve a positive purpose.

In much the same way, I view the gift of living in a democracy where I have the right to have my voice heard. However, in order to make the decisions regarding what is best for my country, and my world, I need to know the truth. Lying to ourselves may serve an immediate purpose, but over the long haul, the baggage of deceit becomes too heavy. The stories we have been told must match. The pieces to the puzzle must fit. As a nation *we are what we do*, and I need to know what we have done. In a democracy, it is not only my right to have my voice heard, but also my responsibility to speak up. This responsibility cannot be taken lightly. I must be aware of what our governments and corporations have done in the past so my thoughts can be shaped for the future. I must ask myself how we arrived at our current position. When we are lost, we need to discover where we are, and how did we get here.

If we are to change our world, we must find the courage to do so. While our society commends individuals for acts of courage and bravery, no single person represents courage more to me than an alcoholic coming to his first meeting of AA. It means he has tried to see past his ego in an effort to take a hard, long look at himself. He has come to see the truth about who and what he really is. It means in his loneliness, he has considered every conceivable escape, including suicide, in an effort to go on. It means, regardless of circumstances, he knows he must change if he wishes to survive. He is at the end of his rope. He is desperate.

As a society are we desperate enough to change? How much longer can we keep going down the road we are on?

In April 2005, I accepted a position in Yemen. It was my first trip to the Middle East, and due to the aftermath of 9/11 and the Iraq invasion, I was extremely nervous about the venture. To further complicate matters, the airline I was booked on deposited me in Sana'a, Yemen's capital, a full twenty-four hours behind schedule. Totally exhausted, I was cleared by Yemen Immigration and then raced to catch my next and last flight, which would take me into Mukullah. From there, it would be a two-hour drive into the desert, and I arrived at my destination a complete and thorough wreck. It had been, without question, the worst trip of my life.

In hindsight, and in addition to the trip itself, there were some other factors that contributed to my anxiety. Late flights and missed connections definitely played a part, but in the weeks to come, I discovered a sense of fear that had become ingrained deep within me. This fear most certainly contributed to my sense of anxiety. As the days passed, I came to see this fear had nothing to do with anything else other than the fact that I was now in the Middle East. So why did I have it? Where did this fear come from?

I had always been proud of the fact that I tried to stay up-to-date on current affairs. International studies and history had been my favorite classes in university, and I had become a bit of a media junkie. I had always believed that the world's problems would be much easier dealt with if people would only educate themselves regarding what was going on around them, and this was accomplished by staying informed. As I searched my soul, I discovered that my fear, fostered in post 9/11 North America, stemmed from a belief that all the people in the Middle East hated all of us in Western society. I had heard the president tell us "You're either with us or against us" and in the vacuum of my ignorance, the message had taken root. The message, largely due to its constant repetition, had been pounded into me by the media sources in North America, and I am embarrassed to admit it, but I had bought it hook, line, and sinker.

However, in my defense, there was little opportunity to hear the other side of the equation. Therefore, if I was ignorant regarding the thoughts and feelings of many people in the Middle East, I was not alone. This fact was explored in a hilarious demonstration when Stephen Colbert hosted the Whitehouse Correspondence dinner in April 2006. At one point,

Colbert offered his congratulations to the six hundred journalists present for doing a great job of telling both sides of the story, "the President's side and the Vice-President's side." I think it is significant, with Bush and their employers looking on, few of the journalists in attendance laughed, and I wondered if Colbert's shot had landed too close to the truth.

What I discovered in Yemen, despite having tremendous oil reserves, was the people were dirt poor and uneducated. I slowly began to see that most of them were decent people and simply wanted to keep a roof over their head and to feed their children. While there may have existed a small percentage of extremists, who would have wished me dead, the majority were good people, who had no intention of doing me or my colleagues any harm. The greatest threat to my safety had nothing to do with politics, but stemmed from the basic fact that as a Caucasian from North America I was much more valuable as a hostage. If there were to be an act of aggression, it would likely be rooted in economics not terrorism.

In my discussions with the local men, I learned that many of them went to the mosque five times a day, and the politics of the day were occasionally part of their religious teachings as it had been for centuries. Being largely uneducated, the masses had historically relied on their religious leaders to provide them with the news of the day and some kind of direction in their lives. The messages they kept receiving, over and over, were that those in the west were infidels. That message had been repeated for centuries, and it was all they knew. Little had changed in Yemen since Moses, and it is possible the same message may have been delivered by the Mullah at the mosque since the crusades. Regardless of the accuracy of the information provided, they, like me, were receiving only one side of the story.

As I began to understand how they thought, and why they thought the way they did, I began to ask myself the same questions. What information were my opinions based on? Despite the fact that we live in what we call a "free society," it immediately became evident that the intense fear I carried with me to Yemen stemmed from a thought process that was programmed by the information I had digested. My "mosque" and the source of the information I had been inundated with was the mass media in North America. The people of Yemen went to the mosque and received their political propaganda, and I turned on CNN. They had no doubt received as much factual information regarding western society from their information source as I had regarding their way of life from my media sources. As I began to see and understand the situation, my fears gradually subsided. These people had a lot more in common with us than CNN or

FOX would have ever given them credit for, and I started to pay attention. I began to question everything I was being told by our governments and media. I worked hard at setting my cynicism aside, and, in an attempt to separate fact from fiction, I relied heavily on the standard axiom of "follow the money". As a result I would learn a great deal and much of it wasn't pleasant.

Fear is a strong motivator, and I asked myself if the general public would be willing to part with billions of their tax dollars if they were not very afraid, regardless of whether that fear is real or imagined? Of course, if the people in Yemen, Iraq, and Afghanistan were portrayed as decent citizens of the world, we would question military invasions and the billions of dollars in expenditures, wouldn't we? I began to wonder why our media rarely informed us of the deaths of innocent people in the countries we invade. Why did we only hear one side of the story? If the mainstream media is not telling us both sides of the story, are they actually involved in perpetuating the fear, which makes us so willing to put our country in economic jeopardy? For example, ask yourself if the media attempted to discover the truth about weapons of mass destruction, or were they more intent on passing along the notion that those weapons and the fear associated with them, actually existed?

This perspective was driven home while I was in Afghanistan in 2009. Upon my meeting a journalist with the BBC, I immediately asked, "When is the media going to start telling people the truth?" "I work for BBC radio," he snapped, "shut your fucking television off!" I laughed and at the same time was grateful to hear his candid perspective. However, as the death toll among young soldiers and innocent Afghan citizens rose, another question rose to the surface: Who benefits by not telling people the truth?

Turn on the evening news on any given night and listen, really listen to what we are being told. Try with all your humanity and compassion to feel how the people in the midst of the stories we are being told feel. Can you imagine how the mother of the two little girls who were taken by their father and murdered feels? How do the mother and wife of a twenty-two-year-old soldier feel upon receiving news of his death? How do the friends and family feel after a drone attack has killed a dozen Pakistanis attending a wedding? How does the woman next door feel after being beaten by her husband in a drunken rage? How does the high school girl feel after going to a party only to be drugged and raped? How does the Afghan family feel after their unarmed fifteen-year-old son is killed for nothing more than sport by a patrol of American soldiers? Are you capable of achieving a level of empathy where you can grasp even a remote sense of their level of pain?

Have we become "comfortably numb" as Pink Floyd might suggest? Have we, as a society, become numb to the pain in our homes, communities, countries, and our world? Is the level of violence the average citizen is exposed to on a daily basis of such a degree that we can no longer identify with, or even care about, our neighbor's pain? Have we, like a drunk numbed out and unable to feel after years of daily drinking, lost our ability to empathize with our fellow man? Are we addicted to violence or do we simply no longer care?

Tucson Congresswoman Gabrielle Giffords miraculously survived being shot in the head by twenty-two-year-old gunman Jared Loughner. He killed six others, including nine-year-old Christina Green, while wounding twelve more. What is interesting about this situation is the public's response to it! Despite all the statistics that indicate you are 20-30percent more likely to be shot and killed if you are carrying a gun, sales of guns saw an immediate 60percent increase in the aftermath of the Tucson shooting. To my way of thinking that is like trying to sober up a drunk by buying him a bottle of bourbon.

I do not wish to be involved in any "right-to-bear-arms" discussion any more than I would suggest that alcohol should be banned. People need to be free to make choices regarding what is best for them, and I support their rights to make those choices. The point I am trying to make is that our attitude, our thought process, regarding violence is reflected in the statistics. We deal with violence by reacting with violence. Is it working? Of course, we have the right to protect ourselves. But we have only to look at history to understand that, as a society, we keep repeating the same mistakes over and over expecting different results. As a recovering alcoholic, I responded to life's difficulties by drinking and was told by the good people in AA that one of the definitions of insanity was doing the same thing over and over expecting different results. So when we know that reacting violently in response to violence rarely has a positive outcome why do we insist, as individuals, communities and countries to continue down that path? Why do we, as individuals living in a free society, where we can exercise free will, continue to make choices with violent outcomes?

So are we addicted to violence? Have we gone numb to the war and violence in this world in much the same way an alcoholic becomes numb as booze takes over his life? Have we gone numb as gangs infiltrate our schools and communities? Living out of fear we buy more guns, bar all our windows, and instruct our children to never open the door or answer the phone. Giving each other the finger on our freeways has become insignificant when compared to the shots that get traded on our way home at the end of a long workday. Can you feel the love? Is this the world you want?

As an alcoholic, I developed an alcoholic thought process. As a result of years of drinking and without realizing it, I slowly became negative and fearful. In order for me to live a happy, productive, and peaceful life, my thought process needed to change. In order to change, I needed to become open-minded enough to listen to what other people had to say. Within a few months, I discovered, not only could I live without alcohol, but also I could love my life without alcohol. I changed. It didn't happen overnight, and today, most of what I need to learn comes from developing a sincere willingness to change and a willingness to listen. In order to survive, I had to give up the idea that my way was right. In exchange, I have been given a great life and a host of new friends, and I am no longer afraid.

Today, there are almost seven billion people on this planet and enough nuclear weapons to destroy ourselves a hundred times over. Throughout the course of history mankind has had the dubious luxury of killing each other off without the threat of extinction. However, today I ask you if we can continue down the same path previous generations have travelled down? Or do we need to change how we think about violence? Perhaps you are one who believes a leopard can't change his spots? Perhaps you think that violence is a basic human behavior that can't be changed. If so, set this book aside and continue on your journey. But I believe we must, and can, change. I believe change is possible because I have seen thousands who have stepped away from death and destruction into a life of hope and peace. I am one of them. I have come to believe.

In his books *Confessions of an Economic Hit Man* and *Hoodwinked,* John Perkins provides a very concise and accurate history of corporate America's involvement in America's foreign policy. I have traveled to many of the countries where Perkins himself was involved with America's takeover of the economies of third-world countries. He was on the coercive cutting edge of globalization, and his books reveal his remorse at the environmental and social costs inflicted upon much of the world so American corporations could profit. Perkins provides an easy-to-understand account of how the system works. While it may appear on the ledgers that the American government is assisting developing nations, the truth is the funds tagged as foreign aid often end up in the accounts of major corporations closely connected to the government, regardless of whether it is a Republican or Democrat administration.

Step One asks us to determine if we are powerless over war and violence and if it is making our lives unmanageable. My research and my extensive travel to numerous countries around the world have opened my eyes. It appears to me that there is more than enough in this world for everyone if those in control are tempted to share. Billions of dollars in oil revenue have been pumped out of the ground in Yemen as locals are paid one dollar a day to dig ditches, often in their bare feet. In Ecuador and Columbia, resistance to oil companies who have destroyed agricultural lands and polluted rivers has been met with military action and assassinations.

An act of violence is preceded by the thought of violence. In 1968, civil rights leader Martin Luther King was killed while trying to end racial discrimination in America. Forty-three years later, in May 2011, I had the opportunity to visit Houston, Texas, for the first time. I arrived on a Sunday night and rented a car. I promptly found a radio station that played great classic rock. The next morning, I hopped in the car to head to my first meeting, and the three people on the morning show began talking about returning to a bar on the weekend they used to visit occasionally. "The place has gone to hell," one of them lamented. "The NWA has taken over. You all know what the NWA stands for folks? WA means 'with attitude' and we all know what the 'N' stands for." I reached over and shut the radio off. My first thought was that most of the DJ's who were on the radio when this music was first aired were preaching love, peace, and an end to war. I wondered about Rodney King and the beating he took at the hands of the LAPD. I wondered if all the good work of Martin Luther King Jr. and others like him had been all for naught. I wondered what direction we, as a society, were going in. Had someone turned the clock back fifty years? And I wondered if this version of "freedom and democracy" is working.

In the spring of 2011, I was in Atlanta having coffee with my dear friend, Anita, who, by the grace of God, has over twenty years without putting a drink or a drug in her system. We were discussing the events in Egypt as thousands of people marched in Tahrir Square in Cairo. What impressed us both was the crowd stopping en masse to pray and Anita said, "The world really needs what we have." I understood immediately what she meant. At the time I had been writing something in a parallel vein, but my work took on a new meaning in that moment as Peace Anonymous and *The Twelve Steps to Peace* were born.

I do not believe in coincidences. As I look back over the past several years, I am impressed by the dozens of people who I have mysteriously crossed paths with and who have inadvertently contributed to this book: military personnel on leave in Thailand, reporters who have stayed at the same hotels, defense contractors who have shared a seat beside me on planes, and, perhaps fittingly, many of my best sources I have met at meetings of AA around the world.

One of the first conversations I had with my children after I quit drinking focused on the principles of love and respect. I told them that many people in our society have been raised with the concept of loving and respecting their parents, and it has become something they have been taught they "should" do. However, in the light of my actions over the course of a decade, I did not feel I had earned my children's love and did not deserve their respect. Love and respect cannot be demanded or coerced; they must be given freely or they are of no value. Most of us have been taught to be patriotic and to love one's country, no matter what. Does that mean we look the other way when problems arise? Does it mean we do not accept responsibility for the damage we have done and the people who have died as we build our empires? "You can't build a wall and expect to live on the other side of memory." We are as sick as our secrets. Have we blindly accepted an attitude of patriotism and love of country, or has our country, exemplified by the actions of its leadership, actually earned our love and respect?

Many of us, as Jack Nicholson so aptly stated in *A Few Good Men*, can't handle the truth! Many of us find it much easier to look the other way and sit in the local coffee shop bitching about those, "Damn Muslims" or the "NWA". Step One is the realization that we cannot continue down the road we are on. Step One asks me, as an individual, to search my soul and ask if the current values and principles at work in our society are acceptable to me. Step One is about accepting my responsibility in the democracy that I live in and to know the truth regarding the actions of my government, at home and around the world. Step One is about being open-minded enough to accept what I find in my search, regardless of how ugly that truth may be.

Recognizing people's disdain for coercion and arm twisting AA adopted, as their approach to spreading their message, the concept of "attraction rather than promotion." People cannot be forced to change, and the goal in AA is to adopt a manner of living that creates peace and happiness. How can we possibly achieve a goal of peace through control or force? Guided by a sincere desire to change and shaped by the principles of honesty, open-mindedness, willingness, and love, millions of alcoholics have changed their lives. Setting aside our learned behaviors, we ask ourselves if there is not a better way. Can this work for you? Can this work for all of us?

If you are open-minded and "can handle the truth," I suggest you pick a spot and dive in. I would suggest reading *Confessions of an Economic Hit Man* and *Hoodwinked* by John Perkins to whet your appetite. I also suggest you check out *Democracy Now, Reader Supported News*, and *Truthout,* which are all online news web sites. Chris Hedges is a Pulitzer Prize winning writer who offers great insight, and Noam Chomsky has written numerous books and is one of the world's most widely quoted contemporary thinkers. These are places to begin with and I also encourage talking to others and developing an open-minded approach while listening to others, whom you may have in the past not necessarily agreed with. We have much to learn from each other and no individual is all right or all wrong, while in the same vein, no political system is all right, or all wrong. The world is getting more crowded and much smaller. If we are to live together, is the development of patience and tolerance goals worthy of our focus?

I also encourage you *not* to believe a single word you read in this book or in any book or website suggested here. You are an intelligent human being, and I encourage you to make up your own mind regarding what is the truth? Sift through the information and all the varied opinions. If you listen to your heart you will find what rings true for you. Travel to the Middle East or Latin America. Go to Cuba. Castro is no saint, but ask the older people in Cuba what life was like under Batista, and you may understand why the Cuban people embraced change in 1957. Ask the people in Columbia, Chile, and Honduras about American interference in their political systems. Do not allow yourself to be heavily influenced by FOX or CNN or any other single media source. My experience tells me you will not get an accurate account in the mainstream media. Do not rely solely on Bush's or Obama's perspective. Do not begrudge those who have done their homework. Listen to them. Honesty, open-mindedness, and a willingness to learn will serve you well if you have the courage to look and understand what we have become. But more important than asking others is asking ourselves the tough questions. Ask yourself why countries which are endowed with significant natural resources have such high levels of poverty and ask yourself where their wealth went? Ask yourself why we have war and who benefits? It is your right as a human being to question everything. And, in your search for the truth remember, above all else: follow the money! There are no coincidences.

Step One asks some tough questions: Do we need to change? Can we continue to live in a world of escalating war and violence? Are we numb to the violence in our world? Are we addicted to violence as a method of resolving our differences? Am I powerless over war and violence and is this making our world unmanageable? Is there a better way?

By myself I am powerless. But I am not alone. There are millions of people who were once as bewildered as I, and together we were able to change. The steps I followed in order to experience changes of mammoth proportion in my life were the same steps taken by millions of people who had gone before me. I had nothing left to lose. I knew things could not continue the way they had in the past. I surrendered and discovered a life beyond my wildest dreams. And I found peace.

Things can change. History does not have to repeat itself. I am living proof.

STEP TWO

**Came to believe that a Power greater than ourselves
could restore us to sanity.**

Focus on the Principle of Faith

For so many years, I prayed, "God, this is Edwene. I'm right
here. Just tell me what you want—anything—and I'll do it.
Whatever you want, I'll be there. I'm right behind you, ready to
go—just give me a sign."

Well, finally I got quiet enough, and I heard God. And what
I heard was, "Edwene, this is God. I'm right here. Just tell me
what you want—anything—and I'll do it. Whatever you want,
I'll be there . . ."

The Four Spiritual Laws of Prosperity A Simple Guide to
Unlimited Abundance

—Edwene Gaines

Then comes a thought that is like A Voice. "Who are you to say
there is no God?" It rings in my head. I can't get rid of it.
—Our Southern Friend from the Big Book of AA

During my first visit to the local detox center I had identified with the
majority of the symptoms pertaining to alcoholism. But despite knowing
alcohol was a problem in my life I had gone back to my old ways. My return
to the detox for my second visit was a humbling experience. Alcohol was
killing me, and I could no longer delude myself regarding who and what I

was. I had to accept the facts; I didn't want to be, but, I was an alcoholic. Besides, if I were to become the world's greatest grandpa, I needed help.

As I walked through the door, Ken took one look at me and asked, "What happened to you?" "I had a fight with my ex-wife," I replied. "You sure showed her, didn't you?" Ken flashed a grin; you know that grin. However, Ken's simple questions illuminated the darkness in which I lived, and perhaps I had learned a little during my first visit here; how could I blame my irrational behavior on someone else?

Step One, admitting that I had a problem and my life was unmanageable was finished, and so was I. I took a close look at my options, and my entire thirty-seven years of existence boiled down to one ultimate question: Did I want to live, or did I want to die? The choice was a lot harder than I'd like to remember. In that moment, sobering up seemed only slightly more appealing than continuing to drink. I was very fearful of the unknown and had no idea what would become of me if I found the courage to face the truth about my alcoholism. Becoming a grandpa swayed me: I chose life.

Despite suffering from very foggy thinking, Step Two generated some questions. What was this Power greater than ourselves thing all about? I also considered myself to be an intelligent, capable human being, and the thought of being insane may have been an issue for some of the others who really needed AA but not me. The rest of the world was a mess, but my ego still had me believing I had a firm grip on the reality. Such was the power of my denial and delusional thinking.

I was bewildered and confused by all this. Ken, without even discussing my thoughts and feelings on the matter, seemed to know the answers to my problems. He suggested I pray. I balked. "Pray to what?" I asked. "Just go pray," he said, "You'll figure it out." I had no concept of what to pray to. My ego tried to step in and tell me real men didn't do stuff like this. I realized it had only been a couple of days since I had fallen off the merry-go-round and, I then remembered, my way didn't work. When I thought I knew the answers, I ended up in detox. I had hit the end of my rope, and perhaps I had more to learn. (In hindsight, I laugh as I had so much more to learn, and still do.) My life was unmanageable as Step One had pointed out and if two to three million people had changed their lives by adopting this lifestyle what did I have to lose? How could I argue? What other choice did I have?

I considered what I knew about religion. Despite being raised by Christian parents, I had also studied a great deal of history and understood the impact religion had in the world of politics and economics. I struggled with its controlling influences. I considered Buddhists, Muslims, Jews, and Christians and wondered who was right and who was wrong? With all these questions rolling around in my head, I knew one simple truth; I was an alcoholic and didn't want to drink anymore. I needed to change. I was desperate. And, in my desperation, I gave some serious consideration to the possibility that perhaps I was wrong about all things spiritual. I had no idea what I was doing but decided to give this prayer thing an honest effort.

My mornings began with me filling up a coffee cup and heading past the detox clientele to the backyard where I would plant my ass on the back steps and watch the sun come up. My prayers began in a confused manner. But within a couple of days, I came to see and believe was that there was a simple rhythm in this world that was undeniable. The sun rose every day at a predictable time. The birds went south and then came back. It seemed man screwed much of the workings of the world up, but if I could take man's impact out of the picture, the entire planet began to resemble a big, beautiful Swiss watch with every part working in conjunction with the next part. There existed a precision I had never been still enough to really notice before, and it was toward this Power that coordinated, so brilliantly, the movements of the world, I directed my first prayers. "Please," I asked the Power that made the sun come up every day, "take away my compulsion to drink alcohol."

And I asked, and I asked, and I asked.

Every morning for ten days I asked. I asked through the course of the day, and I asked when I went to bed at night. I went to programming and learned a great deal regarding my addictive behaviors and how my thought process contributed to my drinking. When programming was over, I asked this Power to take away my desire to drink. My kids would come for a visit, and after they left, I would ask this Power to help keep me sober. I wanted to change. I wanted to be the father I had never been, and the grandfather I hoped I could be, so I asked, again and again. My way did not work, and so I asked the Power of the universe to restore me to sanity and to take away my compulsion to drink.

Despite having met very few people in AA, I knew they had something I wanted and needed. As I prayed and got to know some of these people, my concept of a Higher Power began to evolve. I started to wonder if the collective consciousness of the millions of people, who had learned to live happy, sober lives, could represent a Power greater than me. Was it possible for the membership of AA to represent a Higher Power? The answer to that question seemed obvious. There were millions of them who had resolved the drink issue, and I was one single, solitary drunk. I considered the fact that it had only been a few weeks since I had been wandering around a ditch, looking for the leftovers of last night's beer? Yes, the collective consciousness of the people in AA definitely represented a Power greater than me. I wasn't sure if they had something I wanted, but I most certainly knew something had to change.

We did have a few people from AA come to speak to us at the detox center, and Dave, in particular, helped me tremendously in coming to terms with the question of my sanity. In speaking to our group, he said, "I have never met anyone so stupid that they could not grasp the very simple concepts of change as presented by AA, but I have met a few who were too smart to figure it out." I had always been proud of being a relatively intelligent human being, but Dave explained that intelligence may be detrimental to positive changes in our lives. It was, after all, a simple program. Spirituality couldn't be scientifically analyzed, only experienced. To some intelligence implies self-reliance, but if we were to arrest our alcoholism, we had to be willing to accept help from others and a Higher Power. "Whatever you're thinking, you're wrong," Dave informed me with a grin. I didn't think it was funny, but in hindsight, it was a very helpful suggestion. Its simplicity reminded me that my best thinking kept getting me drunk. It was also frequently suggested we get a sponsor to help us sort out the issues in our lives, which was an idea that appealed to me. After all, if my problems stemmed from how I thought, it only made sense to have someone I could rely on to bounce my thoughts off and help me sort out my life.

It was necessary to see we were part of a larger community and we were not alone. In addition, by relying totally on our own intelligence, we simply reinforced the selfish behavior, which contributed to our misguided thoughts and actions. By relying on our individual brainpower, which is often reflected in our egos, we resist the suggestions of others, especially if we are sensitive to the subject matter of the discussion, which in this case was my sanity. Despite being armed with the knowledge that alcohol was having a very negative impact on my life, I continued to drink heavily. I had to accept that somewhere along the way my thinking had become flawed, which is a fact no human being really wants to embrace. But how else could I explain drinking the house payment, the car payment, the grocery money, and the thirty-seven dollars stashed away in the savings account? How could I explain a couple of nights in jail, hitting ditches while driving drunk, a series of relationships which ended in disasters, and numerous job losses. How else could I come to terms with my disappearing for a decade and abandoning my responsibilities as a father? The list was long and painful. I could no longer hide behind my denial. The fact was staring me in the face—when it came to alcohol I was insane. Getting honors marks in university did nothing to alter the fact that once I started to drink, I had no idea what was going to happen or how long it was going to happen for. There had been moments when I had thought so highly of myself, but the truth was that without a drink in my hand, I didn't know me at all. Who was I really? There was only one way to find out.

Through this process, my ego was being crushed. It was painful to realize that much of what I had thought was unrealistic, selfish, or simply fantasy. I was nursing resentments that were decades old. I was angry, confused, and bewildered. But according to the staff at the detox, I was pretty much an average, run-of-the-mill alcoholic who suffered from selfish, self-centered, alcoholic thinking. I thought I was always right. I thought the rest of the world would be much better off if they did things my way.

I learned that my selfishness and self-centeredness were the root of my trouble. I learned, that as a practicing alcoholic, the anger and resentments that I had carried for years, and had not resolved, would never be resolved if I continued to drink and left unchecked would only drive me back to the bottle. I also learned that for an alcoholic, our maturing process is debilitated and, as a result, alcoholics behave and act childishly. "You are a long way off your path, and it will be a long way back," Ken said. It was a simple statement which spoke to the depth of the despair that I felt when I looked at the wreckage of my past.

I had drunk for years to numb the pain in my life. In the coming days, I was told a lot of things, and I listened. "Doing the same things over and over expecting different results is insane." Or, "it takes a different kind of thinking to solve the problem than the kind of thinking that caused the problem." As I seriously considered the information I was being provided, information which only a few short days ago I would have been insulted to listen to, my ego began to crack and my mind was opening to the truth. The light was beginning to shine in.

Many alcoholics are extremely creative, which is evident in some of the schemes they concocted in order to simply survive the insanity created by their drinking. Every action in my life prior to my arrival in AA was not insane. In fact, I had excelled in certain aspects of my career and in university. I had been a good athlete, and at least my intentions had been good as a husband and a father. The truth is I hid behind my meager successes, and part of my justification for my drinking, both to myself, and when necessary, to others, was based on the fact that I could hold myself up to the world and show everybody that I was cool, successful, or at least talented. My ego took shape, and the "me" I showed the world was quite different from the frightened little boy I was when I was alone with myself. I had to be seen as being in control and having my life "together". As my disease took root, I fell apart on the inside, and I began to descend into full-blown alcoholism. The descent was gradual, and I could not see the insanity of it all. My ego told me I had been a good father, a good employee, and a good student and all of the problems in my life were the fault of others. This supported my denial and prevented me from seeing the truth. The fact that I had convinced myself I was capable and successful prevented me from seeing the cracks, which began to appear in my character. My successes fed my ego and gave me an opportunity to tune out that little voice which continued to whisper I had to quit drinking, and that many of my thoughts and actions were, in fact, insane. Outside, in front of the world, I pretended to be a success, while inside, void of spirit and like a soul-less Rome, I rotted.

So what does all this have to do with war and violence? Despite knowing my drinking was causing all kinds of heartache and was not a positive force in my life I continued to drink. In much the same way, despite being armed with the knowledge of the pain and suffering which will result, we continue, as a culture, to embrace war and violence. Is this insane? Are we addicted to violence? Are we addicted to war?

If so, what are the parameters used to define insanity regarding violence? Is insanity based on the nature of the violent act committed? Is assaulting your spouse in a drunken rage insane, or is it acceptable, depending on the details? Is rape under certain circumstances acceptable and reasonable? Is a Wall Street banker insane when he knowingly invests his client's money in "shitty" investments for the sole purpose of obtaining a commission? Is a brawl at a hockey game an insane act or is it simply the nature of hockey? Is spanking your child an act of insanity? Is insanity based on the number of people you hurt or kill? Or is it based on your method of killing? Perhaps it is the motive for killing that defines the mental status of the perpetrator? Were Charles Manson and Jeffrey Dalmer insane when they committed the atrocities they were incarcerated for? Were Eric Harris and Dylan Klebold insane when they went on their killing spree at Columbine High School in Colorado? Was Jared Loughner insane at the time of his deplorable actions at the Tucson shopping center? Is an eighteen-year-old in combat fatigues insane when he kills the enemy? Is the same eighteen-year-old soldier insane when he kills a defenseless Afghan kid working in a field, simply for sport? Are his commanding officers insane for covering it up? Is the person controlling the drone off his rocker when the unit he controls takes out an innocent wedding party? What are the rules for taking the life of another human being? Is it acceptable if the killing is in self-defense? Is it acceptable for us to invade another country in an effort to gain control of their natural resources so a small group can appreciate huge profits? If that is acceptable then surely it must be acceptable for me, as an individual, to rob a convenience store at gunpoint with the hope of personal gain? Where is the line between "right" behavior and insanity?

Perhaps, if there is a political or military agenda attached, the definition of insanity is based on which side of the agenda your political allegiance resides? Does it make a difference if it is the act of an individual, a group, or an army that determines if an act is insane? I think there would be wide-spread support if we suggested that Idi Amin, Hitler, Pol Pot, Saddam Hussein, and Joseph Stalin were insane. Now how about George W. Bush? Wow, that gets a different response, doesn't it? I heard many of you throw up your hands and lament, "Now, you've gone too far, how can Bush be included on that list?" But I am only asking the question, and what is important here is that we ask ourselves under what parameters do we define our and our society's behaviors. And by what parameters do we judge others? Why is killing of innocent civilians acceptable under an American administration and a deplorable act of terrorism under another? And who determines which regime is deplorable? What makes one person or group guilty of insane behavior and the next one is perfectly acceptable? We label the impoverished fifteen-year-old Palestinian kid, who straps a bomb to his ass and blows up a bus, a coward and a terrorist. In the same breath, we refer to the F-18 pilot, who, with the squeeze of a trigger destroys a defenseless Afghan village as a hero who has sacrificed for his country. Have our levels of acceptance regarding violence changed in the past decade? Is applause regarding state executions acceptable? Are we more tolerant of extreme violence or have we merely become numb and slipped into denial? Is our tolerance of the wholesale death and violence in Afghanistan or Iraq any less insane than it was by the German people, regarding the Nazi atrocities during World War II?

The point of this exercise is quite simple. I was not willing to change my life until I could clearly see that my behavior was insane. Despite the warning signs, until my insanity became unavoidably obvious, why change? While the opinions of others may have planted a seed, I was never going to change my life until I could recognize for myself that I had become a victim of my own delusional and insane thought process. And as wrong as the rest of the world may have been on a number of questions I had to take responsibility for my own thoughts and my actions. I couldn't blame anyone else for my behavior.

The definition of insanity may be different for each and every one of us. But there are numerous questions we can ask the little voice deep within us, regarding our own behavior. Are we not also obligated as members of our society, citizens, or our country, and occupants of the planet in general to make decisions that will have a positive impact on future generations? Are we not all morally obligated to do the right thing? Or do we somehow believe we still have time?

It is not my place to tell you what is insane or what isn't. You must search your own soul and answer those questions for yourself. I believe, and practically all of us would agree, that as an individual, a community, and a country, we have the right and obligation to protect ourselves against violence inflicted upon us by others. We need a police force and a justice system. And we need a military to protect us from the aggression of others. We need to be safe and secure and to not protect ourselves would be equally insane. It then becomes a question of balance and good judgment.

Exactly where does defending ourselves cross the line and our actions become acts of aggression and insanity? When does the right to carry a gun in order to protect ourselves outweigh the safety of the many innocent people we cross paths with on a daily basis? How does defending ourselves and our borders from the aggression of others morph into our invasion of other countries? Despite all the evidence to the contrary where does the idea come from that buying a gun will protect me? I could follow that logic and assume it is a reasonable decision for me to pack around a bottle of bourbon with me everywhere I go just in case I need it. But why would I "need" it when I know the damage it causes in my world? And why would I pick up a gun knowing the damage they cause in my world? Why would I risk destroying my life or the life of another human being? I have come to the conclusion that if I don't buy alcohol or carry alcohol the chances of someone, including myself, getting hurt decrease dramatically. It wasn't always like that, but my thinking has changed and I have come to believe that a Power greater than myself has helped me make that change.

Ask yourself if your actions are insane? Are they creating a positive influence in your relationships with others? Will striking out in anger be a positive act or an act of insanity? If doing the same thing over and over again expecting different results is insane, and one of the basic fundamentals defining addiction, then why do we keep going to war over and over again? Looking at the futility of war is there even such a thing as a "sane" war? If not, why do we continue to support leaders who take us there?

Step Two suggests I "come to believe that a Power greater than ourselves could restore us to sanity". What I do know today, without a single shred of doubt, is that, as a result of Step Two, I have come to experience being restored to a much saner way of life than I ever imagined. Today the emptiness I felt when I watched Phil Donahue that morning so long ago has been filled with faith. I have faith in my friends in AA, and I have faith in this great friend I sometimes call God and sometimes call George.

Can God restore the world to sanity? I don't know. I do know there are three million people who have been restored to sanity. I do know it works like nothing else in the world. Maybe, just maybe, if we as individuals can see our insanity and find enough willingness to ask God for help we may be able to find the peace many of us are looking for. If enough of us ask Him, often enough, it might change the world. We have a choice: continue as we are, hoping that the thinking which caused the problem can somehow solve the problem, or we can seek a spiritual solution that has proven itself capable of significant changes in the hearts and minds of millions of people.

God, as I understand Him, has become a great friend in my world. My God isn't Christian, Jewish, or Muslim. He does not preside over war or football games (although I do think He leans toward the Steelers.) But He has changed my life. It has been over nineteen years since my daughter came to tell me she was pregnant, and I returned to the detox center where Ken suggested I pray. Desperate, I asked and asked for the obsession for alcohol to be taken away. On day number ten, I walked out the gate of that detox. I was full of fear and had no idea what was going to happen to me. As the gate "clanked" shut behind me a feeling I will never forget came over me and the little voice from deep inside whispered, "You will never have to drink again."

I entered the detox with nothing, and I left with everything. Are you willing to believe? Can you believe that there is a solution? Can you believe that peace is achievable? Is this the world you want? If we continue in this direction what will be the result? The prognosis is not good. Based on the direction, my life was going many years ago I was faced with a choice—did I want to live, or did I want to die? Do we change now, or are you not desperate enough yet? The answers to those questions will be waiting for you when the time is right.

Stories like mine are not uncommon in the rooms of AA. We hear stories of desperation and miracles, every day. Bill Wilson, one of AA's founders, in telling his story stated, "Thus I was convinced that God is concerned with us humans when we want Him enough." In our desperation, we were forced to look for solutions, which we would never have considered until we had exhausted every other possibility. People say there are no atheists in fox holes, and it is only in our most desperate moments that we become willing to look at options we would not have otherwise considered. Are we desperate enough yet? Or do we somehow believe we still have time?

God has been referred to in AA circles as an acronym for "group of drunks" or, my favorite, the "gift of desperation." It was obvious I was desperate enough and the certainty of an alcoholic death didn't really appeal to me. However, what did appeal to me was the idea of becoming the best grandpa the world had ever seen. My granddaughter is beautiful. You should see her new puppy.

STEP THREE

**Made a decision to turn our will and our lives
over to the care of God *as we understood Him*.**

Focus on the Principle of Surrender

Surrender doesn't mean you give up. It means you just stop
fighting.

—Sign in an AA Clubroom

I had fought everything and everyone in my efforts to avoid dealing with the destructive nature of my drinking, and it wasn't easy to face the truth and admit I had become my own worst enemy. I was destroying myself, and I was also damaging my relationships with those I love. It became obvious that to continue on my selfish, ego-driven path meant death. The revelation that I had arrived at this juncture in my life, solely as a result of my own thoughts and actions, did not please me. As I surveyed my world, it was indeed humbling to accept that my best efforts had brought me to this place in life.

However, there was, I was told, a solution. I had followed Ken's suggestion, and praying had proven to be a positive experience so I decided to continue to do what was suggested by the people in AA. If my thought process was flawed, I would let them do my thinking for me. My way didn't work, and the people in AA seemed to have the solution I was looking for. Therefore, in an effort to change, I decided to allow this Power greater than myself, as revealed through the collective consciousness of the good people in AA, to be my guide. It was suggested I let go of my need to control things and let the people in AA do what they do best—help drunks like me. And I decided, I would give it an honest effort. It would prove to be the smartest decision I had ever made.

In order to change I had to accept that left to my own devices, I was powerless as described in Step One. I couldn't argue with this fact as I had come to realize I could no longer blame others for my insane actions. If my thought process was the problem, I could clearly understand that utilizing a different thought process, from a Power outside of myself, would be required to do my thinking for me. It only made sense that a different kind of thinking would be required to solve the problem, than the kind of thinking which had caused the problem.

In Step Two, it is suggested I develop a faith in some kind of Power greater than myself, which would relieve me of my insanely destructive thoughts and behaviors, and replace the negative behavior with a more positive approach to living. The people in AA obviously understood my problem, and I had to conclude that through this faith millions had acquired what I so desperately needed. If it worked for them why would it not work for me? I had nothing more left to lose.

Step Three was now asking me to make a decision and invite my new manager into my life. My experience with the gate was still fresh in my mind. "There are two things you need to remember." one old timer mused, "One, there is a God, and two, you're not it." All I had to do was look at the results I had obtained by doing things my way to conclude the old timer was right. Motivated by selfishness, my life had become a disaster. With me in control, I had most certainly made a mess of things. Perhaps God should be the one in charge.

Given that my new manager was God, *as I understood Him,* it meant that I could choose my own concept of God, a God personal to me. I could see that creating positive change would not be easy if my idea of God was that of a vengeful God who would strike me down for the smallest of sins. The suggestion was made that I consider a Higher Power who was kind and loving. Why not make it a God of forgiveness? Why not a God who wants us to be happy, joyous, and free? Why not a God who embraces peace? Why not a God we can ask to fill our hearts with the desire for peace, rather than a God we ask for victory in war? How could a kind and loving God even begin to support war? How could God choose to favor one of His children over another? Each morning, if I ask my kind and loving God to please show me what good I can do in the world the chances are pretty good I won't consider killing anyone.

Another valuable suggestion from the people in AA was to learn everything I could about spirituality in an effort to build this relationship with God. Many in organized religions look to the church's leadership to tell them what and how to believe. While I viewed organized religion as being responsible for at least some of the problems in the world, I had to confess there had also been a great deal of good as a result. One crusty old timer in AA sarcastically mentioned, "Perhaps the greatest gift of organized religion was building all of them churches so we could have AA meetings in the basements." I was told nothing is all good or all bad, and it was suggested that I keep an open-mind in my search and grab on to whatever works for me. The rest I could let go of and perhaps it will be of benefit to others.

AA suggested direct communication with this Higher Power. Prayer and meditation were strongly encouraged, and I spent a great deal of time taking long walks with my dad's delusional springer spaniel. My life had been like a hurricane of insanity, and the walks helped me as I was learning to be still. I prayed as I walked, and if I paid attention, I would hear what I needed to hear. I knew the small voice inside me had tried in vain for many years to guide me away from the insanity of drinking, and I had been unwilling to listen. My God used many other sources. A song on the radio would trigger my emotions, and I would see an event of my past in a different light. A book I needed to read would be offered on loan. Or a movie would hit me in a way it never could have in the past. However, most often what I needed to hear would be offered by someone at an AA meeting or at coffee after the meetings. The void inside me slowly began to fill as the answers I was looking for began to simply "appear" as a direct result of my sincere desire to change.

I read a lot of books on spirituality and, in particular, *Conversations with God* by Neale Donald Walsch opened my eyes. Walsch's approach made sense to me, and I came to believe God comes to us in a number of different ways, and that He has a great sense of humor. There was no vengeful God whose wrath I would feel if I strayed from the path. There was no hell, other than the one that had come out of the bottle and lived in my own mind. Everything I had ever thought about God before coming to AA began to change, and I began to find some peace.

I believe the greatest gift of AA was the encouragement I received in developing a personal relationship with God, *as I understood Him.* Unencumbered by religious dogma or peer pressure, I have a choice in what

I believe, which I find is not only more fulfilling, but it invites me to be a willing participant in my own spirituality and to become truly involved. Shakespeare wrote "To Thine Own Self Be True," and those words are inscribed on the medallions given out in AA when sobriety anniversaries are celebrated. I believe my goal in life is to become the person my soul, my God, wants me to be, and a clear picture of who I really was could not be obtained if my perspective was altered chemically.

Occasionally my relationship with my God reveals some discrepancies with our cultural views and laws. For example, we are all aware of the Ten Commandments, one of which is "Thou shall not kill". We are told we live in a Christian society, which abides by Christian values, and our politicians consistently offer Christian rhetoric when expressing our values as a culture. If we are so Christian it seems strange we have all this killing? Why do we have state-sanctioned executions? Why do we have wars? As a spiritual entity, when I ask my God about the correct approach to war I think of Muhammad Ali having the courage to not take the "step forward" when being inducted into the army to fight in a war that violated his principles. As a conscientious objector, Ali's courage to follow his inner voice and do what he believed was the right thing helped spark a generation to rise up in defiance of the American government and demand an end to the war in Vietnam.

Should we all, each and every one of us, not be conscientious in our life's decisions, especially those regarding the taking of another life? Who am I to condemn another man his right to believe as he will? When we talk about God and country, which comes first? Why would anyone assume the government has the authority to determine what my relationship to my God should look like? What if, when we speak of God and country, we realize Muhammad Ali's action were completely in line with his belief system? Who has the power to legislate the will of God, especially when it comes to a God of "my" understanding? Is it possible the government was wrong in their desire to control the actions of one man? And would the Vietnam War have even occurred if Ali's desire to truly listen and act according to his conscience was the acceptable practice of every responsible adult as opposed to following blindly in what history would write as a dark chapter in America's past.

What would be the result if our culture taught us to accept being personally and spiritually responsible to a kind and loving God, and to align our will and our actions with His? Would this be translated into a moral code where perhaps our focus shifted away from being so profit motivated to a focus more in harmony with simply doing the right thing for no other reason than because it is the right thing to do? Three million alcoholics changed due to a simple desire to stop drinking and to be of service to other human beings. As a result, they develop a manner of living which is not easy but is so much better than anything they had before, and they found peace in the process. We let go of our old ways of doing things, which damaged our lives and those of others, in order to grab on to a spiritual way of life and do the "next right thing". The proof is tangible, and if you asked any of those three million, I am sure you would hear the benefits of having a personal relationship with a Higher Power. The values and principles created by living according to God's will, not mine, have had a remarkable impact in my life, and I am incredibly grateful as a result.

As a society what are our values? Could a Wall Street banker knowingly sell "shitty" investments after sincerely asking God to guide him in an effort to be honest and of maximum service to his fellow man? Could a corporate CEO work in concert with politicians and knowingly, at taxpayer's expense, invade a country in an effort to reap huge personal financial gain, if he had to rely on God's blessing to do so? However, the best question to ask may be: Would the people, armed with the knowledge that they are ultimately responsible for the actions of their government, after searching their souls and asking their God for direction, tolerate a system that would allow these things to happen? Does your God, the same one you ask to look after your children, really want us to kill so a few can profit?

When our politicians speak of God and country, it often appears God enters into the equation only when it is politically or financially beneficial to the parties involved. It is as if God is kept waiting in the wings in case He is needed and only gets on stage when His presence is necessary to finalize the deal. I often wonder had the individuals involved embraced a sincere desire to be of service to their fellow man and invited God into the decision-making process on Wall Street, what would our economy look like today? Would we be in the mess we are in? Had we followed the direction of a kind and loving God would we have even considered invading Iraq? Would the people have stood for it? Would a kind and loving God have us take care of our poor and our sick? If we ask God to help us liberate Afghanistan, do we show up with guns, or do we show up with food, medicine, and a desire to help?

Recently, I was on a small local bus on Grand Cayman Island where, within a week, five murders had taken place in the same small neighborhood. The victims, and the perpetrators, were all very young men and had grown up together. Despite knowing each other since they could crawl, they were now killing each other in a drug-related gang activity. The discussion on the bus focused on the violence and the helplessness many of the people felt, having known those involved their entire lives. There was, however, a woman from Texas who stated, "It's all in God's hands. He has a plan."

Many of us conveniently avoid the responsibility of looking at our world in such a manner. We see inequality, violence, and corruption, and look the other way. If it is God's responsibility to resolve the issue, then perhaps it is also reasonable to assume that God is responsible for creating the problem in the first place. But God wasn't killing those kids. Their actions were a result of their thought process, and it was their choice. And we all have a choice. While I may have been born with a genetic predisposition toward alcoholism, I am most certainly not going to throw my hands up in the air and suggest God poured that stuff down my throat. If I remember correctly, I was a very willing participant in those insane festivities.

What I do believe today is a Higher Power will help us make better decisions in our own lives, when we are willing to ask and are actually sincere about changing our current practices. Whether you are on your knees praying to a Christian God, walking through the forest talking to The Great Creator, seeking assistance from a group of AA members, or simply searching your own conscience, knowledge of the right thing to do will reveal itself. The answers will arrive if you are sincere and unselfish in your request.

My favorite AA bumper sticker reads "Shit Happens—So Does Miracles". There are some amazing miracles which have happened in my life as a result of the Twelve Steps of AA, and I consider my simply being alive to be one of them. In fact, the term "miracle" frequently gets tossed around the tables of AA, which may be why my friend Anita suggested the world needs what we, in AA, have. Doesn't the world need a miracle? If a belief, a faith in a Higher Power can impact the lives of three million drunks why will that Power not help you, if you sincerely open your heart to those possibilities? Can you imagine the kind of world we could have if a majority of the world's population started their day by seeking direction from a kind and loving God?

As I began working on this book, I was struck by the parallels in many areas between violence and alcoholism. The issue of control lies at the heart of both of them. An alcoholic works hard at hiding his drinking, often from his spouse and his boss. He knows there is something wrong but does not want to appear different. He attempts to control how he appears in public so people will not know of his drinking. He selfishly hoards his booze and controls the family's finances. In his selfishness, he attempts to control the lives of those around him to suit his wants and desires. When people resist, and they often do, he becomes angry and frustrated. If only people would do things his way, everything would be great. As an alcoholic, my need to control, in hindsight, was obvious. My ex-wife and a couple of girlfriends didn't see the need to conform to my control policies. The courts in my custody situation didn't go along with me either. And the police on more than one occasion thought their methods were superior to mine. Living my way did nothing but create chaos for me and those I professed to love. I had to give up control, and I had to surrender.

But isn't control what violence is all about? Whether it is domestic violence, or the invasion of another country, someone feels the need to exert control over another. We delude ourselves into believing that it is in the best interests of the people. For example, we were going to liberate the oppressed people of Iraq, but I most certainly didn't meet any Iraqis who felt "liberated" during my visit there. The Afghan people, after twenty years of fighting the Russians, have had an American led international force in their country for another decade. It adds up to thirty years of occupation for the Afghan people. The cost in human and financial terms has been enormous, and the Afghan people are not willing to submit to U.S. control any more than they were willing to submit to the Russians.

Alcoholics are also famous for their ability to deceive. When we were drinking, many of us were incapable of telling the truth and, even when the truth would not have altered the impact of our circumstances, we often chose to lie as a matter of habit. We would say anything that would justify or rationalize our usually hidden agenda. Nothing was sacred except having our selfish demands met. Think about the schoolyard bully who wants your kid's milk money. He may justify his actions because that is what somebody did to him. Think about the abusive husband who has convinced himself, that, had his wife only listened, she wouldn't have the black eye. Think about the number of lives lost and the huge cost to the taxpayers if we would have insisted on some real evidence, rather than the concocted stories regarding weapons of mass destruction and importing uranium for the purpose of manufacturing of nuclear weapons. What if, as a people, we asked our God if killing and controlling each other really is His will for us, or if perhaps, there is a better way? Trust me, He will answer if you stop what you're doing, become still, and really listen.

Despite what society, the president, or the media might have to tell us about what is good and right for us I have to make the decisions in my life based on how I think and feel. If the next-door neighbor tells me to pick up a drink, I am not going to listen. If the president tells me to pick up a drink, I am not going to listen. But what will I decide to do if the president tells me to pick up a gun, knowing I must accept the responsibility for the outcome of my actions. Deferring that responsibility to others or blaming others for the outcome of my decisions was also part of my insanity. I must be responsible for the thoughts and actions, or inactions, which affect my life and my world. Muhammad Ali understood this and must have spent a great deal of time searching inside himself for God's will, knowing he would be facing serious consequences for his actions. Ultimately he found the courage and the spiritual conviction to follow his inner voice, and in the process, he has earned the respect of many, while being vilified by a few. But Ali must have also known that his inner peace would have been jeopardized, had he not acted in concert with his soul. We are what we do, and Ali obviously valued being a man of peace.

We all have choices. Do we follow the mandates of our elected officials, who may have a personal motive for war, or do we search our souls and listen intently for the right answer to reveal itself? It is up to you. If, in moments of quiet reflection, you come to believe that the killing of others is the right thing to do, then you must live with the consequences of your actions. Or, as in Ali's case, he searched his soul and faced harsh public criticism and dire legal consequences for having the conviction to follow his inner voice, a decision he is no doubt grateful for today. Each situation may require serious contemplation based on its own circumstances. But ultimately we, as individuals, must accept responsibility for our own actions, and it is up to you to decide if you pay heed to the voice of your own soul, the rhetoric of our political leaders, or the guys down at the corner bar.

Despite our technical capabilities, which at first glance would suggest that as a culture we should be thriving, we are faced with innumerable problems in our world. Many are hungry, even though we have enough food. Many lack education despite the fact that we have the resources to provide all the children in the world with schooling. Over-population and the environment are high on the list of issues, which must be addressed. What would God have us do? What good can I do in the world today? Am I being selfish or do I have an honest desire to help others? Why is there no limit to defense budgets, while so few resources are made available to actually help those in need? What are my responsibilities as a citizen, not only of this country, but of this world?

What really prevents us from doing the right thing? Making a decision, to do as a kind and loving God would have you do, may be a start. It would be much easier if we could free ourselves of thought processes, behaviors, and painful experiences, which no longer serve a positive purpose. We might wish to take a hard look at ourselves in an effort to expose where we had gone wrong and develop a willingness to learn from our past mistakes. It is not an easy thing to do, but the lessons are invaluable. In fact, it is only when we conduct a fearless and moral inventory, and become willing to accept the truth about ourselves, is change really possible.

Step Four is next.

STEP FOUR

Made a searching and fearless moral inventory of ourselves.

Focus on the Principle of Honesty.

Having a heartfelt desire to kill another human being is not normal.

—Joyous James, Recovering Alcoholic and
twenty-year Military Veteran

We want to find exactly how, when, and where our natural desires have warped us. We wish to look squarely at the unhappiness this has caused others and ourselves. By discovering what our emotional deformities are, we can move toward their correction.

—Twelve Steps and Twelve Traditions

Note: Step Four has a tendency to evoke some powerful emotions and Steps Five through Nine are designed to help us deal with these emotions. I suggest that once you begin down the Step Four path, you make a conscious decision to proceed through to Step Nine as quickly as possible. I would also suggest the reader find others to either work through these steps with, or at least a trusting person to confide in. As you proceed, I ask you to have some courage to look honestly and objectively at yourself and the world we live in and have some faith that things can change for the better, because they can. We cannot solve our problems if we are reluctant to look at them, and perhaps our greatest lessons come from our willingness to look at ourselves and our world. After watching those in AA change during the past few years, I believe I can safely say that embracing our problems is much more beneficial than all attempts at avoiding them.

In addition, I also wish to point out that the goal here is not a political one. I don't think it matters if your perspective is liberal or conservative, left or right. What we are concerned with is searching our souls and discovering the truth regarding the world we live in, with a goal of making the decisions necessary to create a peaceful world. Those decisions can only be made by honestly, and objectively, looking at who we are, because, after all, we are what we do.

*

What do we mean when we talk of a "fearless and thorough moral inventory?"

The goal of a business manager when taking an inventory of his business is to develop a clear understanding of the circumstances which impact his business. It is only by conducting an honest and thorough inventory can he discover the truth regarding his operations. Any attempt at avoiding or denying the facts would render the inventory process pointless as he would be only fooling himself. Therefore, the only feasible approach is to conduct an honest and thorough appraisal of his stock-in-trade in an effort to learn everything possible regarding the status of his operations. Based on his discoveries, he will be able to see which aspects of the business are valuable, what needs to be changed and what the business would be better off without.

The goal of our conducting a searching and fearless moral inventory is very similar and is essentially a fact finding mission to discover what makes us tick. We are attempting to take an honest look at our behaviors and actions of the past to determine what characteristics in our make-up have served us well and what was detrimental. For people who are new to the fellowship of AA, nothing is more daunting than the prospects of conducting a fearless and thorough moral inventory. And experience has taught me nothing is more rewarding.

Alcoholics come from every conceivable economic, ethnic, and religious background, and we are people, who under most circumstances, would not have mixed. But it was our disease which brought us together, and in the process it was easy to see, despite our differences, how much we had in common. All of us, and I was no different, arrived at AA full of fear and shame. The concept of delving into our past and coming face to face with what we have done and who we have become is a challenge some can't cope with. Their inability to honestly look at themselves and accept what they find is too overwhelming, and many return to drinking, only to die from the disease of alcoholism. It takes courage to do Step Four.

The rooms of AA are full of people who have suffered childhood abandonment, sexual, and/or physical abuse. Many have come from alcoholic homes and are the result of generations of alcoholism. And many of us have lied, cheated, and stolen to feed our addictions. We have lost the trust of families and employers. "We become what we do," Megan Stack reminds us, and as we come out of the fog created by years of drinking, we must accept who and what we have become, regardless of how painful that process might be. Those things we would never want exposed to the world are the things, which will eventually poison our thoughts and drive us back to the bottle. We had to be free of the old way of thinking, and by taking an honest inventory we are able to see what is in our make-up that is valuable and what we need to change. We were full of fear, and we discover we are only as sick as our secrets. And I remember those intense feelings of loneliness and fear, but I also remember the feelings of hope as I looked around the rooms of AA with the realization that I was no longer alone. As uncomfortable and fearful as I was, I also knew the answers didn't come out of a bottle. "If we keep doing what we've been doing, we will keep getting what we've been getting," I was told. Therefore, I couldn't go back to drinking. The solution, my only viable option, was AA and the steps. So I did my best to set my fear aside and, renewing my commitment to become the world's greatest grandpa, I decided to forge ahead.

There were numerous items which gnawed at my soul and left me feeling deeply ashamed. The goal of Step Four is to bring these things to light, to put them on paper and look at them in an effort to understand them. When they are extracted from our hearts and minds and placed on a piece of paper in the light of day, our souls begin to heal. If we can make peace with the events of our past, then there is hope for the future. We are changing, and dragging around the sack of misery that fueled my drinking had no place in my life if I wished to be happy, joyous, and free in the future. I needed to go back through my life and face the painful circumstances that had created in me the need to drink. History, I was told, does not have to repeat itself.

This is not a superficial undertaking. We could not peel back the cover, take a peek inside, and be satisfied with the results. Like the businessman who cannot afford to fool himself regarding the values of his business, it is necessary to conduct a thorough accounting of our lives. The Big Book of Alcoholic Anonymous states, "Half measures availed us nothing," and nowhere was that statement of more value than when we arrived at Step Four.

One thing that became immediately obvious to me had been my propensity to blame others. It was easy to see how I would never assume the responsibility for my life if every problem was always someone else's fault. I was angry, and I blamed the courts, my ex-wife, teachers, parents, siblings, police, and employers, everybody but myself, for the circumstances I found myself in. The truth is life isn't always fair, but rather than simply accepting the fact that there were times when things did not go my way I immersed myself in a cocktail of resentment and self-pity, and I drank in an effort to deal with those feelings. Regardless of any injustices, which may have occurred in my life due to the actions of others, I had to learn to accept the responsibility for my reaction to those events. And my reaction to losing custody of my children was to run away from home and get drunk for a decade in an effort to kill the pain. My reaction to almost anything and everything painful was to drink. In hindsight, it seems extremely childish, but at that moment, the pain of these events was extremely real and overwhelming.

The death of my sister, however, was a different kettle of fish. I didn't blame others for her death. I blamed myself. The weight I carried as a result of her death fueled my drinking for years, and I will never forget my father looking me in the eye and asking the fateful question, "Why did you build the raft?"

I have carried that moment with me my entire life, and it was only in sobriety, courtesy of Step Four, that I have been given the tools and the ability to deal with that pain. As I looked back at my life, I could see that my drinking started shortly after the day my sister drowned. At the time, I thought drinking was a rite of passage, and I was drinking to party and have fun with my friends. But today I believe that once I experienced the pain-numbing effects of alcohol, I became, at least at an emotional level, someone other than the architect of Barb's death. I chose to circumvent the slow, natural, healing process with the more immediate method of dealing with my pain—by drowning Barb's memory in a reservoir of alcohol.

In addition, I didn't realize that many of the life decisions I would make in later years would be tempered by the events of that day and, of course, influenced by my drinking. Today, despite the fact I have been sober for nineteen years and my father has been dead for fifteen years, I realize that many of the choices I had made were not based on what was best for me but, instead, were decisions based on winning back my father's approval. I loved him and that day at the reservoir had placed a huge wall between him and me. I believe I had failed him in mammoth proportions by building the raft, and winning back his approval became paramount in my mind. The truth, revealed so obviously by Step Four, was my father lost two children that day—a daughter to the waters of the reservoir and a son to alcohol. My disappearance wasn't quite as obvious as it did not occur immediately, and, knowing my father, had either of us been able to realize the full impact his asking me "why I built the raft?" I am sure he would have forgiven me immediately. But that discussion, due to my drinking and an inability to see the reality of the situation in its proper perspective, never happened. I was two years sober when my father had a major stroke, and it has taken much longer for me to sift through the emotions and events of my sister's death. It was a big onion for me to peel, and I am still not sure if the job is finished, or if it ever will be. I do, however, find it much easier to live in peace today knowing I have done, or am at least willing to do, everything possible to resolve the issue rather than trying to bury it or drink it away.

The truth is that at thirteen I did what teenage boys all over the world do-I built a raft. Yes, my actions caused great pain, and I had feelings of immense guilt and shame. Even though it was over forty years ago, I still remember the days following Barb's death very clearly. I remember the emptiness, the hurt, and the overwhelming weight of simply being alive. I remember feeling responsible for the empty chair at the dinner table and the loss of someone who was deeply loved. I remember feeling responsible for my mother's pain and her sense of loss, which is still evident today.

And then I met alcohol, and all those feelings of guilt and remorse were numbed. The pain did not vanish entirely, but, at the very least, it was pushed deep down and out of sight. I went from feeling responsible for the most heinous of crimes to feeling like the life of the party, and who wouldn't want that? Alcohol became my coping mechanism, my medication, and my catalyst for healing. Even though I didn't realize it at the time, change was always my goal, and alcohol changed everything.

Of course, at thirteen, I didn't have the ability, or the desire, to see the truth. I couldn't see that the fun-loving party guy was really a wounded child who was only trying to cope with a very painful experience, and the alcohol induced state of euphoria was a mask, behind which that child hid.

The negative effects of alcohol in my life were almost immediate. The year following Barb's death, I had failing grades in school, and relationships with others were suddenly strained. I remember feeling empty and extremely lonely as I began to use alcohol to fill the hole in my life, a process which made me at least believe I was a complete human being. It worked almost instantly, and it continued to work, although I had to keep increasing the dosage, for a long, long time. And my rate of consumption would continue to increase because in the coming years, I would acquire more guilt, more shame, and more negative feelings, usually as a direct result of my behavior when I drank. The spiral down had begun.

While Barb's death was a very painful experience, my failure was not in building the raft, but in my inability to accept the responsibility for my reaction to the events of that day. Barb's death did not give me an excuse, drunk or sober, to behave in an unacceptable manner. It would have been easy to simply justify the exploits of the subsequent twenty-four years on Barb's death, but that would have been nothing more than a simple act of rationalization. How, in 1990, could I blame my inability to pay my bills or be a father to my children, on the events of a single day in 1969? I needed to go deeper. I needed to be fearless and thorough in cataloguing the events of my life in an effort to see exactly how my business of living had gone off-track. I needed to accept ownership of how I had lived, the things I had done, and the things that I had failed to do. I needed to see the flaws in my character in an effort to understand who and what I was. While my sister's death may have marked the point where I had gone off the path, I had over two decades of drinking to be held accountable for, and while the task was intimidating, Step Four would prove to be the one of the greatest things I could ever do for myself and for the people I loved.

As I worked on the step, I began to see my entire life resembled a mass of character defects. I was raging with anger and full of resentment. Dishonesty had run rampant in my life as I had lied, cheated, and stole from family and friends in order to drink. My thinking had been either grandiose, where in my mind I captained ventures which catapulted me into wealth and fame, or I had considered myself the lowest life form on the planet. I had no concept of humility and rarely, if ever, did I see myself as I truly was. In fact, without a drink in my hand, I had no idea who I truly was. I was full of fear largely due to the fact, as the Big Book points out, that "self-reliance had failed me," and as a result I had no faith or confidence in myself. And yet, through all this, I remained very judgmental and had all the correct opinions on every issue facing mankind. I thought

I knew all the answers to all the world's problems, and I strongly identified with the term "bankrupt idealist". And blocking my path, while defending all these character defects, was an ego wrapped in selfishness, which simply didn't want to give up center stage, much less admit to being wrong about anything. Thank God for pain.

It was painful, and humbling, to realize doing things my way had brought me to this point. The Big Book of AA states, "The first requirement is that we be convinced that any life run on self-will can hardly be a success." I had to admit I had worked very hard at trying to get the world to do things my way, and my way, motivated by selfishness and a need to control others, didn't work. As my ego began to crumble, the people in AA explained that I had been carrying these defects for a long time, and there was only one way to get rid of them. I had to document each one and accept the responsibility for my actions in conjunction with it. It did not matter what my ex-wife or an old boss had done to me. I had no control over them. There was only one person I could change, and that person was me. It was only when I had documented and accepted where my character defects had caused problems for others and myself, could I ask God to remove them. There was no guarantee they would be removed, and the only other option was to continue carrying the weight with the possibility that the burden would drive me back to the bottle. I reflected on my progress to this point and realized that God had already removed my obsession with alcohol. I had not had a drink for a few months, which I was very happy about, and any real desire to drink had been removed and no longer existed. Perhaps there was hope in the other areas of my life.

I, who had never experienced any kind of spiritual development, was now praying every day, for no other reason than it seemed to be working. The spiritual aspects I had been encouraged to grab onto were filling the vacuum created by the absence of alcohol, and based on everything that had happened thus far, I had no reason to doubt anything the people in AA had suggested. I struggled to find some courage and then picked up my pen and got down to business.

I listed the people, institutions, and organizations with which I had developed resentments. I examined each one in an effort to learn what had created the feelings of ill will. However, what was more difficult, and much more important, was the need for me to see, and accept, where I had been at fault. What had I done to add to the problem? What had been my motives? Had I approached situations with an attitude of mutual benefit and service to others, or had I been greedy and selfish? Did I have expectations of a particular outcome? Did I want everything to be my way, or had I willingly listened to the wants and needs of others?

As I considered the events of my past, the anger rose in my chest. The circumstances around the custody case had always provoked intense anger and a deep sense of betrayal. I had held Linda, my ex-wife, responsible, but I had also believed that there had been some kind of deal struck between Linda's father and my lawyer. I had never received a bill from my lawyer, which I considered an interesting fact. However, what was even more interesting was that Linda, in the years since we had been separated, had purchased two houses, and my original lawyer had handled the legal work on both purchases – for free! All this added to my sense of betrayal. Accepting that others had done me wrong, as they often had, was easy, but was I going to further complicate matters by drinking in an insane manner? How was that kind of reaction going to resolve anything?

My anger surrounding the custody issue had triggered my drinking in the past, and it frightened me. I had to be rid of these resentments or I was afraid I would get drunk. Someone in the fellowship pointed out to me a story in the back of AA's Big Book called *Freedom From Bondage* and suggested I read it. At one point, the woman who had written the story quoted a passage from a magazine which she had found beneficial in dealing with her resentments:

> "If you have a resentment you want to be free of, if you will pray for that person or that thing you resent, you will be free. If you will ask in prayer for everything you want for yourself to be given to them, you will be free. Ask for their health, their prosperity, their happiness, and you will be free. Even when you don't really want it for them and your prayers are only words and you don't mean it, go ahead and do it anyway. Do it every day for two weeks, and you will find you have come to mean it and you want it for them, and you will realize that where you used to feel bitterness and resentment and hatred, you now feel compassionate understanding and love."

A lump rose in my throat. I didn't want to drink anymore, but I didn't want to feel this intense rage inside me either. Ten years had passed since my children had gone to live with Linda, and there was nothing I could do to change that. Being drunk and angry was killing me, and some wise ass in an AA meeting stated, "My having a resentment was like me drinking

poison hoping to kill someone else." It was another analogy I couldn't argue
with, and I could clearly see how my anger was having a negative effect on
my life, whereas the people I was angry with were not only unaware of
the rage I carried, but also they simply didn't seem to care. So I got on my
knees and asked that Linda and my in-laws be given everything I wanted
for myself. I asked for their happiness, health, and prosperity. For the
record, I will state that I hated those initial attempts as they ran contrary
to everything I had ever thought or believed, but I really didn't want to
drink anymore so I prayed for my in-laws frequently. With each attempt,
it did get easier, and slowly I began to develop some sympathy for them
and could see that they, like me, were terribly defective human beings. I
arrived at the point where I asked myself, had I been in their shoes, would
I have done anything different? Two weeks later, the rage had dissipated
significantly. As my load lightened, I began to adopt a sense of forgiveness,
which was a much kinder feeling than the anger it had replaced. Once
again the solution to my problem had appeared courtesy of a suggestion
from someone in AA. The other aspect to this solution, which didn't go
unnoticed, was my inability to resolve the problem myself, and relief came
only after getting on my knees and asking God for help. I still had no idea
what this Power I was praying to looked like, or where it came from, but I
could no longer argue with the results.

As I documented the circumstances of my life, what was revealed to
me were the problems surrounding my relationships with other people. I
had spent two nights in jail on two separate occasions because of violent
behaviors involving relationships with women. I had been extremely drunk
on both occasions, which was no excuse, and I had to look at the underlying
thought process, which had caused my insane emotional behavior. I had to
look at the problems I had encountered at work where relationships with
co-workers and employers had gone off-track. The fact, which loomed large
and I could not deny, was that in every circumstance, which had caused
me grief, I had wanted to be in control. Despite the fact that I may have
had good intentions when I had demanded my way, others had retaliated,
often causing me a much greater sense of pain and anguish, to which my
reaction was to try harder. And the harder I tried, the worse the situation
became. "When you find yourself in a hole," I was told, "it might be wise
if you just stop digging?"

By the time I had sifted through the years of my drinking, I had drawn
some conclusions regarding my moral inventory. The truth was, and still
is, that I am a tremendously imperfect human being. I had demanded

perfection in others while failing miserably myself. There were countless situations where I had not been honest or responsible. I had been selfish and self-centered, and my drinking had prevented me from growing up on an emotional level. I had not always acted appropriately and with integrity. There were numerous instances in my life where I had lied in an effort to get my way, and there were numerous situations where I had failed to disclose an important piece of information, which would have profoundly changed the events of the moment. These acts of omission were as morally depraved as any lie or act I may have been responsible for. The fact is I had lived a life nearly void of any moral principles and had consistently blamed others in an effort to justify my actions. While my sister's death may have provided me with an understanding of why I had embraced alcohol, I also had to accept responsibility for all the actions, which had transpired since that time. I didn't want to drink the rent money, but I did. I didn't want to hit my girlfriend, but I did. I didn't want to disappear from my children's lives and get drunk for a decade, but I did. I didn't want to call my boss an asshole . . . well maybe I did, but I shouldn't have, and you see there is always room for improvement. It did, however, become clear to me we are what we do, and I was a selfish drunk who lied, cheated, stole, and used people, while shirking the responsibility for my actions.

I also came to see that I didn't want to be the person I had become. I wanted to be respected by my children. I didn't want to be selfish, and I wanted to contribute to society in a positive manner. If we are what we do, then perhaps if I did something different I would change and become the person I had always hoped to become.

The other major block in my life was fear. Fear gets a bad rap in our society. No man wants to admit being afraid, but each and every one of us, regardless of how big, wealthy, or strong we appear to be, suffers from this crippling emotion. It seems it is not the fear as much as our complete inability to acknowledge it. As a result, the fear gets the upper hand, and we would rather react in a drastic, violent, or negative manner than simply accept the fact and admit, even to ourselves, we are afraid. There is nothing more ego deflating than admitting we are afraid, which is perhaps why we do not want to do it. We have a perception that it is weak to be afraid, when the fact is we are simply acknowledging the truth. After years of listening to grown men being honest about their thoughts and feelings in AA, there is no doubt we all have a difficult time dealing with this emotion, and I wonder how many wars have been fought, how many people have died, due to fear-based reactions. Fear sells guns. Fear sells violence. While our leadership may be motivated by power or greed, it is fear, real or perceived, which motivates us to send our children off to war.

When I came to terms with who and what I had become by conducting a fearless and thorough moral inventory, I realized Ken had been right and, "I was a long way off my path." The fear I felt when I looked at the task in front of me was overwhelming. "We change, one day at a time," I was told. One day was all I had to focus on. I had to work on being honest, respectful, and living with integrity for only one day and then do it again tomorrow. And one day at a time for the past nineteen years, I have managed to do that. Some days it feels like I have made no progress, and other days I no longer recognize the alcoholic mug, staring back at me in the mirror. You see I still am an alcoholic. And I will always be. I can never delude myself regarding my human condition, and in asking God for help on a daily basis, I have been graced with a daily reprieve from my need to drink. It is only by trying to live by right principles can I maintain any kind of spiritual balance in my life. I recognize that dishonesty, fear, and resentment will have a negative impact on my spirituality and my sobriety and may lead me back to the bottle, which is no longer an option for me as I see quite clearly that for me, to drink is to die. I recognize I must at least try to meet God halfway if I am going to experience any hope of being happy, joyous, and free.

So exactly what does my illustrious drinking career have to do with peace?

The point is very simple, and it is all about change. When Sarah became sick and tired of my antics and walked out in disgust many years ago, she lamented, "A leopard can't change his spots!" Years later, when I was approximately fifteen years sober, I called her. I hadn't talked to her in years, and it was good to hear her voice. I reminded her of her statement, and then I asked her, "If I can't change my spots, what am I supposed to do with all these stripes?" You see I have changed. In fact, I can't believe I am the same person. The spots are nearly gone, and I have been given another life, a much different life, as a result of the Twelve Steps. My life, which was full of chaos, pain, and nights in jail, is over. I have been given a set of spiritual tools which have allowed me to change, and change at depth. And I am not alone. I am a member of my community and am committed to being of service to my fellow man. So you see the point of this entire exercise is simple: if I can change, so can you and so can our world. Today I belong to an organization, which has transformed millions of people whose lives were insane, often violent and chaotic. The world is screaming for a solution to peace, and we have been fortunate enough to have been given that gift.

However, here is the kicker. I needed to bottom out. I needed to arrive at a point in my life where I knew I could no longer live the way I had been living. I needed to want change so desperately that I would go to any length to get it. I had to grasp, deep in my soul, an understanding that I needed to change and that I could no longer continue living as I had been living. And in order to grab onto this new way of life I had to become willing to honestly look at who and what I was. I had to be willing to be fearless and thorough to discover exactly what made me tick.

So exactly how badly do you want peace? What motivates you? Are you more concerned about dividends than you are about peace? Are you capable of looking at your life and seeing past your ego to what your true values are? Are you selfish, greedy, controlling, and fearful? Do you rationalize and justify your acts of dishonesty? Are you honest in all of your affairs? Do you tell the truth? Do you delude yourself by believing if you keep your thoughts and actions a secret you are doing okay because you have not actually told a lie and therefore your actions are acceptable? Are you intent on judging and blaming others? Are you capable of looking inside yourself and coming to terms with exactly what you find?

As we make an effort to become responsible for the moral principles in our own lives I ask you to consider this: We live in what we wish to believe is a democracy. In a democracy, the people provide the voice which directs the country and the politicians are supposed to be servants of the people. Therefore, you, the people, are ultimately responsible for your government. If it is your responsibility, perhaps you might like to know what your government is doing out there in the world on your behalf? Is it acting responsibly? Is it conducting your business on the world stage in a manner, which reflects your values and makes you proud? Do you know? Is conducting a fearless and moral inventory to discover the truth regarding the actions of your government a worthwhile exercise? Is your government honest? Does it treat the citizens it is obligated to serve, and others, with respect? Does it function with integrity? Are you being lied to? Is the government stealing from you? Is your government obligated to do what is in the best interests of the people? If you are paying for this government do you believe you are entitled to know the truth?

Many people do not wish to look at the truth, and I understand it is not an easy thing to do. It is difficult to do a moral and fearless inventory, especially when we do not really want to know the truth. In the rooms of

AA, we refer to the practice of avoiding reality at all costs as "denial" and the basic characteristic of denial is that it has a shelf life. You can only pretend the problem doesn't exist for so long before it lands in your lap and demands your attention. It is similar to chronic alcoholism in that it does not solve itself and will only get worse until you decide to address it. There is no running away, so you either face the issues today or you will be forced to face them tomorrow. You cannot build a wall and live on the other side of it.

Part of my goal surrounding Step Four is to provide you with a few well-documented examples while encouraging you to do more, much more, of your own homework. Please do not take my word for anything. I have my own thoughts and opinions based on a great deal of reading and traveling, and my intent in Step Four is not to pass judgment on anything, or anyone. The goal is to make observations and see where our behaviors have added to the problem. While I can't do a thing about the actions of other countries, I do have a responsibility to know and direct what are our respective democracies are doing, especially if those actions are counter-productive in creating a peaceful world? I also believe it is truly important for each and every one of you to make your own observations and decide for yourself what you believe is the correct path for your country to follow. But in order to make informed choices, you must know the truth. If you are, as an individual, ultimately responsible for your government is it not realistic for you to be aware of how your government really functions? Is it not important to know what your government does and why?

If you wish to read an excellent example of a Step Four, I invite you to read *Confessions of an Economic Hit Man,* and the sequel, *Hoodwinked,* by John Perkins. These books were never intended to be a Step Four as described here, but what Perkins has achieved is an honest and revealing account of his involvement in implementing American foreign policy. He explains in simple, easy-to-understand detail, the truth of his involvement with American corporations, the American government, and international financial institutions who worked together with a goal of controlling the economies of many Third World countries. His accounts detail how the American government has been involved in overthrowing democratically elected governments and how the CIA has been involved in assassinations, usually with profit for corporations, and their shareholders as the only goal. What is, however, most impressive in Perkins' accounts is how he changed his life and became dedicated to creating positive change in the world. His work left Perkins with a troubled conscience, and he ultimately left his profitable career as an Economic Hit Man and is now an advocate for peace, social justice, and the environment. You see a leopard *can* change his spots, and Perkins is an example of the change, which is possible when we become informed and are willing to make different choices. But in order for us to change the direction western nations are heading, we must first become aware of who we are and what we have done. This requires some work. It requires an honest appraisal. It requires a thorough and fearless moral inventory. And it isn't pretty.

I have often heard business owners lament as to how they suffer sleepless nights, worrying about their business, the risk involved, and the welfare of their employees. For those reasons, if they become successful, they deserve to make a lot of money. Nobody here begrudges anyone a decent living. However, they seem to miss the fact that there are also millions of people all over the world who lay awake at night, wondering how they are going to feed, clothe, shelter, educate, and keep their children safe from the bombs being lobbed in their direction, and I rarely hear anyone being interviewed from the Harvard School of Business talk about their welfare. As well, before we go any further, I wish to state that there are a huge number of corporations which function with a reasonable degree of morality. Not all businesses and corporations are intent on war or destroying the environment. Not all corporations are involved in assassinations and overthrowing governments. While many on the current political scene may bash corporate America as being immoral that is not the intent here, but we do need to look at the truth. The world needs corporations, but the idea that the only thing corporations are obligated to do, at any cost, is provide a return on investment for shareholders *must* change. If peace is the goal, we, as citizens, must insure our governments and corporations be morally obligated in creating peace. If governments or corporations need to kill, steal, threaten, or coerce people in order to profit, then they have crossed the line. People must come before profit. And if you turn on the evening news and hear some kind of justification for the killing of people, primarily innocent people, I suggest you widen your search in an effort to obtain a more balanced perspective of the news. If people need to die in order for a corporation to make a profit, we may want to consider pressuring our government to stop doing business with that corporation. And if our government is working in concert with these corporations who dehumanize and kill, then we, who live in democracies, are obligated to pressure our governments to change. These are your governments, and you are responsible for them.

This takes us back into the realm of fear, and our world is immersed in it. I ask you this: Are you more willing as a taxpayer to see your tax dollar being spent to protect you, when there are explosions going off all around you? Would the American people have been willing to part with billions of dollars in tax money to invade Iraq, had 9/11 not happened? Did the fear created by 9/11 not also create the circumstances which allowed numerous, politically well-connected corporations, to partake in the spoils of war in Iraq? The average citizen would never have stood still for their tax dollars to be spent in the manner they were, had the people of America not feared for their safety. So is the fear real, or is it manufactured? Is it part of a propaganda campaign designed to free your money from your wallet? Do we create enemies so there is someone to buy our bombs? Perhaps, after all my traveling, I am being cynical, but just a few days ago, there were more people killed by bombs in Kabul, and my immediate gut reaction was that those responsible were the CIA, not the Taliban or Al-Queda. And, if I am cynical, I am cynical for one major reason: this business of war follows a pattern which has been well established over the course of the last few decades. The pattern has resulted in huge windfall profits for a very select group of people, who incidentally have expressed little loyalty or concern for people on either side of the ocean. You might also find the same people on the top of the campaign contributor's list for a significant number of our elected representatives as they seem to have a vested interest in who runs our governments. This is just an observation, and I encourage you to follow the money and prove me wrong. God, how I wish I were wrong.

The simple exercise of following the money will usually reveal all you need to know about the truth. And the truth is rarely discussed in the mainstream media. For example, the actions of Julian Asange, the founder of Wikileaks, have been scrutinized for months, and he has caused quite a stir in his desire to provide the people of the world with the truth. One would think in a democratic, open society, our governments and legal institutions would embrace the truth, but not so with Asange. Why not? Is it because Asange shines a light on a system many believe to be designed for the benefit of a few and at the expense of many? Much of what he offers reveals not only embarrassing information surrounding our corporate and government leaders but also potential information that could result in civil and/or criminal charges being brought against those in power. Many view the charges against Asange as an attempt to silence a man whose greatest crime may be knowing too many secrets, and I wonder if it is the truth, or the need to cover it up, which is the greatest concern to those in power. We are only as sick as our secrets.

As we honestly begin to delve deeper into our fearless and moral inventory, there are some concerns, which we need to address regarding how our society looks at problems. The propensity in our world to find one small issue with which to discredit an entire proposal is common and may be part of our denial. We discredit eight years of a presidency with a stain on a dress. We discredit a singer's entire life due to one single act of indiscretion. It works in the other direction as well, and for years, I tried to convince myself, because of an occasional good deed, my moral fiber was unquestionable, and this allowed my drunken behavior to continue. How often do we consider someone who gave millions to charity to be a person of good moral fiber, and we forget the damage he has done in accumulating the wealth? Is an axe murderer who contributes to the Boy Scouts a pillar of the community? You may wish to entirely discredit what is being said here, but does that not feed into the entire argument regarding our reluctance to honestly look at ourselves. "Identify, don't compare," the people of AA suggested. Instead of trying to discover where people who suggest our system is flawed are wrong, perhaps in an effort to make the world a better place, we may wish to hear them out. After all, if our system is so free and democratic, it should be quite capable of surviving the thorough scrutiny of its citizens.

The point is we, as individuals, honestly want to learn as much as we can about the government we are responsible for in an effort to have the best country imaginable for the sake of our children and our grandchildren. And we accomplish this not by discrediting, but by embracing the thoughts of all as we look for the grain of truth in what they have to offer. I too used to think I was always right until I realized that my alcoholism stemmed from a very warped thought process and not only my sobriety, but also my serenity, came only as a result of my willingness to listen to the thoughts of others and to see where they were right.

After being around for over seventy-five years, AA continues to suggest, and I concur, that alcoholism is a "spiritual malady". If alcoholism can be considered an insane condition which requires spiritual intervention, what can be said of war? If, at worst, alcoholism can be frowned on as something undesirable in our culture, how can we possibly embrace actions which result in the deaths of thousands of people all over the world, year in and year out? If we view addiction as being depraved, how can we possibly embrace war as something positive? Unless, of course, you follow the money!

The president may speak into the microphone and assure the people, "God is on our side." But I am not convinced God has anything to do with war, and I wonder if the action is not more akin to an alcoholic ego trying to justify some selfish, immoral action as opposed to doing God's good work. Simply watching recent headlines brings forth a stream of questions: How can we as a society consider debating the moral correctness of torture, abortion, or capital punishment at home while our armies are killing innocent people all over the world? How can you blindly consider war an act of patriotism without even reading a book in an attempt to discover the truth behind it all? Why do we, like sheep, believe what we are being told as we head off to war when we know, deep in our souls, that killing another human being is a soulless act of depravity and considered insane in almost all circumstances outside of self-defense? Why, in a society with all our technological capabilities, coupled with millions of people who have no desire to harm anyone, are we constantly at war? Why are we not thriving? What is in the water that creates our need to kill each other? What is the flaw in our character which creates this insane desire? Are we not addicted to the power of greed and control? Are we responding from our souls to the world's needs or do our reactions stem from our selfish, self-centered ego?

To exemplify this flaw, I will provide you with a few, well-documented cases, which can easily be verified. Please bear in mind that to do a thorough examination regarding the history of America's foreign policy would take volumes, and what is contained in these pages barely scratches the surface. There is so much more to learn, and similar discoveries can be obtained by a look at the history of any country, although the international implications will not compare to America's global influence. Again I wish to stress that this is not about passing judgment, and my only desire is to cast some light on a handful of situations from the past in order to illustrate a pattern as to just how we have arrived at our current place in history. Many of you may become upset and will be unable to grasp the reality here, and you may wish to discredit any or all of this. That is fine, and it only means we continue killing each other as we have for centuries and nothing changes. But haven't we evolved past that? Doesn't slipping into denial only defer the problem, and I ask you if it is better to face the truth now or wait until it demands your attention? The problem will not go away by itself. Our world will continue down the path it is on until the citizens decide it is time to set things right. You see, I believe we can change, and we can do it in peace if we act together. And we act now.

*

The Banana Massacre, which forms part of the backdrop in Gabriel Garcia Marquez's brilliant novel *One Hundred Years of Solitude,* occurred on December 06, 1928, in Cienga, Columbia. Employees of the United Fruit Company (UFC), at the time based in Cincinnati, had been on strike for a month. Their demands included an eight-hour, six-day work week and a written contract. The UFC petitioned the United-States government who threatened Columbia with invasion if the Columbian government did not protect the interests of the UFC. Bowing to pressure from the American government, the Columbian army set up machine guns at the corner of the square which was occupied by the strikers and opened fire. Reports of casualties range from 47 to 2,000 deaths. However, a telegram from US Bogotá Embassy to the US Secretary of State, dated December 29, 1928, stated between five and six hundred strikers and one soldier had died.[1]

While even one death is significant, the involvement of American fruit companies in South and Central America will continue to be an interesting focal point of American foreign policy.

*

One of the benefits of conducting an honest and fearless moral inventory is it discloses our humanity, and I begin to ask myself how I would feel if I were placed in a similar situation. The inventory assists in the development of empathy and an ability to identify with others. When I begin to accept the reality of my behavior, I begin to understand the reaction others may have to it. I have learned the hard way that mistreating others can result in decades, and, perhaps, a lifetime of mistrust and ill feelings.

The world reeled in 1979 when Mohammad Reza Pahlavi, the Shah of Iran, was forced into exile by the Ayatollah Khomeini during the Islamic Revolution. Khomeini was installed as the Supreme Leader of the Islamic Republic of Iran and was overwhelmingly supported in a national referendum by the Iranian people. A few months later, a group of Iranian students took US Embassy personnel hostage, labeling them CIA spies, and held 52 of them for 444 days. The hostage taking had not been approved

---

[1]   Wikipedia, The Banana Massacre, http://en.wikipedia.org/wiki/Banana_massacre

by Khomeini, but he did support it once the action had taken place. It was a precarious situation for many months, and the hostages were finally set free in January 1981.[2]

Today the political relationship with Iran is stressful. There is a great deal of saber rattling and talk of war, and President Mahmoud Ahmadinejad is accused of attempting to build nuclear weapons. An Iran with nuclear weapons is something the United States, and many other countries in the west, considers a serious threat, which, of course, it is. But the question looms large: Why do Iran and so many other countries in the Middle East, and around the world, have such a serious hatred of the United States?

My understanding of Iran's position has been clarified, *not condoned*, by simply understanding the events surrounding the CIA's overthrowing of Mohammed Mossadegh, Iran's democratically elected Prime Minister, in 1953. Mossadegh, who incidentally was Time's "Man of the Year" in 1951, promised the Iranian people a greater share of the revenue from the Iranian oil industry, which he subsequently nationalized. This action infuriated both the British and the Americans.

> After Mossadegh nationalized oil, the CIA's director, Allen Dulles, demanded action. However, because of Iran's proximity to the USSR, President Eisenhower ruled against risking a nuclear war by launching an invasion. Instead, a CIA agent named Kermit Roosevelt, Teddy's grandson, was dispatched with several million dollars. He hired a band of thugs to disrupt the country. Riots and violent demonstrations followed, creating the impression that Mossadegh was both unpopular and inept. In 1953 he was overthrown, imprisoned for a while, and then spent the rest of his life under house arrest. The CIA's Mohammad Reza Pahlavi, was brought in and crowned the Shahanshah ("King of Kings"). [3]

It was the first time the United States had overthrown a democratically elected government and in the process some lessons were learned.

> Washington learned that one man with a few million dollars could accomplish a task that previously had been left to armies and had cost billions. Roosevelt had transformed Iran into

---

[2]   Wikipeadia, Iran, (2) http://en.wikipedia.org/wiki/Iran

[3]   John Perkins, *Hoodwinked* (New York: Broadway Books, 2009) 40

a US puppet, and he had done it without risking a war with the Russians—or, for that matter, without most of the world, including U.S. citizens, having any notion that we had brought a democracy to its knees.[4]

The problem, of course, is that the situation did not remain a secret forever, and many in Iran and throughout the world deeply resented the American and British meddling in Iran's internal affairs. The situation engendered a lack of trust, which still exists today throughout all the Middle East. But when we are only aware of half the story, it is difficult to understand all the implications. The actions of the students who took innocent American Embassy employees hostage was a deplorable act and created a great deal of anger within America. It does, however, become much easier to understand why there exists so much animosity within Iran toward the United States when the American orchestrated coup is added to the mix. The 1953 coup which removed Mossadegh, a democratically elected leader, is a fact which I have never heard discussed by the media, despite all the rhetoric surrounding Iran's political agenda over the course of the last three decades. A willingness to honestly appraise the current political situation is incomplete without a thorough understanding of the CIA's involvement in Iran. The information does not make either side in the argument right or wrong, but the information provides clarity and understanding, which is necessary for peace to become a real possibility.

*

Having found a way to control Iran, and their oil resources, without having to invade was a feather in the cap for the CIA. It was also accomplished without incurring the wrath of the Russians who had emerged from the Second World War with nuclear capabilities. Iran, however, was only one country, and the American government was searching for ways to control the resources of the Third World without provoking the Soviets.

In *Confessions of an Economic Hit Man*, John Perkins goes into great detail to explain one of the methods utilized by the American government, in conjunction with American corporations, in securing the resources of many countries by simply controlling them economically. In the era following WW II, the Russians viewed many of the actions of the United

---

[4]   Perkins, *Hoodwinked*, 41

States in the international arena to be acts of aggression. To counter this, the American government secretly invited a few corporate leaders into the inner sanctum of the government to assist in covertly implementing foreign policy. This way, when the Russians questioned any particular actions, the government could point at the respective companies and absolve themselves of any responsibility. The concept and logic was sound; the only drawback was that it put the foxes in with the chickens.

After being interviewed by the National Security Agency, John Perkins was hired as Chief Economist by Chas. T. Main, Inc., in 1971. His major responsibility was to draft economic proposals, which would encourage resource rich, Third World governments, to assume significant debt in order to build infrastructure projects. Government leaders in these countries were interested in creating societies similar to those in the west. Power generation, roads, and water and sewer projects were viewed as advancement. The accuracy of Perkins' proposals was never questioned by the western financial institutions, and Perkins was encouraged by his superiors to make lofty and exaggerated predictions regarding increased GDP and ROI for these Third World countries.

The system worked well. For example, a government would receive a proposal from Perkins stating that if the government borrowed $4 billion from the International Monetary Fund (IMF) to build a power station and transmission system, the spin-off economic growth would be more than sufficient to repay the loan for the project. However, because the loan was guaranteed by an American bank, the work had to be done by American engineering and construction companies such as Bechtel, Stone and Webster, and General Electric, who amassed fortunes on these projects. Sooner or later the day always came, when the Third World government, which was supposed to benefit from the industrial growth in their country, came to the realization that the economic forecast provided by Perkins, or other Economic Hit Men had been exaggerated, and they could not repay the loan. The debt would then be used against them and leveraged to gain access to the wealth of natural resources their country had to offer. "Hmmm, you can't repay your loan? You have oil, don't you?" would be a typical response. The financial burden would be passed onto the already impoverished citizens of these Third World countries and, despite living in a country with huge natural wealth, so much of their economy would go to servicing the debt there would be no funds available for schools, health care, or housing. In addition, some of the funds provided for these projects would be entered into the books as "aid" for the country in question leading American citizens to conclude their government had conducted a benevolent act in order to assist those in less-developed nations, when, in fact, it would be American multinational corporations working in those countries who had received the funds.

Perkins writes:

> Economic hit men (EHMs) are highly paid professionals who cheat countries around the globe out of trillions of dollars. They funnel money from the World Bank, the U.S. Agency for International Development (USAID), and other foreign "aid" organizations into the coffers of huge corporations and the pockets of a few wealthy families who control the planet's natural resources. Their tools include fraudulent financial reports, rigged elections, payoffs, extortion, sex, and murder. They play a game as old as empire, but one that has taken on new and terrifying dimensions during this time of globalization.
>
> I should know; I was an EHM.[5]

Ecuador was a country which had been burdened with huge debt at the hands of the international banks, which had made great promises of economic prosperity for the nation. The country experienced a flurry of growth, but it seemed that multinational oil companies, engineering firms, and construction companies were enjoying the profits and the people of Ecuador were experiencing the debt.

Ecuador's debt had been incurred during the 1970s when Ecuador had been ruled by a military dictatorship friendly to American interests. The government changed in 1979 when Jamie Roldos, a charismatic lawyer and university professor, was democratically elected, and inaugurated as president. Roldos strongly supported the rights of the citizens of Ecuador and believed, with some merit, the people of Ecuador had been coerced into a bad deal, which he intended to set right. Roldos was not a communist but simply believed that it was the right of the people of Ecuador, as a free and sovereign nation, to chart their own course, free of outside influence. His objectives included obtaining a much greater share of Ecuador's oil

---

[5]   John Perkins, *Confessions of an Economic Hit Man* (san Francisco, Berrett-Koehler, 2004), 9

revenue for the benefit of the people, which meant he would have to go head to head with Texaco, the major player in Ecuador's oil industry.

By 1981, Roldos had presented the government of Ecuador with a new hydrocarbons law which, once passed, would redefine the relationship between foreign owned oil companies and the government of Ecuador. The law basically outlined the changes Roldos wanted, and in essence, it stated the citizens of Ecuador would come first in the development of Ecuador's oil industry. As the new law was being debated, but before it was passed, Roldos publicly informed all foreign interests that they would either comply with what was in the best interests of the people of Ecuador, or they could leave. On May 24, 1981, he left Quito for a small community in southern Ecuador and died when his plane crashed.

Roldos had been warned of a threat on his life and had employed the use of a decoy plane. One of his security advisors strongly recommended he use the decoy plane, which was the one that crashed. Newspapers and many international observers of the situation in Ecuador immediately blamed the CIA, although nothing was ever proven.

*

While Roldos had been trying to sort out the oil industry, his friend Omar Torrijos, the democratically elected president of Panama, had been busy sorting out issues surrounding the Canal Zone of Panama.

Like Roldos, Torrijos was a charismatic man who was well loved by the people of Panama. And like Roldos, Torrijos was not a communist, but he was intent on providing the people of Panama with an opportunity for economic self-determination, free from outside influence. For years, the people of Panama had sought the control of the Panama Canal, and in 1977, Torrijos had managed to negotiate a treaty with President Jimmy Carter, which would turn control of the Canal Zone over to the government of Panama. The people of Panama responded with the largest turnout in history as 96% of Panamanians turned out to vote in a referendum as the Carter—Torrijos Treaty was ratified.[6]

However, not everyone in Washington was happy with the treaty, especially in the Republican camp. Not only the canal, but the entire

---

[6]   Wikipedia, Torrijos-Carter Treaties, http://en.wikipedia.org/wiki/
      Torrijos%E2%80%93Carter_Treaties

Canal Zone, including the School of the Americas, which was a training center operated by the U.S. military, would revert to Panamanian control according to the terms of the treaty. The School of the Americas was an institution well-known within Latin America.

> These facilities were hated by Latin-Americans—except for the wealthy ones who benefitted from them. They were known to provide schooling for right-wing death squads and the torturers who had turned so many nations into totalitarian regimes. Torrijos made it clear that he did not want training centers located in Panama—and that he considered the Canal Zone to be within his borders. [7]

When Reagan won his bid for the presidency in 1980, one of his goals was to renegotiate the canal treaty, which Torrijos refused. On July 31, 1981, only weeks after Roldos' plane had crashed in Ecuador, Torrijos died in a very similar plane crash. Torrijos was replaced by a much more pliable General Manuel Noriega, who incidentally, was also a graduate of the School of the Americas.

In 1982, when Perkins had begun writing *Confessions of an Economic Hit Man,* many tried to convince him it would not be wise to continue. However, the following passage was written by Perkins at the beginning of those pages:

> The book was dedicated to the presidents of two countries, men who had been my clients, whom I had respected and thought of as kindred spirits—Jaime Roldos, president of Ecuador and Omar Torrijos, president of Panama. Both had just died in fiery plane crashes. Their deaths were not accidental. They were assassinated because they opposed the fraternity of corporate, government, and banking heads whose goal is global empire. We EHMs failed to bring Roldos and Torrijos around, and the other type of hit men, the CIA-sanctioned jackals who were always right behind us, stepped in.[8]

*

---

7   Perkins, *Confessions of an Economic Hit Man,* 89
8   Perkins, *Confessions of an Economic Hit Man,* 9

For much of the twentieth century, Chile was a model of a Latin American democracy. In 1975, the Church Report (a study of covert operations in Chile by the CIA and other U.S. government institutions) stated:

> Chile defies simplistic North American stereotypes of Latin America. With more than two-thirds of its population living in cities, and a 1970 per capita GNP of $760, Chile is one of the most urbanized and industrialized countries in Latin America. Nearly all of the Chilean population is literate.

When the 1970, presidential election took place the people of Chile elected Salvador Allende as their president. Allende won despite the *"extensive and continuous"* involvement of the CIA in Chile from 1963 through 1973. The 1970 election was Allende's fourth bid for the office, and he had become a well-known political figure throughout the country. So why was the United States so interested in Chile's political situation?[9]

Allende's previous campaigns had focused on land reform and the nationalization of major industries, in the center of which was Chile's copper mining industry. American mining companies, such as Anaconda and Kennecott, were raking in enormous profits, and Allende was seeking a redistribution of wealth.[10]

The 1964 election which was won by Eduardo Frei Montalva of the Christian Democrats as the American government, through the CIA, had paid for more than half of Frei's campaign in an effort to keep Allende from winning.[11]

But it was a different story in 1970 as no winner of an absolute majority was established, and according to the Chilean Constitution, a runoff election would be required. President Richard Nixon and Secretary of State Henry Kissinger tried in vain to make sure Allende would not

---

[9]   U.S. Dept. of State, Church Report—Covert Action in Chile 1963-1973, http://foia.state.gov/Reports/ChurchReport.asp

[10] The Third World Traveler, Chile: Hardball, excerpted from the book The Price of Power: Kissinger in the Nixon Whitehouse by Seymour M. Hersch, 1983, http://www.thirdworldtraveler.com/Kissinger/Chile_Hardball_TPOP.html

[11] Wikipedia, Chilean presidential election, 1964, http://en.wikipedia.org/wiki/Chilean_presidential_election,_1964

assume control of the country but to no avail and in November of 1970 Allende was appointed president, a fact which enraged Nixon. The United States had spent millions, trying to keep Allende out of office in an effort to protect American interests in Chile. An Allende victory in Chile posed no military threat, and Nixon's concerns were focused primarily on the potential economic loss for American corporations as stated by Seymour Hersh in the Price of Power:

> There is compelling evidence that Nixon's tough stance against Allende in 1970 was principally shaped by his concern for the future of the American corporations whose assets, he believed, would be seized by an Allende government. His intelligence agencies, while quick to condemn the spread of Marxism in Latin America, reported that Allende posed no threat to national security. Three days after the popular election, the CIA told the White House in a formal Intelligence Memorandum that, as summarized by the Senate Intelligence Committee, the United States "had no vital interests within Chile, the world military balance of power would not be significantly altered by an Allende regime, and an Allende victory in Chile would not pose any likely threat to the peace of the region."[12]

The Nixon administration and the CIA had aligned themselves with General Pinochet and, despite the evidence indicating Allende posed no threat, the coup which overthrew the Allende government took place on September 11, 1973. There exist varying accounts of Allende's demise. Some say he committed suicide, whereas others say he was murdered during the coup. With Allende out of the way, Pinochet didn't waste any time exercising his authority:

> Following the September 11, 1973, coup, the military Junta, led by General Augusto Pinochet, moved quickly to consolidate its newly acquired power. Political parties were banned, Congress was put in indefinite recess, press censorship was instituted,

---

[12]   The Third World Traveler, Chile: Hardball, excerpted from the book The Price of Power: Kissinger in the Nixon Whitehouse by Seymour M. Hersch, 1983, http://www.thirdworldtraveler.com/Kissinger/Chile_Hardball_TPOP.html

supporters of Allende and others deemed opponents of the new
regime were jailed, and elections were put off indefinitely.[13]

Space does not permit a full account of the events in Chile throughout the
sixties and seventies. The information overwhelmingly seems to suggest that
the CIA spent millions of dollars attempting to keep Allende out of office,
primarily in an effort to protect American corporate investment. The coup
which resulted in Allende's death and brought Pinochet to power was a direct
result of covert action taken by the CIA and came after years of instability in
Chile, which the CIA was largely responsible for. While it is unclear if the
assassination of Allende was ever ordered by Nixon or CIA Director Richard
Helms, there seems to be no denial on the part of U.S. officials that Allende's
demise would be a welcome event.[14] In addition, it seems that Nixon and
Kissinger may have abused their power in bypassing the State Department
and the Forty Committee, which was responsible for oversight on covert
operations. The Church Report states, with reference to the 1964 election:

> Half a decade later, in 1970, the CIA engaged in another special
> effort, this time at the express request of President Nixon and
> under the injunction not to inform the Departments of State
> or Defense or the Ambassador of the project. Nor was the Forty
> Committee ever informed. The CIA attempted, directly, to
> foment a military coup in Chile.[15]

In the days and weeks to follow, the political landscape in Chile under
Pinochet changed dramatically. A democratically elected president had
been overthrown by a U.S. supported regime. Pinochet declared himself
president, suspended congress, and subsequently banned political parties,
freedom of speech, habeas corpus, and trade unions.[16]

---

[13]   U.S. Dept. of State, Church Report—Covert Action in Chile 1963-1973,
       http://foia.state.gov/Reports/ChurchReport.asp

[14]   The Third World Traveler, Chile: Hardball, excerpted from the book The Price
       of Power: Kissinger in the Nixon Whitehouse by Seymour M. Hersch, 1983,
       http://www.thirdworldtraveler.com/Kissinger/Chile_Hardball_TPOP.html

[15]   U.S. Dept. of State, Church Report—Covert Action in Chile 1963-1973,
       http://foia.state.gov/Reports/ChurchReport.asp

[16]   Wikipedia, Augusto Pinochet, (16) http://rationalwiki.org/wiki/
       Augusto_Pinochet

Perhaps what Pinochet will be forever remembered for is the brutal human rights violations committed against the people of Chile following the coup. Thousands "disappeared" in the days following the coup, and the Santiago soccer stadium witnessed thousands of murders. I have personally talked to people who lived close to the stadium, and they struggled to sleep as gunfire would erupt through the night. It was only in time, they would learn the nature of the gunfire was due to the summary executions and senseless murders of thousands of citizens whose only crime was their political support of Allende.

> The Human Rights Violations during the Military government of Chile refer to all acts of human rights abuses, persecution of opponents, political repression and state terrorism committed by the Chilean armed forces and the Police, government agents and civilians in the service of security agencies, during the dictatorship of Augusto Pinochet in Chile since September 11, 1973, until March 11, 1990.
>
> According to the Commission of Truth and Reconciliation (Rettig Commission) and the National Commission on Political Imprisonment and Torture (Valech Commission), the number of direct victims of human rights violations in Chile, it accounts for at least 35,000 people: 28,000 were tortured, 2,279 were executed and around 1,248 continued as Disappeared. In addition some of 200,000 people have suffered exile and an unknown number (hundreds of thousands) would have gone through clandestine centers and illegal detention.[17]

Chile had been a stable democracy for decades and on September 16, 1973, as the people of Chile were preparing for the runoff election which would ultimately choose who the next president of Chile would be, Henry Kissinger addressed the press and stated, "I have yet to meet somebody who firmly believes that if Allende wins, there is likely to be another free election in Chile."

---

[17]   Wikipedia, Human Rights Violations during the military government of Chile, (17) http://en.wikipedia.org/wiki/ Human_rights_violations_during_the_Military_government_of_Chile

In the coming months, Salvador Allende, the democratically elected
leader would be dead, and the U.S. supported Pinochet would take
control of Chile. Thousands would be tortured or killed, and it would be
seventeen years before the people of Chile would experience another "free
election".[18]

*

In the same manner, the people of the Middle East have never forgotten
the 1953 coup orchestrated by the CIA in Iran; there is a tremendous
amount of history regarding U.S. covert activity, which lives in the hearts
and minds of the people in Latin America. And in the center of much of
the controversy, we find the United Fruit Company which would go on to
become Chiquita Brands International.

However, United Fruit is not the only multinational with an interesting
past in Central and South America. In 2002, a court in Nicaragua along
with Chiquita ordered Dole Fruit and Dow Chemical to pay $489 million
in damages to workers, who had been injured or developed serious
health-threatening conditions due to contact with Nemagon, a pesticide
which had been banned years earlier in the United States and was proven to
cause serious health problems. In addition to the personal health concerns,
many hold the multinationals responsible for the severe contamination and
pollution of the fresh water system, which the people of Nicaragua rely on
for potable water.[19]

What is interesting about United Fruit/Chiquita is the consistency
with which the company seems to be at the center of volatile issues
within Central and South America, and their political connections within
Washington. With the memory of the Banana Massacre in 1928 not yet
forgotten by farm workers in Latin America, United Fruit would be involved
in the 1954 coup which would see the democratically elected government
of Guatemalan President Jacobo Arbenz overthrown in a covert action
orchestrated by the CIA.[20]

---

[18]   U.S. Dept. of State, Church Report—Covert Action in Chile 1963-1973,
       http://foia.state.gov/Reports/ChurchReport.asp

[19]   Perkins, *Hoodwinked*, 172

[20]   Wikipedia, 1951 Guatemalan coup d' etat, http://en.wikipedia.org/
       wiki/1954_Guatemalan_coup_d'%C3%A9tat

From 1931-1944, Guatemala was led by a pro-American dictator named Jorge Ubico. Under the Ubico administration, United Fruit prospered. It became the largest land-owner in Guatemala and received generous tax exemptions. In 1944, Ubico was overthrown by a civilian revolt, and the new president, Juan Arevalo, instituted many reforms beneficial to the people of Guatemala. Arvalo's democratically elected successor, Jacobo Arbenz, would continue with reforms, and by 1952, he had legalized unions and had introduced agrarian land reform, which expropriated land that was not in use for the benefit of thousands of rural families. The UFC, being the country's largest land owner, was naturally affected by these reforms, despite the fact that the company only used a small percentage of the land they owned. A month after Dwight D. Eisenhower was sworn into office, the Guatemalan government expropriated 40percent of United Fruit's land. Subsequently, Eisenhower approved a covert operation code named Operation PBFortune, which would fund and supply arms to paramilitary groups opposed to Arbenz.[21]

In a study conducted by the Americas Program of the Interhemispheric Resource Center, Lisa Viscidi writes:

> Under the guise of combating communism, the U.S. government ordered a CIA-orchestrated coup to oust Arbenz in 1954. The democratically elected president was replaced by a U.S.-backed general who annulled the majority of the land expropriations, returning the territory to its previous owners. In the following decades a civil war ensued, pitting military dictatorships against a leftist guerilla insurgency. The best lands were rewarded to military officers and rich land-owners tied to the military regimes, thus cementing the system of inequitable land distribution.[22]

While Operation PBFortune was sold as a CIA operation to overthrow Arbenz and stop the spread of communism, it was followed by Operation PBHistory:

---

[21]   Frontline World, Timeline: Guatemala's History of Violence, http://www. pbs.org/frontlineworld/stories/guatemala704/history/timeline.html#

[22]   Lisa Viscidi, A History of Land in Guatemala: Conflict and Hope for Reform, September 17, 2004, http://www.nisgua.org/themes_campaigns/ land_rights/Background/A%20History%20of%20Land%20in%20 Guatemala%20091704.pdf

Afterwards there was an operation, Operation PBHistory, whose
objective was to gather and analyze documents from the Árbenz
government that would incriminate Árbenz as a Communist
Puppet. This Operation found no evidence to support such
a strong claim; the Árbenz government was found to not
have been "infiltrated" by communists, but simply allowed
communists the democratic right of party-formation and
political participation.[23]

Considering there was no Communist threat, what would have
motivated the CIA to spend millions of American tax dollars to overthrow
a democratically elected government, while pushing Guatemala into a
long civil war, which would subsequently cause the deaths of thousands
of citizens? While United Fruit had enjoyed substantial, but perhaps
questionable and unwarranted gains during the Ubico dictatorship, why
were they so opposed to the land expropriation by the democratically
elected Arbenz government when, according to the UFC's own website,
UFC was to be compensated according to the company's stated value for
the land, which was not even being utilized.

Using the Agrarian Reform Act the Arbenz government declares
that 209,842 acres of uncultivated lands of United Fruit
should be expropriated and distributed to landless peasants.
The Guatemalan government promises the company an
indemnification of $627,572 in governmental bonds. The value
of this indemnification was based on the company's declared tax
value of the land.[24]

Perhaps the management of United Fruit didn't consider the
compensation package adequate, but what further muddies the water is
UFC's shareholder situation in 1954. One would think there is a major
conflict of interest when the CIA, at American tax-payers' expense,
overthrows a democratically elected government of a Third World country

---

[23]   Wikipedia, 1954 Guatemalan coup d' etat, http://en.wikipedia.org/
       wiki/1954_Guatemalan_coup_d'%C3%A9tat
[24]   United Fruit Historical Society, http://www.unitedfruit.org/chron.htm

when the Secretary of State, John Foster Dulles and his brother, CIA Director Allen Dulles, were both shareholders of United Fruit.[25]

With no communist threat present, is it possible the coup was based solely on economic gain? And if so, is it also conceivable that top-ranking officials within the government utilized the CIA to send a message to Third World governments around the world that the United States would not tolerate sovereign nations from implementing policies which would place the interests of their citizens ahead of those of American multinational corporations?

The aftermath of the Guatemalan coup isn't pretty. The U.S. supported Colonel Carlos Castillo assumed control of Guatemala as thousands were imprisoned with no right to appeal. In an effort to combat the dictatorship which had been imposed on them as a result of the 1954 coup, the people revolted and the country was mired in civil war from 1960-1996. Forty thousand to fifty thousand people disappeared, and an estimated two hundred thousand were killed. Initially the war, which pitted middle-class intellectuals, students, and farmers against U.S.-trained soldiers with CIA support, did not go well for the people. In 1960, a small group of military officers revolted and hid in the countryside after the failed attempt to overthrow the government. This group, called MR-13, reached out to Fidel Castro in Cuba for support, perhaps because they had nowhere else to go. In an effort to combat MR-13, the United States sent in Green Berets to instruct the Guatemalan military on counterinsurgency techniques. The civil war continued and:

> In November 1965, U.S. security adviser John P. Longan arrived to Guatemala and with a Guatemalan Army élite launched Operation Cleanup a death squad that throughout the year 1966 effected kidnappings and assassinations constituting "the first systematic wave of collective counterinsurgent 'disappearances' in Latin America" that killed the leaders of Guatemala's labor unions and peasant federations during Árbenz Government. In 1966, soon after President Julio Cesar Mendez Montenegro (1966-70) assumed office, the Guatemalan Army launched a counter-insurgency campaign that successfully combated and

---

25   Wikipedia, 1954 Guatemalan coup d' etat, http://en.wikipedia.org/wiki/1954_Guatemalan_coup_d'%C3%A9tat

dispersed the left-wing guerrilla organizations fighting in the mountains and country.[26]

The war, if you remember, had originated due to some unused land being expropriated from the UFC by the democratically elected government in Guatemala. By the end, there were over two hundred thousand dead. The conflict, as described in a report of the Archbishop's Office for Human Rights (ODHAG), states that "almost 90percent of the atrocities and over 400 massacres" were attributed to the U.S. backed Guatemalan army with the guerillas being responsible for less than the remaining 5percent. [27]

*

In June 2009, the democratically elected president, Manuel Zelaya, of Honduras was overthrown in a military coup. While various media outlets in the U.S. ran stories suggesting the coup was due to Zelaya's desire to extend presidential term limits, common consensus in Latin America suggests the coup was engineered by Chiquita and Dole Food, who had openly criticized Zelaya for advocating a 60percent increase in the minimum wage for the benefit of the Honduran people working on the plantations. In *Hoodwinked*, John Perkins quotes a conversation he had with a Panamanian bank vice president, who wished to remain anonymous, shortly after the coup:

> "Every multinational knows that if Honduras raises its hourly rates, the rest of Latin America and the Caribbean will have to follow. Haiti and Honduras have always set the bottom line for minimum wages. The big companies are determined to stop what they call a 'leftist revolt' in this hemisphere. In throwing out Zelaya, they are sending frightening messages to all the other presidents who are trying to raise the living standards of their people."

The same people suggested a similar situation in Haiti, where "coincidentally," Jean-Bertrand Aristide had been overthrown by the CIA for attempting to raise the minimum wage from $1.00 to $2.40 per day.[28]

[26] Wikipedia, Guatemalan Civil War, http://en.wikipedia.org/wiki/ Guatemalan_Civil_War
[27] United Fruit Historical Society, http://www.unitedfruit.org/chron.htm
[28] Perkins, Hoodwinked, 212-213

In *Hoodwinked*, Perkins also quotes the *Los Angeles Times* from July 23, 2009, in reference to the Zeyala coup:

> What happened in Honduras is a classic Latin American coup in another sense: Gen. Romeo Vasquez, who led it, is an alumnus of the United States' School of the Americas (renamed the Western Institute for Security Cooperation). The school is best known for producing Latin American officers who have committed major human rights abuses, including military coups.[29]

*

There is little about the process of Step Four that generates a warm, fuzzy feeling in any of us. In fact, Noam Chomsky, Professor Emeritus at MIT and an author of over 100 books, many dealing with international politics, has stated, "I think we can be reasonably confident that if the American population had the slightest idea of what is being done in their name, they would be utterly appalled." Most of us want to think well of our respective countries and will do everything conceivable to avoid looking at the evidence, regardless of how overwhelming it is. Our pride stands in the way, and perhaps the only thing more painful than conducting a fearless and thorough moral inventory is the process of accepting the truth about our discoveries.

In the last few pages, I have attempted to document a few of the more well-known and easy-to-confirm cases in an effort to simply illustrate how one may approach Step Four in order to develop an honest assessment of western society's involvement in some of the world's affairs. Many of us will try to rationalize and justify our actions as matters of national security or acts necessary to deter the advancement of communism. However, it frequently appears the violent actions taken by our governments were directed at democratically elected leaders of sovereign nations who were simply intent on doing what was in the best interests of their constituents. While their actions may have resulted in a negative financial impact on a few multinational corporations, do those circumstances provide adequate justification to overthrow governments and create civil wars which result in the deaths of thousands? I will let you be the judge and only encourage you to do your homework so you can provide a balanced assessment of the situations in question. The internet is loaded with information that will

---

[29]   Perkins, Hoodwinked, 215

never be disclosed in the mainstream media, and there are hundreds of books available in your local library. Much of the information I have based my work on has come from actual government documents, and I again encourage you to conduct your own searches in an effort to learn as much as possible so you can make informed decisions regarding what is in the best interests of your country and our world.

*

Step Four is about clearly seeing and accepting our part regarding the problems of the world, and before we move on, there are a few additional points I would like to discuss. The first involves one of my favorite places on the planet: Columbia. I fell in love with Columbia long before I got there. In *A Hundred Years of Solitude,* Gabriel Garcia Marquez paints a magical picture of this country and when I finally arrived it was like seeing the country for a second time. The scenery is magnificent and may only take a backseat to the warmth and passion of the people.

Most of us are aware of Columbia's troubled past regarding the drug trade. There are also deep political divisions in the country, which has been the basis for a significant amount of internal violence in the past century. In Marquez's autobiography, *Living to Tell the Tale,* he provides a colorful description of the night in 1948 when Robert Gaitan, the charismatic populist liberal leader, was assassinated in Bogota. Gaitan's political career began after gaining popularity as a lawyer and defender of worker's rights after he took on the United Fruit Company following the 1928 Banana Massacre. In addition to Marquez, in the crowd that night was Fidel Castro and numerous representatives of the CIA. Gaitan's daughter, Gloria, believes the CIA was ultimately responsible for the death of her father, but a riot erupted upon Gaitan's being shot, and the murderer was beaten to death by the crowd. The riot would morph into a decade of Columbian history known as *La Violencia,* which pitted liberals against conservatives, and occasionally, brother against brother. *La Violencia* is estimated to have resulted in the deaths of over three hundred thousand people.[30]

Armed with a small glimpse into the volatile history in Columbia, we arrive at 2007 where Chiquita Brands International entered a guilty plea

---

[30] Wikipedia, Jorge Eliecer Gaitan Ayala, http://en.wikipedia.org/wiki/Jorge_Eli%C3%A9cer_Gait%C3%A1n_Ayala

and agreed to pay a $25 million fine for violating a U.S. anti-terrorist law prohibiting companies from doing business with terrorist organizations. Chiquita has stated it paid the United Self-Defense Forces of Columbia (AUC) $1.7 million between 1997 and 2004 for protection of its workers.

> It was here, in northern Colombia's lush banana-growing region that Chiquita Brands International, the $655 million fruit giant, slipped into a blood-soaked scandal. Between 1997 and 2004, Chiquita gave $1.7 million to the AUC, whose death squads destroyed unions, terrorized workers, and killed thousands of civilians. Chiquita's top officials admit approving the payments but say they thought that if they didn't pay up, the AUC would kill its employees and attack its facilities. Because the U.S. State Department has labeled the AUC a terrorist organization, federal prosecutors charged Chiquita in March with engaging in transactions with terrorists. In an agreement with the Justice Department, Chiquita pleaded guilty and will pay a $25 million fine.[31]

In 2010, families of those killed by AUC while working for Chiquita filed a civil suit in a Florida court holding Chiquita responsible for the deaths of their family members. Paramilitary groups are being blamed for over fifty thousand deaths, and AUC is alleged to have massacred and tortured dozens, but most notably in a town called Mapiripan in 1997. In addition to the $1.7 million Chiquita, paid the AUC it also stored in their warehouses, and then delivered to the terrorist organization, three thousand AK-47 assault rifles and five million rounds of ammunition, which makes one wonder where a banana company would find three thousand AK-47's.[32]

Chiquita isn't the only company being scrutinized in recent history for their business practices in Columbia.

---

[31] Portfolio.com, The Banana War, http://www.portfolio.com/news-markets/international-news/portfolio/2007/09/17/Chiquita-Death-Squads/

[32] Amercias on msnbc.com, Bananas, Columbian death squads and a billion dollar lawsuit, http://www.msnbc.msn.com/id/43221200/ns/world_news-americas/t/bananas-colombian-death-squads-billion-dollar-lawsuit/

The widening scandal may engulf other U.S. firms doing business in Colombia. Two jailed leaders of the AUC (which agreed to disband last year [2006]) have testified in Colombian courts that many multinational corporations operating in Colombia paid them off. Congressman Bill Delahunt, a Democrat from Massachusetts who is leading a House subcommittee investigation, told me he plans to call the Coca-Cola Co., Nestlé, Occidental Petroleum, and Drummond (an Alabama mining outfit), among others, into congressional hearings to explore accusations that they or their business partners also funded the AUC or other groups. "We want to know," Delahunt says, "if American companies are fueling the violence that has beset Colombia for decades." All four companies deny they funded paramilitaries. Delahunt says, "If a company did not participate, it's unfair to let allegations sit out there. But we'll find out the truth."[33]

In an article originally published in *Dollars and Sense* magazine in 2003, writer Madeline Baran describes the situation in Columbia with regard to Coca Cola and the relationship between unions and corporations in general.

Activists say at least eight union activists have been killed by paramilitaries at Colombian Coca-Cola facilities since 1989. And plaintiffs in a recent series of lawsuits hold Coca-Cola and two of its bottlers responsible for the violence, alleging "systematic intimidation, kidnapping, detention, and murder of trade unionists in Colombia, South America at the hands of paramilitaries working as agents of corporations doing business in that country."

The murders of Coke bottling workers are part of a larger pattern of anti-union violence in Colombia. Since 1986, over 3,800 trade unionists have been murdered in the country, making it the most dangerous place to organize in the world. Three out of

[33] Portfolio.com, The Banana War, http://www.portfolio.com/news-markets/international-news/portfolio/2007/09/17/Chiquita-Death-Squads/

every five people killed worldwide for trade union activities are from Colombia.[34]

While Chiquita has stated the payments to AUC were for "protection" of employees, the company does have a long history of being anti-worker and/or anti-union, and much of the violence conducted by AUC was directed at union leaders. Chiquita also has a long history of being well connected politically:

> Several of Chiquita's former directors and legal advisors are tightly linked to the U.S. federal government. Roderick Hills, the former director and head of Chiquita's audit committee, previously served as a legal advisor to President Gerald Ford and as President of the Board of the Securities and Exchange Commission between 1975 and 1977. Joseph Whitehouse Hagin, Vice President of Chiquita from 1991-2000, served as Deputy Campaign Manager in George W. Bush's 2000 campaign and Deputy Chief of Staff at the White House for George W. Bush from 2001-2008.

> Eric H. Holder Jr., President-Elect Barak Obama's nominee (now in office)for U.S. Attorney General and deputy attorney general in the Clinton administration, was the lead defense attorney for Chiquita Brands during the Department of Justice's indictment of the company for making payments to terrorist groups in Colombia as well as in several lawsuits filed against Chiquita for alleged human rights violations committed in Colombia by Chiquita-financed terrorist groups.

> Carl H. Lindner Jr., President of the Board from 1984 to 2002 and CEO of the company from 1984 to 2001, is a major Republican donor; according to Mother Jones, between 2000 and 2004, Lindner donated more to PACs, individual candidates, and parties than any other American individual. In

---

[34] Madeline Baran, The Third World Traveler: Stop Killer Coke, Dollars and Sense Magazine, Nvemeber/December, 2003, http://www.thirdworldtraveler. com/Transnational_corps/Stop_Killer_Coke_Colombia.html

particular, Lindner was a major donor and fund-raiser for the 2008 McCain campaign and the Republican Party.[35]

As a point of interest in 1969, the Zapata Corporation gained controlling interest in United Fruit. And in 1969 controlling interest of Zapata (which would go on to become the Harbinger Group) was owned by future CIA Director and President of the United States George H. W. Bush.[36]

*

In the spring of 2011, I was on a Halliburton site in Iraq when one of the management people informed us that, "The government of Iraq had awarded Halliburton a management contract which would see Halliburton get a commission for every barrel of oil that came out of the ground in Iraq." While I have not been able to confirm the existence of such a contract, there is no doubt that Halliburton is a huge player in the Iraqi oilfield where estimates of oil reserves exceed 350 billion barrels and at $100-$150 per barrel that translates into a staggering sum of cash.[37]

Halliburton's involvement during the Iraq invasion is well-known and well-documented. The oil services company received billions in government contracts during the war, and it is no coincidence Halliburton would receive such a contract from the Iraq government. However, when one considers the chronological order of events, and the involvement of the CIA and military in conjunction with other corporations, questions do arise.

Dick Cheney was a career politician and had no experience in the private sector, and yet he became the CEO at Halliburton after serving as Secretary of Defense under George H. W. Bush. When George W. Bush was elected as president in 2000, it was common knowledge Iraq was a target. What is also interesting is the well-known relationship between the Bush family and the Saudi oil elite, which, of course, includes the Bin

[35]   Sourcewatch, Chiquita Brands International, Inc., http://www.sourcewatch.
       org/index.php?title=Chiquita_Brands_International,_Inc.

[36]   Jim Down, Chiquita, Newsfinder, http://www.newsfinder.org/site/readings/
       chiquita/

[37]   Wikipedia, Oil Reserves, (37) http://en.wikipedia.org/wiki/
       Oil_reserves_in_Iraq

Laden family. Saudi, which is arguably America's greatest ally in the Middle East, is also the source of significant funding for terrorist organizations.[38]

Regardless of who was responsible for the attack on the World Trade Center on September 11, 2001, the tragedy became a convenient platform to launch a political and military assault on Iraq. Like the unsubstantiated "communist" threats of previous administrations in Latin America, Saddam Hussein's alleged involvement in 9/11, weapons of mass destruction, or attempts to manufacturer nuclear weapons were proven to have no basis. Is it conceivable Iraq was invaded solely for the oil? And if you follow the money, I wonder why the profit from the Iraqi oilfields only find its way into a few select pockets, despite the fact the American people paid dearly as their nation was forced to the edge of bankruptcy and the lives of thousands of their children lost. Would it not be much more equitable if the spoils of war were at least equitably shared by the American people, who financed the undertaking, instead of going into the pockets of a corporation who invested nothing only to be placed in a position to profit in billions?

*

Typically, when conducting a Step Four, a pattern is revealed. For example, as a result of doing my Step Four, I was able to clearly see, while I did not get into trouble every time I drank, I was drinking every time I got into trouble. I came to see how my self-serving attempts at controlling people, places, and circumstances to suit my wants and needs ended in calamity and destroyed relationships, despite my being convinced doing everything my way was really in the best interests of everybody concerned. And when things went wrong, which was all the time, I justified my behavior by blaming everybody else. The pattern was obvious when, instead of looking at a single incident, I stepped back and looked at the big picture. My world was a mess because of the actions and behaviors I had taken. I had to get honest and accept the truth of who and what I was. And the wreckage of my past left no doubt that I had created the chaos in my life and much of the chaos in the lives of others. As much as I would have liked to, I could not blame anyone else for my actions.

---

[38]   Alex Spillius, The Telegraph, Wikileaks: Saudis 'chief funders of al-Qaeda', http://www.telegraph.co.uk/news/worldnews/wikileaks/8182847/Wikileaks-Saudis-chief-funders-of-al-Qaeda.html

What is the pattern and what are the facts when we conduct a fearless and thorough moral inventory of our society? What is obvious and irrefutable is thousands of people, mostly in Third World countries, who had no reason or means to fight back, have died so a handful of people could profit. Despite our rhetoric regarding freedom and democracy we have overthrown democratically elected governments and replaced them with brutal dictators sympathetic to the desires of American corporations. Millions of people all over the world have watched the wealth of their countries stolen, often at gunpoint, by American corporations, supported by American governments, with high-profile government officials often leading the charge.

These are not judgments, but simple and non-refutable observations. And I sincerely wish I were wrong, but like my drinking, I cannot deny the truth by pretending the evidence is not real. The information to support everything within these pages is readily available, and there is much, much more, as I have only scratched the surface in an effort to illustrate we are not saints and have done more than our fair share in creating the violence, which has led to the deaths of millions. Nothing here is a secret. In my travels, I have met some extraordinary people. There are hundreds of Vietnam vets living in Thailand and Cambodia who are more than willing to tell their stories. I have had numerous discussions with business and military professionals in airports, on planes, and on the ground in the Middle East and Afghanistan, and the consistency of their stories has only encouraged me to write this book. When I ask those who were there, the truth regarding American foreign policy the answer, off the record, I consistently get is, "Weapons, oil, and drugs."

"Remember when you used to hear about the Columbian drug cartel every night on the news?" an Army officer on leave asked me as he nursed his beer in a Phuket bar. "Of course," I respond. "When was the last time you heard anything on the news about the cartel?" he inquired. I thought for a moment and responded, "It's been years," I said. "Supply of cocaine dry up?" he asked. "No," I answered, based on the front line knowledge I had from my involvement in helping others in the addiction circles, "There is more cocaine out there than ever." "So why don't you ever hear about it?" he asked. "You tell me," I said. "The right people are running the business in Columbia, which is why you never hear about it. What do you think we want out of Afghanistan?" The penny dropped, but he continued, "There's billions of dollars' worth of opium grown in Afghanistan every year. Why do you think we're there?"

A year later, I found myself in Columbia, and the more I asked the more I came to believe the good officer had steered me straight. The story on the street in Columbia consistently indicated involvement by the CIA in the cocaine industry. Subsequently I did some follow-up homework and was surprised, and disappointed, to discover that since the Afghan invasion things have changed in the opium business. Please do not misconstrue this as somehow supportive of the Taliban. Nothing could be further from the truth. However, it seems the Taliban hates the drug business and had banned the cultivation of opium poppies. As a result, the United-Nation Drug Control Monitoring group in their 2001 Annual Opium Poppy Survey reported:

> In July 2000 the Taleban authorities banned the cultivation of opium poppy throughout all areas under their control. In November/December 2000, reports from Afghanistan suggested vigorous implementation of the ban by the authorities. Early in February this year, UNDCP carried out a Preassessment Survey to obtain an early quantitative assessment of the area of poppy cultivation, and to determine the degree of compliance with the ban. Subsequently, in May 2001, a delegation of UNDCP major donors undertook a mission to the main poppy cultivating areas of Afghanistan to, *inter alia*, assess the effectiveness of the ban first hand. Both the Pre-assessment Survey and the UNDCP Donor Mission observed the near total success of the ban in eliminating poppy cultivation in Taleban controlled areas. This finding has been confirmed by the Annual Opium Poppy Survey.

The report goes on to state that in 2001, the year the American led coalition invaded Afghanistan, a total of 7,606 hectares of land was utilized in Afghanistan for poppy production which was down 91 percent from the year before and almost all former poppy growing provinces having no, or only small areas, under cultivation due to the poppy ban.[39]

By 2007, the UN reported land under cultivation for opium poppies was up from the 2001 low of 7,606 hectares to 193,000 hectares in 2007,

---

[39] United Nations international Drug Control Program, Afghanistan Annual Opium Poppy Survey 2001, http://www.unodc.org/pdf/publications/report_2001-10-16_1.pdf

which translates into an increase of over 2400 percent. The latest figures for 2011 indicate 131,000 hectares were cultivated for the poppy crop.[40]

In 2008, American Free Press wrote:

> Afghanistan now supplies over 90 percent of the world's heroin, generating nearly $200 billion in revenue. Since the U.S. invasion on October 7, 2001, opium output has increased 33-fold (to over 8,250 metric tons a year).[41]

The CIA's involvement in the drug business is nothing new. Air America, a front company for the CIA, smuggled drugs for Chiang Kai-Shek. The Iran Contra Affair witnessed cocaine being shipped into the USA and sold on the street and the proceeds going back to the U.S. supported Contras, all with the CIA's knowledge.[42]

While it is well-known that major oil companies are profiting from the taxpayer's investment in Iraq, it is somewhat more difficult to determine who exactly profits from the Afghan drug trade. But several indicators point toward at least some degree of CIA involvement. There is a huge amount of money at stake, and you have to admit that a 2400percent increase since the invasion, represents substantial market growth and an excellent return on investment. (Don't tell Wall Street.)I can see a multitude of investors wanting a piece of that action. The Huffington Post reports:

> "When the history of U.S. involvement in Afghanistan is written, Washington's sordid involvement in the heroin trade and its alliance with drug lords and war criminals of the Afghan Communist Party will be one of the most shameful chapters."[43]

*

---

40 United Nations Office on Drugs and Crime, Afghanistan Opium Survey 2011, http://www.unodc.org/documents/crop-monitoring/Afghanistan/ Executive_Summary_2011_web.pdf

41 Victor Thorn, Rawa News, CIA, Heroin Still Rule Day in Afghanistan, http://www.rawa.org/temp/runews/2008/11/24/cia-heroin-still-rule-day-in-afghanistan.html

42 Wikipedia, CIA Drug Trafficking, http://en.wikipedia.org/wiki/ CIA_drug_trafficking

43 The Huffington Post, October 15, 2008

I am beyond disgust as I took a few minutes to watch a video of a group of marines urinating on some bloodied corpses in Afghanistan. What is wrong with us? Who gave us the right to be so incredibly condescending and selfish and stupid? Who gave us the right to disrespect the people of this world to such an extent that we are hated around the world solely due to the selfish and ignorant actions of a few greedy, manipulative bastards? America is full of wonderful people whose reputations are being destroyed all over the world, and whose only fault is either naively believing the myth surrounding the "goodness" of America's foreign policy or simply looking the other way in an effort to deny the obvious. And so again I ask the question: Can we continue in this manner? Do we need to change? Is this how you want your world to be?

*

One of the greatest motivators in this world is fear. In earlier pages I discussed the fear I experienced during my first trip to the Middle East and how that fear was generated based solely on the rhetoric surrounding the events of 9/11 and the Iraq invasion. Consider for a moment the numerous changes in our world, things we would have considered serious violations of our human rights and personal freedoms a few short years ago, which have transpired since 9/11 as a result of fear.

During the writing of this book, friends and family have stated their concern for my well-being. Their worries include the possibility that I will be shot, put on the no-fly list, audited, never work again, incarcerated in Guantanamo Bay, my book will be banned, or a bunch of cocaine will appear in my luggage, despite the fact that I have been clean and sober for almost two decades and have no desire to go back to that way of life. Are these fears realistic? Are they possible? When I consider the millions of people who have died or had their lives destroyed for attempting to change the status quo, I would be a fool to think I am beyond reach. But I know I am not alone, and we must reach past the fear in order to succeed and achieve peace.

So is the fear real or imagined? Is the fear an honest response and a result of seeing the truth in our world? Or is the fear based on propaganda designed to see billions of tax dollars invested to invade countries, only to discover, in hindsight, that those who orchestrated the plan are filling their pockets with billions of dollars in resource wealth and drug money. Or is it possible our tax dollars fill one pocket during the invasion and the resource wealth of these Third World countries fill the other? Do the people get the bill and lose their children at war, while a select few garner massive profits?

How convenient! When the Berlin Wall came down many people around the world believed we had a real shot at peace, only to discover the hideous terrorist threat which seemed to be simply waiting in the wings. And, as a result, a few politically well-connected individuals are accumulating a huge amount of wealth. How extremely convenient!

When we are afraid we will do anything to feel safe. We will send our children to war. We will bankrupt our country; we will willingly accept being frisked at airports, having our phones tapped, jeopardize our constitutional rights, and sacrifice the right to speak freely regarding the concerns in our hearts. "You are either with us or against us," we are instructed by our leaders and to disagree is translated by many into being unquestionably unpatriotic. If you exercise your democratic right and question the leadership, you are branded a conspiracy theorist, a communist, or a socialist. Perhaps the simple truth is, as one follows the money, which consistently seems to wind up in the same pockets that we, the public, have been duped by the same people who managed to steal the wealth of Guatemala, Columbia, and Ecuador.

As a result of my travels, I do know the media in North America has done a wonderful job in shielding us from the truth. I am not sure if I consider myself fortunate for discovering a different version of the story, and I often wonder if remaining ignorant is not an easier way to live. After digesting hundreds of discussions, books, and observations, my mind is swamped with unanswerable questions. For example, while we know some Saudis helped finance, and possibly even create the Taliban and al-Qaeda, is there a chance Eisenhower was right and "we do create enemies so there is someone to buy our bombs?" Consider for a moment the deaths of thousands of people in Third World countries where multinational corporations and western governments have flexed their muscles. Add to the mix the close relationship between corporations who benefit in war and our political leadership, and given the fact that billions of dollars from oil, drugs, and other ventures are involved, is it a stretch to speculate that the entire system of death and deception is motivated by the greed of a few? I do not suggest a detailed conspiracy, but I do wonder if "business as usual" has, in the terms of addiction, finally "bottomed out" and shunned all its moral values in the pursuit of selfish self-interest, much in the same manner in which I used to pursue a drink. I also hope and pray that we are getting closer to our last drunk and we wake up some morning to discover we are killing ourselves and we can no longer continue to do the same things over and over expecting different results. The nonsense has to end.

This is not an assault on capitalism. In fact, I embrace capitalism. I believe it is the only economic system that allows for individuals and societies to prosper, grow, and develop. But is this wild-west, winner-take-all approach, where those willing to buy political favors manipulate the system, kill, imprison, or torture those who stand in opposition, the kind of world we want to live in? I ask you, is killing millions of innocent people for profit acceptable? What are the principles with which we conduct ourselves? What are our values? Step Four invites us to set aside our propensity, like little kids in a sandbox, to blame our selfish behaviors on the actions of others. It is not Saddam Hussein's fault our military showed up on his doorstep and killed thousands of his countrymen. Those are our ridiculous actions, and it is time we accepted responsibility for the things we do all over the world in the name of freedom and democracy.

Are the citizens of western society capable of shutting off their televisions long enough to conduct a fearless and thorough moral inventory of their "democracies"? Can you honestly look at our actions and determine where we have gone off-track? Where is the line? What is the truth? Forget, for a moment the actions of others, and ask yourself, where have we been at fault?

One of the beautiful things about a twelve-step group is that it provides a safe place for us as individuals to discuss the things in life which trouble us on an emotional level, and I realize many of you will find this information uncomfortable and perhaps appalling—it is. I believe one would have to be disconnected at a soul level not be upset and angry, which may be precisely the point. However, let me also congratulate you for having the courage to look inside as nothing will change if we continue to look the other way. These problems must be embraced.

Before we conclude Step Four, I wish to disclose a small piece of information I uncovered as a result of my research. Had I discovered John Stockwell at the beginning, I may have considered it the ranting of a disgruntled employee. However, Stockwell's story is concise and consistent with the thousands of pages available from a variety of public and private sources when one stops to connect all the dots. After considering Stockwell's disturbing conclusions, you may wish to discount what he offers; however, if you accept only 10percent of what he suggests as being factual, I believe you will develop a knot in your gut in much the same manner I did.

Stockwell spent thirteen years as an employee of the CIA, beginning as a marine in 1964. He became a task force commander and sat on a subcommittee of the National Security Council. He met routinely with CIA Director, Bill Colby, Secretary of State, Henry Kissinger, and a variety of Generals and was awarded the medal of merit before he resigned. When he left the CIA, he was the highest ranking officer to leave the agency and go public, and his first book *In Search of Enemies* was published in 1976. Stockwell claimed the actions of the CIA were "counterproductive" to national security and that the secret wars conducted by the agency were of no benefit to the United States. Stockwell believed that the CIA's goal was to keep the world unstable in order to justify the leadership's spending of huge sums of money on defense, and the American people were encouraged to "hate and fear" as enemies were created to insure the defense budgets remained high. As the cold war with the Soviets flourished, Stockwell is quoted to have said, "If the Soviet Union were to disappear off the face of the map, the United States would quickly seek out new enemies to justify its own military-industrial complex." (Again shortly after the Berlin Wall came down to signify the end of the Cold War and the Communist threat, the terrorist organizations in the Middle East began to blossom. Is this a coincidence when one considers there are billions of dollars involved?)[44]

In an effort to summarize John Stockwell's expertise in the many areas in which he served, I will provide you with excerpts taken from his lecture *The Secret Wars of the CIA,* which was written in 1987. It is disturbing, but I encourage those with a sincere desire to grasp the impact of America's foreign policy to read the document in its entirety. In addition, there are a significant number of videotaped interviews of Stockwell available on You Tube.

Despite Stockwell having the best of intentions, his raising concerns about the actions the CIA was taking were ignored, and his position threatened. Something else that becomes clear in reading Stockwell's accounts is the opinion other countries around the world may have of America and some of the reasoning behind those feelings. It had long been America's stand that America's military responses in many Third World countries were to counter communist threats. Stockwell negates these theories and suggests the exact opposite were true as countries may have reached out to the Soviets or the Cubans in an effort to combat the threat America posed. He exposes the depth of the propaganda machine and the cover-ups, which form the lies, not only to the public, but also between the CIA and other government agencies. Near the end of Stockwell's CIA

---

44   Wikipedia, John Stockwell, http://en.wikipedia.org/wiki/John_Stockwell

career, he is sent to Angola as the task-force commander and he describes the process, which was totally unnecessary, that would result in the deaths of thousands of people and the obvious lack of concern exhibited by the politicians involved:

"I had been designated as the task-force commander that would run this secret war [in Angola in 1975 and 1976] . . . and what I figured out was that in this job, I would sit on a sub-committee of the National Security Council, this office that Larry Devlin has told me about where they had access to all the information about Angola, about the whole world, and I would finally understand national security. And I couldn't resist the opportunity to know. I knew the CIA was not a worthwhile organization, I had learned that the hard way. But the question was where did the U.S. government fit into this thing, and I had a chance to see for myself in the next big secret war . . .

I wanted to know if wise men were making difficult decisions based on truly important, threatening information, threatening to our national security interests. If that had been the case, I still planned to get out of the CIA, but I would know that the system, the invisible government, our national security complex, was in fact justified and worth while. And so I took the job . . . Suffice it to say I wouldn't be standing in front of you tonight if I had found these wise men making these tough decisions. What I found, quite frankly, was fat old men sleeping through sub-committee meetings of the NSC in which we were making decisions that were killing people in Africa. I mean literally. Senior ambassador Ed Mulcahy . . . would go to sleep in nearly every one of these meetings . . .

You can change the names in my book [about Angola] and you've got Nicaragua . . . the basic structure, all the way through including the mining of harbors, we addressed all these issues. The point is that the U.S. led the way at every step of the escalation of the fighting. We said it was the Soviets and the Cubans that were doing it. It was the U.S. that was escalating the fighting. There would have been no war if we hadn't gone in first. We put arms in, they put arms in. We put advisors in, they answered with advisors. We put in Zairian para-commando battalions, they put in Cuban army troops. We brought in the S. African army, they brought in the Cuban army. And they pushed us away. They blew us away because we were lying, we were covering ourselves with lies, and they were telling the truth. And it was not a war that we could fight. We didn't have interests there that should have been defended that way.

There was never a study run that evaluated the MPLA, FNLA and UNITA, the three movements in the country, to decide which one was the better one. The assistant secretary of state for African affairs, Nathaniel Davis, no bleeding-heart liberal (he was known by some people in the business as the butcher of Santiago), he said we should stay out of the conflict and work with whoever eventually won, and that was obviously the MPLA. Our consul in Luanda, Tom Killoran, vigorously argued that the MPLA was the best qualified to run the country and the friendliest to the U.S.

We brushed these people aside, forced Matt Davis to resign, and proceeded with our war. The MPLA said they wanted to be our friends, they didn't want to be pushed into the arms of the Soviet Union; they begged us not to fight them, they wanted to work with us. We said they wanted a cheap victory, they wanted a walk-over, they wanted to be un-opposed, that we wouldn't give them a cheap victory, we would make them earn it, so to speak. And we did. 10,000 Africans died and they won the victory that they were winning anyway.

Now, the most significant thing that I got out of all this, in addition to the fact that our rationales were basically false, was that we lied. To just about everybody involved. One third of my staff in this task force that I put together in Washington, commanding this global operation, pulling strings all over the world to focus pressure onto Angola, and military activities into Angola, one third of my staff was propagandists, who were working, in every way they could to create this picture of Cubans raping Angolans, Cubans and Soviets introducing arms into the conflict, Cubans and Russians trying to take over the world.

Our ambassador to the United Nations, Patrick Moynihan, he read continuous statements of our position to the Security Council, the general assembly, and the press conferences, saying the Russians and Cubans were responsible for the conflict, and that we were staying out, and that we deplored the militarization of the conflict.

And every statement he made was false. And every statement he made was originated in the sub-committee of the NSC that I sat on as we managed this thing. The state department press person read these position papers daily to the press. We would write papers for him. Four paragraphs. We would call him on the phone and say, "call us ten minutes before you go on; the situation could change overnight, we'll tell you which paragraph to read." And all four paragraphs would be false. Nothing to do with the truth. Designed to play on events, to create this impression of Soviet and Cuban aggression in Angola. When they were in fact responding to our initiatives.

And the CIA director was required by law to brief the Congress. This CIA director Bill Colby—the same one that dumped our people in Vietnam—he gave thirty-six briefings of the Congress, the oversight committees, about what we were doing in Angola. And he lied. At thirty-six formal briefings. And such lies are perjury, and it's a felony to lie to the Congress.

He lied about our relationship with South Africa. We were working closely with the South African army, giving them our arms, coordinating battles with them, giving them fuel for their tanks and armored cars. He said we were staying well away from them. They were concerned about these white mercenaries that were appearing in Angola, a very sensitive issue, hiring whites to go into a black African country, to help you impose your will on that black African country by killing the blacks, a very sensitive issue. The Congress was concerned we might be involved in that, and he assured them we had nothing to do with it.

We had in fact formed four little mercenary armies and delivered them into Angola to do this dirty business for the CIA. And he lied to them about that. They asked if we were putting arms into the conflict, and he said no, and we were. They asked if we had advisors inside the country, and he said 'no, we had people going in to look at the situation and coming back out'. We had twenty-four people sleeping inside the country, training in the use of weapons, installing communications systems, planning battles, and he said, we didn't have anybody inside the country.

In summary about Angola, without U.S. intervention, 10,000 people would be alive that were killed in the thing. The outcome might have been peaceful, or at least much less bloody. The MPLA was winning when we went in, and they went ahead and won, which was, according to our consul, the best thing for the country.

At the end of this thing the Cubans were entrenched in Angola, seen in the eyes of much of the world as being the heroes that saved these people from the CIA and S. African forces. We had allied the U.S. literally and in the eyes of the world with the S. African army, and that's illegal, and it's impolitic. We had hired white mercenaries and eventually been identified with them. And that's illegal, and it's impolitic. And our lies had been visible lies. We were caught out on those lies. And the world saw the U.S. as liars."[45]

Stockwell describes the outcomes in a variety of other countries where the CIA conducted covert actions. None of these countries had the capability of hurting the United States in anyway, and yet the outcomes revealed huge human casualties:

"We're talking about ten to twenty thousand covert actions [the CIA has performed since 1961]. What I found was that lots and lots of people have been killed in these things . . . Some of them are very, very bloody.

---

[45]   John Stockwell, America's Third World War, How 6 Million People Were Killed In CIA Secret Wars Against Third World Countries, http://www. informationclearinghouse.info/article4068.htm

The Indonesian covert action of 1965, reported by Ralph McGehee, who was in that area division, and had documents on his desk, in his custody about that operation. He said that one of the documents concluded that this was a model operation that should be copied elsewhere in the world. Not only did it eliminate the effective communist party (Indonesian communist party), it also eliminated the entire segment of the population that tended to support the communist party—the ethnic Chinese, Indonesian Chinese. And the CIA's report put the number of dead at 800,000 killed. And that was one covert action. We're talking about 1 to 3 million people killed in these things.

Two of these things have led us directly into bloody wars. There was a covert action against China, destabilizing China, for many, many years, with a propaganda campaign to work up a mood, a feeling in this country, of the evils of communist China, and attacking them, as we're doing in Nicaragua today, with an army that was being launched against them to parachute in and boat in and destabilize the country. And this led us directly into the Korean war.

U.S. intelligence officers worked over Vietnam for a total of twenty-five years, with greater and greater involvement, massive propaganda, deceiving the American people about what was happening. Panicking people in Vietnam to create migrations to the south so they could photograph it and show how people were fleeing communism. And on and on, until they got us into the Vietnam war, and 2,000,000 people were killed.

There is a mood, a sentiment in Washington, by our leadership today, for the past four years, that a good communist is a dead communist. If you're killing 1 to 3 million communists, that's great. President Reagan has gone public and said he would reduce the Soviet Union to a pile of ashes. The problem, though, is that these people killed by our national security activities are not communists. They're not Russians, they're not KGB. In the field we used to play chess with the KGB officers, and have drinks with them. It was like professional football players—we would knock heads on Sunday, maybe in an operation, and then Tuesday you're at a banquet together drinking toasts and talking.

The people that are Dying in these things are people of the third world. That's the common denominator that you come up with. People of the third world. People that have the misfortune of being born in the Metumba mountains of the Congo, in the jungles of Southeast Asia, and now in the hills of northern Nicaragua. Far more Catholics than communists, far more Buddhists than communists. Most of them couldn't give you an intelligent definition of communism, or of capitalism."[46]

In the past few years, largely due to America's conduct in Guantanamo Bay and Abu Graib, the dehumanizing topic regarding the merits of torture has been discussed. According to Stockwell, throughout Central and South America during the sixties and seventies, the CIA and other agencies representing the American government were actively involved in the practice:

"We had the `public safety program' going throughout Central and Latin America for twenty-six years, in which we taught them to break up subversion by interrogating people. Interrogation, including torture, the way the CIA taught it. Dan Metrione, the famous exponent of these things, did seven years in Brazil and 3 in Uruguay, teaching interrogation, teaching torture. He was supposed to be the master of the business, how to apply the right amount of pain, at just the right times, in order to get the response you want from the individual.

They developed a wire. They gave them crank generators, with `U.S. AID' written on the side, so the people even knew where these things came from. They developed a wire that was strong enough to carry the current and fine enough to fit between the teeth, so you could put one wire between the teeth and the other one in or around the genitals and you could crank and submit the individual to the greatest amount of pain, supposedly, that the human body can register.

---

[46]   John Stockwell, America's Third World War, How 6 Million People Were Killed In CIA Secret Wars Against Third World Countries, http://www. informationclearinghouse.info/article4068.htm

Now how do you teach torture? Dan Mitrione: 'I can teach you about torture, but sooner or later you'll have to get involved. You'll have to lay on your hands and try it yourselves.'

. . . All they [the guinea pigs, beggars from off the streets] could do was lie there and scream. And when they would collapse, they would bring in doctors and shoot them up with vitamin B and rest them up for the next class. And when they would die, they would mutilate the bodies and throw them out on the streets, to terrify the population so they would be afraid of the police and the government.

And this is what the CIA was teaching them to do. And one of the women who was in this program for two years—tortured in Brazil for two years—she testified internationally when she eventually got out. She said, 'The most horrible thing about it was in fact, that the people doing the torture were not raving psychopaths.' She couldn't break mental contact with them the way you could if they were psychopath. They were very ordinary people . . .

There's a lesson in all this. And the lesson is that it isn't only Gestapo maniacs, or KGB maniacs, that do inhuman things to other people, it's people that do inhuman things to other people. And we are responsible for doing these things, on a massive basis, to people of the world today. And we do it in a way that gives us this plausible denial to our own consciences; we create a CIA, a secret police, we give them a vast budget, and we let them go and run these programs in our name, and we pretend like we don't know it's going on, although the information is there for us to know; and we pretend like it's okay because we're fighting some vague communist threat. And we're just as responsible for these 1 to 3 million people we've slaughtered and for all the people we've tortured and made miserable, as the Gestapo was the people that they've slaughtered and killed. Genocide is genocide! "[47]

---

[47]   John Stockwell, America's Third World War, How 6 Million People Were Killed In CIA Secret Wars Against Third World Countries, http://www.informationclearinghouse.info/article4068.htm

Incidentally, Dan Mitrione, former police officer and FBI agent, had moved to Uruguay under USAID and ran the office of public safety (public safety—you have to love the irony) where he taught local police officials the fine art of torture. His claim to fame was using homeless people as guinea pigs for his torture instructions and is alleged to have tortured four beggars to death. The government at the time in Uruguay was dealing with an urban guerilla group called Tupamoros, who kidnapped Metrione, and he was found dead a short time later having been shot twice in the head.[48]

Stockwell urges those who are interested in seeking the truth not to take his word for anything and encourages the public to read in order to confirm his statements. In addition to his lecture *The Secret War of the CIA*, Stockwell has also published two books, *The Secret Wars of the CIA* and *The Praetorian Guard.*

*

When it comes to documenting the collusion between governments and corporations, Step Four could take decades to write. The relationship between the financial sector and the political leadership in Washington, which led up to the economic collapse in 2008, has been a story extremely well-told in Charles Ferguson's documentary, *Inside Job.* Of primary concern to all of us, should be the changes in legislation which led to the collapse, the unethical practices of the banking industry in the management of public funds, Washington's use of public money to bail out a system mired in corruption, the reluctance by the political leadership to pass legislation, which would protect investors in the future, and the lack of willingness to hold accountable those individuals in the financial sector who were responsible. In addition, we must always remember to follow the money, and we will discover that the banking industry has paid out millions to lobbyists and in campaign contributions, which, no doubt, will place their concerns ahead of the taxpayers whenever legislation is being changed or introduced.[49]

Another excellent piece of film describes the legal battle Dr. Stanislaw Burzynski, a bio-chemist and physician, has had with the FDA in his efforts

---

[48]   Wikipedia, Dan Mitrone, http://en.wikipedia.org/wiki/Dan_Mitrione
[49]   Charles H. Ferguson, Director, Inside Job, 2010, http://www.sonyclassics. com/insidejob/

to provide patients with his promising work in the treatment of cancer. It seems the government, through the FDA, is determined to protect the financial interests of major pharmaceutical corporations by doing everything they can to prevent Burzynski from continuing his practice. It seems that nobody can deny Burzynski's work has shown great promise and has saved a lot of lives already. However, the FDA has brought Burzynski before several grand juries in an attempt to charge him with something and have been able to accomplish little other than racking up significant debt in legal costs and wasting Burzynski's valuable time. The only problem, it appears, is that none of the major pharmaceutical companies, who incidentally spend millions on lobbyists and practically own the FDA, will share in the profits from Burzynski's breakthrough technology and are using the FDA to maintain the status quo and keep Burzynski from practicing outside of Texas. The drawback, of course, is that millions of people the world over will not have access to the new medical treatments, but the suffering of people does not seem to concern the FDA, and once again corporate greed seems to be the fundamental principle at work here.[50]

*

The concept of taking a moral inventory is to allow us to clearly see the character defects in our thought process, which led to our demise, with a goal of changing our behavior. Step Four is not about blaming but is simply a process we go through to discover what works and what doesn't. If the thought does, in fact, precede the action, then what kind of thought encourages us to invade a country, overthrow a democratically elected government, bomb defenseless villages, steal another country's oil, support a system which encourages fraudulent behavior by our political and banking institutions, and spend billions on defense contracts while failing to properly educate and provide health care for our children? We are encouraged to "support our troops", but how do we do that without supporting the corporations who will profit from the oil they steal in a Third World country, with millions of impoverished people, as a result of the invasion we funded?

So what is the thought process, and what are the values we as a society possess, which supports these actions? Do we believe we are being patriotic,

---

[50]   Eric Merola, Director, Burzynski The Movie, 2011, http://www.
burzynskimovie.com/

or would a patriot insist on acting more benevolent? Are we protecting our rights and freedoms, or are we selling out to corporate interests? Are we bravely facing down a terrorist threat, or are we reacting with fear based on the propaganda, unsubstantiated by any hard evidence, we are being told by the media? What motivates you, and what motivates us as a nation to do the things we do? Can you take a fearless and thorough look at yourself and your country? What kind of world do you want? What kind of world does your inner voice, your God voice, want for you?

Conducting a fearless and moral inventory is not a pleasant process; however, it is an extremely valuable exercise. Numerous questions come to mind, and each of us must answer them for ourselves. Is war working? Is the killing of others necessary for our peace and security, or is this war really an exercise in economics, for the benefit of a few? If liberating the Iraqi people was the goal, I often wonder what would have transpired, had we arrived at the Iraqi border with hundreds of trucks filled with food and clothing, instead of our weapons of mass destruction.

The following was originally published in the *Guardian* following a rather violent confrontation between police and those involved in the Occupy Wall Street movement. The article succinctly illustrates why we cannot expect our politicians to correct the system without pressure from the people. Clearly, when the opportunity to accumulate substantial personal wealth would be jeopardized by walking away from corporate sponsorship, why would our elected representatives want to change that? Why would they want to kill the goose that laid the golden egg?

But wait: why on earth would Congress advise violent militarized reactions against its own peaceful constituents? The answer is straightforward: in recent years, members of Congress have started entering the system as members of the middle class (or upper middle class)—but they are leaving DC privy to vast personal wealth, as we see from the "scandal" of presidential contender Newt Gingrich's having been paid $1.8 m for a few hours' "consulting" to special interests. The inflated fees to lawmakers who turn lobbyists are common knowledge, but the notion that congressmen and women are legislating their own companies' profits is less widely known—and if the books were to be opened, they would surely reveal corruption on a Wall Street spectrum. Indeed, we do already know that congresspeople are massively profiting from trading on non-public information they have on companies about which they are legislating—a form of insider trading that sent Martha Stewart to jail.[51]

*

America is without doubt the greatest country in the history of the human race. The technological advancements alone have been staggering, but those successes would never have been possible if it were not for the concepts of freedom, democracy, and the opportunity to dream huge dreams. Attached to our dreams was the knowledge that our successes would result, not only in benefits for mankind, but in financial reward as well. Our beliefs, our faith, and trust in ourselves and each other formed the foundation which put man on the moon.

As America's successes grew, the world's people became envious and looked to America for leadership. People from all over the world flocked to America, often leaving behind the violence, poverty, and oppression of their homelands, to embrace the concept of freedom and democracy. But what happens in a democracy when the voice of the people is lost to the "chi-ching" of corporate campaign funds? Is there anything wrong with a system which almost guarantees our elected officials will become millionaires in office simply by supporting corporate interests, rather than the best interests of their constituents? It seems everyone connected to government is making a great deal of money, and I wonder where the benefit is for the taxpayer with all our global economic and military undertakings. Or does he simply get the bill? Is this democracy by the people, for the people?

And what about the American people, who worked hard, supported the system, and the country they believed and trusted in? They didn't ask for this. This wasn't part of their democracy, their American dream. These actions, many of them covert, were taken without their blessing, without their knowledge, and with no debate. And many of those actions taken with their knowledge were based on lies and deceit. These were the actions of a government that they, or their forefathers, thought they had left behind when they came to America.

Imagine for a moment a president being elected with a mandate of change. We all know control of the government and electoral system has gradually been usurped and has become subservient to those with wealth

---

[51]   Naomi Wolfe, The shocking truth about the crackdown on Occupy, The Guardian, Nov. 25, 2011, http://www.guardian.co.uk/commentisfree/cifamerica/2011/nov/25/shocking-truth-about-crackdown-occupy

and power; we know the game is rigged. And then along comes a man who seeks the office of the president and is committed to changing the system. He wins by an overwhelming majority, and we all go back to our caves thinking our job is done. But the new president hits a wall—the money wall. Those who hold great wealth circle the wagons and what the President discovers is that the other elected representatives, whose support he desperately needs in order to pass the legislation, which places the power back in the hands of the people, are reluctant to go along with the new deal. It seems many of them have had their campaigns paid for by corporations, corporations who have no desire to change. There is too much money at stake. Knowing the change is necessary, and having the mandate of the people, where does the President go for support now? After all, he is only one man, and, even if he is the president, by himself he can do little.

Change requires the support of the people. The CIA actions in Angola, Honduras, Columbia, and Nicaragua were not carried out with the knowledge of the people of America. These actions were done covertly, and we are only as sick as our secrets. The overthrowing of numerous governments around the world has happened without the consent of the American people. If the people were told anything, rarely was it the truth. Has the trust between the government and the people been violated as a result of these lies and the violent actions of our governments? Unfortunately, people around the world hold America responsible for these acts of violence, but how can the American people be held accountable for the actions of the CIA and a few corporations who have acted covertly? However, it may be the responsibility of the American people to change their government and address the issues that threaten peace in our world. And by conducting a Step Four, we can see the truth and discover what it is within our system which must be changed.

America is the greatest proponent of capitalism in the world. For decades, we have heard the cry for free trade and global competition. But competition requires a semblance of order and fairness. It is not fair to show up for the pick-up game with Kobe Bryant and Lebron James on your team. Is it fair when an economic superpower threatens Third World countries with economic sanctions when their governments are simply trying to help their citizens? And I ask you if it is fair and humane, or is it an act of depravity, to send in the CIA and/or the military to overthrow democratically elected governments in order to secure the wealth of the world's resources for the benefit of a few? Is it acceptable for our governments to assist corporations who covertly hire death squads to overthrow governments and kill workers whose only interest is starting a union so they may earn a decent living and feed their children? Is this the capitalism you wish us to embrace? Is this competition or is it extortion? Have we not crossed the line?

Peace requires a level of trust. Covert actions may have had a place in the past, but we live in a different world today. Nobody trusts the schoolyard bully. He may get your milk money and everybody on the playground may be afraid, but he does not get your respect. And you know, deep down inside, that what goes round comes round. People in Cambodia, Indonesia, Palestine, Chile, and in every corner of the world know the truth because they have witnessed major corporations, supported by government, stealing the wealth of their countries. I ask you to ask yourself if this is acceptable? What kind of world you wish to live in?

Change must come from the people. The president alone can't do it. That is why it is only by working together can we create the world we, the people, want. That is why we must go back through our lives and the history of our political endeavors, and learn from our past mistakes so history does not repeat itself. Doing the same thing over and over expecting different results is insane and, as talk of invading Iran intensifies, I wonder where our trusted leadership will take us? Perhaps it is time to be still and search deep within ourselves for a new direction. The answers will come if you listen.

The reality, the truth of Step Four, reveals our dark side. We can turn away, slip into denial, and allow the behavior to continue. Or we can learn some very valuable lessons from our past. We can continue to allow our governments and corporations to exploit and kill as they attempt to control the way of the world, or we can find God within and amongst ourselves as we try to free ourselves from the bondage of greed, self-centeredness, and our need to control. Are we capable of listening to those of other countries who, fearing repercussion, have been afraid to speak? Are we willing to learn from our mistakes, or do we continue to repeat them?

America has the opportunity to lead the world into the future and must decide whether it will lead by fear and at the point of a gun, or will it lead in peace? Can we as a society continue to conduct ourselves as we have in the past, or do we need to change? The government will not do it for you. The choice is yours.

STEP FIVE

Admitted to God, to ourselves, and to another human being the exact nature of our wrongs.

Focus on the principle of integrity.

> To be persuasive we must be believable; to be believable we must be credible; to be credible we must be truthful.
>
> —Edward R. Murrow

> Have the courage to say no. Have the courage to face the truth. Do the right thing because it is right. These are the magic keys to living your life with integrity.
>
> —W. Clement Stone

> When people do not want to see something, they get mad at the one who shows them. They kill the messenger.
>
> —Julia Cameron (The Artist's *Way*)

After spending most of my life drinking in an attempt to avoid looking at myself, Step Four was not a pleasant undertaking. There is no shortcut, no easier, softer way. And there was little to be pleased with as I looked back at my life. I had lied to the world. This ego I had created and behind which I hid was, I thought, smart, capable, and charming. To lie to the world was one thing, but my biggest problem was that I believed the story too. Step Four shattered any illusion I may have had about myself, and a few short years later, I have nothing but gratitude for the process of dealing with the character defects within my thought process which created my need to drink.

"Step Five is easy," the old timer pointed out to me, "You and God both know what you did, all you have to do is tell someone else." That made sense. I knew it was my secrets which had caused me the greatest problem, and I knew in order to be happy, joyous, and free, I had to get those skeletons out of my closet. While meetings were a great place to talk about many of life's issues, we all harbored more intimate details we did not wish to share publically. But our secrets, and I was no different, fueled many of our fears and much of our delusional thinking. We are only as sick as our secrets, and in order to get well, the secrets had to go.

Let's be honest; nobody comes to AA because they want too. As my life spiraled into hell, I thought AA was my last step down, but the reality was, it was the first step up. My life was a mess, and I hated myself for many of the things I had done and for many of the things I hadn't done. I think the lowest point of my life came after I had honestly faced the truth as described by my Step Four without the benefit of my medication. I was no longer emotionally numb. For the first time in my life, I had to "feel" what it was like to be me, and those feelings were not pleasant. It helped to realize Step Four wasn't designed to punish me; it was designed to teach me some very valuable lessons. The greatest lesson, of course, is that if a particular action didn't create a positive outcome, I didn't have to continue doing it. And why, I asked myself, would I want to go through the painful exercise of conducting a fearless and thorough moral inventory of myself without the benefit of learning everything I could from the exercise? When you're going through hell, keep going.

It seemed the more I could clearly see the wreckage of my past, the more I realized how messed up I was and the more committed I became to my new way of living. The more willing I was to accept responsibility for my actions, and stop blaming others, the more honest, open-minded, and willing to change I would become. The more I could rid myself of negative thought, the more room I would have in my heart for gratitude. The more I could let go of my selfishness and begin thinking of others, the more humility I would acquire. If I could see how my behavior was creating chaos in the lives of others, perhaps I would stop feeling the need to control people, places, and situations and learn to accept and tolerate others as they were. If I were to have an impact on the lives of others, perhaps setting a good example, rather than attempting to manipulate and control them, would provide more positive results. As I began to see that my behavior was having a long-term, negative impact on my own life, as well as the lives of others, I considered letting go of the character deflects, which fed my insane and selfish thought process, and tried being an example of a decent human being. Attraction, rather than promotion, was an interesting concept.

As difficult as it was to look at myself, the saving grace in all this came, once again, from my new friends in AA. "Step Four is cleaning your house, and Step Five is taking out the garbage," it was explained. "If being happy is your goal, how can you possibly be happy with all those thoughts of guilt and remorse rolling around inside your head? You need to tell someone, you need to let it out," I was told as my sponsor made preparations for me to do my Step Five.

Step Four had been a lot of work, and I wasn't very happy with the realization, once I could see past the denial and the self-justification, of who I was. Step Five, however, filled me with fear and the last thing I wanted to do was tell anyone the things I had done in my past. As I neared the end of writing my Step Four, my sponsor informed me he had made an appointment for me to meet a priest, a Catholic priest, to do my Step Five. I had grown up in a small, protestant, farming community, and if the one thing people in my community held dear it was a simple, sincere, dislike for the Catholic community ten miles down the road. As childish as it seems today, they were not to be trusted. The fear, which was completely unsubstantiated, kept me awake the entire night before my meeting with the priest, and I arrived at his office the next morning full of apprehension.

My memory of that meeting is vague, but it did not go well. However, there were some valuable lessons to be learned as a result. In hindsight, it is amazing to see the extent my unrealistic fears were having in my life. I sat in front of this man who was taking time out of his life to help me, but I wouldn't let him because I was frozen by fear. It had gotten easier for me to sit in a room full of alcoholics and discuss my life because I felt a bond with them. They were messed up drunks like I was. But I felt that I had nothing in common with this priest who, in my mind, was so much closer to God than I ever imagined anyone could be. (Today, I realize we are all very imperfect people, and regardless of whether you are a priest, a goat herder, a CEO, or a union representative we all have a right to be here.) As I attempted to test the waters with what I considered to be serious admissions of guilt for the heinous acts in my past, he committed a heinous act of his own; he yawned. I sat in his office believing I was such a badass human being and my story of sex, drugs, and rock 'n' roll, which was causing me no end of heartache, was either boring this man to death, or he was waiting for me to quit screwing around and tell him what I needed to tell him. The priest, in his wisdom, finally realized our meeting wasn't producing the desired results, and he suggested I come back another day. "We will do the right thing when the pain is great enough," I was told later by my sponsor. And perhaps the truth is I simply wasn't ready to do this step, but the good thing was a small piece of the fear I had lived with for years had been dealt with. I had made a beginning, however haltingly, to discuss my character defects with another human being, and I would continue to build from there.

Despite my struggles, the benefits of Step Five were obvious to me. I was full of guilt and shame and had to get rid of it, or I was going to go back to drinking. I did another Step Five a few months later, although I was still reluctant to let all my secrets go. As a result, I left that meeting feeling that I was still, somehow, not finished. There were bits of personal history I did not want anyone to know, and the weight I continued to carry continued to trouble me.

They say business and politics makes for strange bedfellows. Well, AA brings us in touch with people whom we never thought we would be associated with. A couple of years after my initial botched Step Five, I became friends with, of all people, a Catholic Priest, and it was with him that I was finally able to sit down and disclose the remaining secrets I had held so close. "A lot of us have been through similar situations," he replied upon hearing me out, "Please don't let it worry you any longer." In a symbolic gesture, we burned the pages which contained my Step Four and a chapter in my life came to an end.

I left his office understanding freedom. I was still responsible for the events of my past, but somehow the weight, the emotional burden, had been lifted, and I felt free. I could look the world in the eye, and finally feel like I was part of the human race. Those in AA refer to it as a "spiritual awakening". I was connected. Nothing had changed, and yet everything had changed. It was similar to the experience I'd had when the gate "clanked" shut as I left detox a couple of years earlier. Something within me had changed, and it was good.

There is nothing complicated about Step Five, but it does take courage to tell another human being the exact nature of your wrongs. My error in Step Five occurred in simply not trusting the process and taking so long to accomplish this difficult but relatively simple step. I was so deeply ashamed of myself, and the one person impacted negatively by my reluctance to tell the truth was me. And I am amazed at how my negative behavior, despite being directed at you, hurts me. So if I treat you like shit . . . You got it. I am what I do.

My friend Scott suggests to people the first order of business is to tell the person they are doing their Step Five with the absolute worst thing they have ever done in their life. All the rest of the garbage then pales in comparison and will simply pour out. The release of the shame and guilt is evident in the behavior of my friends in AA. They are alive and well, and still completely nuts, but sober. The laughter is real, and they have learned to laugh at themselves. They laugh about the nights they were unable to crawl over the lines in the middle of the road. They laugh about the insanity of chartering an airplane to look for a car they had lost when on a drunk and ran out of gas in the middle of nowhere. They laugh about the time they woke up in a hotel and called the front desk to ask what town they were in. They look at their past and laugh because they can't believe they were those same people. They can't believe they've changed. And, realizing we have cried enough and that we have a choice, we choose laughter.

In addition to Step Five, I have also sought the benefits of therapy in an effort to deal with the deeper emotions surrounding my sister's death. AA is not an organization of professionals. They are very good at helping people, but there are also times when professional help is necessary. The interesting aspect of the relationship between a therapist and a patient involves a substantial amount of soul searching and a willingness to discuss the emotional aspects of our lives. How does that differ from Steps Four and Five? An honest and sincere acknowledgement of our past thoughts and actions, coupled with a desire to discuss these circumstances with another human being, forms the essence of Four and Five. And the realization that keeping secrets from someone I am paying to help me sort out my life makes no sense whatsoever. I have a pretty clean slate today, although I do seem to continually come up against new fears. This I view as a positive thing and believe if I were not coming up against new problems I would not be growing and learning.

When I came to AA, I was told my past would become my greatest asset. Change takes time, faith, and a willingness to trust. I knew my actions and my way of living were not working. The small voice inside me had been whispering for years, and I knew drinking was killing me. I had become so incredibly unhappy and was afraid to trust God or the people in AA. I was afraid of anyone and anything but all that has changed as a result of these steps.

By the time I had finished Step Five, the world looked like a different place, but the world hadn't changed. My past was still there. But everything looked different. And then I realized what it was: like millions of others before me, I had changed.

*

We are fighting a war on terror, and yet I ask you, who are the terrorists? When I put myself in the shoes of the average person in Ethiopia, Columbia, Cambodia, Indonesia, Iraq, in fact every Third World country in the world, who do they fear the most? Regardless of the spin you may hear, are our goals benevolent, or are they selfish? Yes, occasionally we may do something helpful, but that is not our true nature. The American, British, and Canadian governments, militaries, and corporations head to the Third World to take their oil, gold, fruit, drugs, and anything else of value. They will buy, overthrow, or kill the political leadership to get what they want, and the only benefit the people of those nations may actually experience are a handful of very poorly paid jobs. Where is our integrity? What is wrong with us? The issue may be summed up in the words of Bishop Desmond Tutu:

> When the missionaries came to Africa they had the Bible and we had the land. They said, "Let us pray." We closed our eyes. When we opened them we had the Bible and they had the land.

Our governments are supposed to protect the people in a democracy. Some will argue that protecting the rights of an individual and allowing that individual to purchase the support of legislators is freedom. Some will argue that banking institutions, who pay well-connected lobbyists and make huge campaign contributions, are entitled to have friendly governments change the laws designed to protect citizens and prevent economic collapse, in order for them to enhance their bottom line. There are those who believe our governments must do everything possible to insure our oil supply is uninterrupted and, therefore, condone the invasion of Third World countries and the subsequent deaths of thousands of people to insure our needs are met. But are our needs being met at the expense of others?

The truth is we are living a lie, and we know it. The harder we try to convince ourselves that we are living in a democracy, the more this thing unravels. Governments stopped working on behalf of the people a long time ago. The illusion must be smashed so we can get on with putting our world back together. This is not about liberals and conservatives, or left versus right. It is about the truth. It is about being honest. It is about integrity. And it is about our children and their future.

Does our economy cater to the military? If you are poor one of the only ways to get an education is to join the military. When the economy collapses due to the actions of the greed-motivated banking industry, perhaps the only place left for you to turn in an effort to feed yourself is the military. In your heart and soul, you don't want to kill anyone. You know the invasions of Iraq and Afghanistan are wrong choices for you as an individual to support, but you need to eat. And you find yourself in Iraq-killing innocent people and watching some of your own die as well, all so a corporate entity ran and directed by a handful of well-connected, politically savvy individuals can control the world's oil industry. The half-time show honors military veterans, many of whom have never stopped to "follow the money" in an effort to understand why they did four tours to the Middle East. They believed they were being patriotic. They believed they were serving their country. They believed the propaganda, and they believed anyone who spoke out against the war were communists or socialists. Their intent was honorable, and they have my greatest respect, but I ask, were they serving their country or serving a board of directors?

In fact, faced with an overwhelming economic or military threat from America, were we not forcing people in the Third World to do everything possible to save themselves and protect their families? In some cases we pushed people, many of whom didn't know the difference between communism and capitalism, into the arms of the communists as they struggled simply to survive. They were seeking help anywhere they could in an effort to escape the bloodshed we delivered to their doorstep. I wish it were not true. I wish we were killing for freedom and democracy. I wish our intentions were honorable. I wish I could somehow believe we were killing for peace, but I can't get there, not anymore. The thought precedes the action. The motive has been repeated time and time again. It is the same song that has played for years in places like Honduras, Guatemala, Chile, Iran, Indonesia, The Congo, Angola, and everywhere else in the world where there existed anything of value the corporate world wanted to selfishly exploit.

Let go of your denial. Sit quietly for an hour, a day, or a week. Shut off your television and examine carefully the events of the past. Are we the terrorists? I am sorry, and I know this is not pleasant and I wish it were not true. I wish more than anything, it was not true. But it is what it is. We are what we do. Like the moment of clarity when an alcoholic wakes up and can suddenly see the futility in living as he has been living, we ask ourselves where does this end? At what point does this stop? Can it continue or do the seven billion people in this world become enslaved to serve the handful of extremely wealthy? Is this the freedom and democracy you have been telling me about?

As painful as it is, we have to clearly see how the greed-driven, winner take all, killing to control attitude simply must go. The party is over, and as frightening as it may be, we must find another way. Our way, our way of thinking, has to change because to continue will be the end of us all. Step Five asks us to tell another human being. I suggest you tell *every* human being.

It seems that when it comes to the exact nature of our wrongs nothing gets in the way of doing the right thing quite like our addiction to power, control, and greed. While Step Four asked us to take an honest look at our values and the errors we have made, Step Five invites us to discuss our short-comings, with God and another human being. There is nothing wrong with profit, but where does profit morph into greed? Most of us like sex, but would we condone rape? When well-connected corporations utilize the military and other taxpayer funded institutions for their personal gain haven't they gone too far? Our elected officials initially arrive in office as average citizens and leave office with their pockets full due to corporate sponsorship. Government supports their corporate sponsors, many of whom have garnered their wealth due to their relationship with elected officials in the first place. These corporations have risen to places of prominence in our society due to the receipt of taxpayer dollars and have then used that money to purchase even more influence with the government. The money flows in a circle and the only part the taxpayer plays in this game is it's his money, but what is in his best interests is no longer a concern for our political leaders.

These steps have the potential to bring people together peacefully, in an effort to change their world, and AA may be the most democratic organization in this world. Every single member has a voice, and the combination of those voices creates what is referred to as the "collective conscience" of AA. The organization is largely directed by the AA traditions and Tradition Two states, "For our group purpose there is but one ultimate authority—a loving God as He may express Himself in our group conscience. Our leaders are but trusted servants; they do not govern."

Therefore, with every member having an equal voice and guided by the principles of love and service, doing the right thing, because it is the right thing to do, becomes paramount. We are trying to let go of our selfish ways, and our decisions are reflected in Tradition One which states, "Our common welfare should come first; personal recovery depends upon AA unity." Therefore, we realize that it in our best interests to be involved in the decision making and also, by placing the best interests of the group ahead of our own selfish interests, we insure that AA will be there to help others in the years to come.

Financially AA is self-supporting, obtaining all its funds from contributions of those it serves. We were not very responsible people in our drinking days, and we decline outside contributions because our recovery is our responsibility, and we do not wish to have what is in our best interests influenced by outside sources. In their wisdom, the founding fathers (ironically Bill Wilson had been a Wall Street banker) of AA recognized that money had the potential to influence decisions, which could ultimately have a negative impact on the organization. Therefore, contributions are severely limited so favors within AA cannot be bought. It is suggested that our financial resources at the local level be kept to a minimum and that we maintain only a "prudent reserve" to meet immediate expenditures. We pass any excess funds on to our international organization, which helps AA grow and prosper all over the world, which, at the same time, relieves the vast majority of the membership of any temptation to divert the cash flow.

Occasionally, there will be a story regarding a member of AA, who has fallen on hard times. At one time, my home group had a large safe with a mail slot cut into it. We would pass the hat at meetings, put the money in an envelope, and drop in through the slot and into the safe. Several months passed, and someone decided to open the safe and take the money to the bank. Upon opening the safe, we discovered there were only a few envelopes. We gave it some thought and realized one young member who had the combination, had decided to go back out drinking, and ended up in jail for a short time. He had been seen on the streets a few days prior, and we wondered if he was the guy who stole the money. The interesting thing is that we all had a good laugh about it. We recognized that his actions could have been duplicated by any one of us had we decided to revert back to our old way of life and we were grateful not to be him. There was no anger and if anything we were all grateful for the lesson.

"Don't the American people know what their government and corporations are doing?" I have been frequently asked by people all over the world. Those in the Third World ask almost reluctantly as if what they are asking is a stupid question. What seems so obvious to them, they believe, must be obvious to all of the world's people, and they further conclude that the American people simply don't care. It isn't fair that the American people are viewed harshly by our global neighbors due to the covert actions of the government and American corporations. My experience is that people in America, Iraq, Afghanistan, Yemen, Columbia, and Cuba are all good people, but their governments I hold suspect. And it seems that at the heart of every issue with government, whether the leader is communist, fascist, or a democratically elected president lays the ability to control and direct the country's wealth and finances. If you wish to understand the "exact nature" of the problem, follow the money.

Are we not letting the fox in with the chickens when we have corporations, unrestrained from any moral obligation and whose only goal is a return on their investment, allowed to lobby and invest billions in campaigns with a publicly funded government? Is it acceptable that these corporations happen to be involved in military or covert actions funded by taxpayer dollars, in which thousands die and countries are left in ruin? Do you expect your elected officials, who are on the payroll and have their campaigns funded by the same corporations, to suddenly drop the bag of money on the way to the bank and decide to do the right thing?

We need government, but we need government to protect the interests of the majority of people, not campaign financiers. The people in AA had the wisdom to recognize that money could sway our ability to do the right thing. People often say we need to get the government out of business. I wonder if our interests wouldn't be better served if we got business out of government. The truth we all know deep down inside is that as long as corporations are allowed to financially influence our publicly funded system, government officials will be tempted to do the wrong thing. The people are paying for their government, and it is the people the government is obligated to protect.

We are not killing for peace. We are not even killing for profit. We are killing for greed. Perhaps there exists rare occasions where war has been unavoidable. These issues can be discussed with a myriad of opinions. Ask yourself and ask your God: Is war insane? Has war created the desired results? Why would we continue to pursue war if it doesn't produce the outcome we desire? Is war an undertaking necessary for our well-being? Or is war a selfish act employed by egocentric and selfish individuals' intent on personally benefiting politically and economically? As the wealth of the world seems to consistently end up in the pockets of the same people as a result of war, why do we, the public, continually support it? Does the government, who controls both the military and the finances necessary to mobilize our armies, really work on behalf of the people? And if they are not working in the best interests of the people when are they going to tell us the truth? Do we not have the power to decide? Can we become conscientious objectors and make sure those elected to work in our best interests are, in fact, doing just that?

We, in the west, have attempted to colonize much of the world. Our actions have been motivated by selfishness and greed. Millions of people have died, and our environment has been negatively impacted. We have trusted our leadership to do the right thing—and they have—for themselves and their financial backers. They have stolen your wealth and the wealth of much of the world, and in the process our democracies, our voices, have been lost.

What values do you want to see in our culture? Do you want honesty and integrity? Do you want to see your children in good schools with a roof over their heads and food in their bellies? In many of what should be the richest countries in the world children have no schools, doctors, or shoes as American corporations, supported by the American government, siphon the wealth of those countries into their offshore bank accounts. And we wonder why they hate us as the same corporations have worked in conjunction with the same government to abscond with the wealth of the American people. Can you see the truth here? Can you see the game is rigged?

Is the world we leave behind for our children more important than Wall Street bonuses and corporate dividends? I have often said that nothing will change in this world as long as we place money at the top of our list of values. Yes, the economy is important, but there are a lot of countries in the world that seem to have solid economies, while providing their citizens with excellent education, good health care, and a reasonably peaceful existence. I struggle with the logic that we can spend billions on defense and nothing on schools and infrastructure. It seems senseless of course, until you follow the money.

Examine other cultures. Read. Share the truth, your truth, with others and with your elected representatives. Establish a Peace Anonymous group and invite your elected representatives to your meetings. See which ones are sincerely interested in changing the system. Look for alternatives. Seek the truth. Seek peace. Seek change. Seek a God of your own understanding. Develop a personal relationship with that little voice inside and listen to it. I am quite confident that the vast majority of us have the desire to do the right thing.

Step Five is about values, about motives. What values motivated us to think the thoughts and take the actions that brought us to where we are today? If we are what we do, perhaps it is time we do something else. Perhaps it's time we changed?

In summary, when it comes to personal issues, we searched for a trusted confident who we could share our deepest and darkest concerns with in an attempt to lighten our load. With regard to our nations and the politics of the day, we seek the transparency in government which makes democracies actually democratic. And when we discover the lies and deceit, often disguised as secret or issues of nation security, which have resulted in wars and other acts of violence, who do we tell? Perhaps there have been enough secrets. Perhaps we should tell everybody.

Step Five suggests we discuss, not where others and other countries are at fault, but where did *we* go wrong. It asks us to admit to God, to ourselves, and to another human being the exact nature of *our* wrongs. So talk to each other. Share your experience, strength, and hope with each other. Practice non-violence, but practice it together. Be informed. Be honest. Be at peace.

STEP SIX

Were entirely ready to have God remove these defects of character.

Focus on the Principle of Acceptance.

> And acceptance is the answer to all my problems today. When I am disturbed, it is because I find some person, place, thing or situation—some fact of my life—unacceptable to me, and I can find no serenity until I accept that person, place, thing or situation as being exactly the way it is supposed to be at this moment.
>
> —Dr. Paul O. (*Big Book of AA*)

There is nothing complicated about the Twelve Steps. While it is easy to know and understand these steps, it is another thing entirely to live them, and they must be lived. It seems that Step Four was the most work, and Step Five created the greatest fear, but Step Six, I believe, is the most difficult because it requires a consistency that is extremely difficult to maintain on a daily basis. Are you ready, on a daily basis to be entirely ready to have God remove your intolerance, greed, resentments, fear, and desire to control others?

There is very little written about Step Six in the Big Book of AA, but the step essentially asks us if we are prepared to do whatever is necessary to change. When we realized doing things our way wasn't working we decided, in Step Three, to "turn our will and out life over to the care of God, *as we understood Him.*" We then, in an effort to understand exactly what our problem was, honestly documented our character defects in Step Four. And in Step Five, we sought to relieve ourselves of the emotional burden these defects had caused us by letting go of our secrets and facing our defects.

Step Six asks us to become entirely ready to let go of those defects. We are still responsible for our actions and know we cannot change the past. However, by accepting ownership of our defects, we became empowered to do with them as we wished. We had a choice. We discovered we could be honest, kind, and loving, and, with God's help, we could change and let go of our old ways.

In an effort to change, we are learning to accept our imperfections and our character defects. And we are learning to accept God, *as we understand Him,* into our lives in a way that perhaps no religion could teach us. On an ever increasing scale, many of us are searching deep inside ourselves in search of a greater spiritual understanding. The voice of our souls may be buried under addiction, abuse, or other worldly clamors, which seem to take precedence in our lives. However, more and more of us are learning to be still and learning to listen to the voice. We are turning to meditation, yoga, and other spiritual endeavors as we discover a connection with the Great What Is. Some may continue to scoff, but for those who know and understand, there is no going back. The poster reads:

No God, No Peace
Know God, Know Peace

I have been a member of AA for nineteen years now, and many people who have tried to sober up during this time have died from the disease of alcoholism. Why am I still alive? Why, when I repeatedly asked the Power that made the sun come up to remove from me the obsession to drink was it removed from me? Why was I blessed with this gift? If I would have asked one less time would it have made a difference? Was I, perhaps for the first time in my life, sincere in my desire to change? Was I more sincere than the others who died? Or was I simply, for the first time in my life "entirely ready" to let God in? Why is it that the desire to drink simply vanished the moment that gate "clanked" shut? Some of you may think I am being overly dramatic here, but those in AA understand exactly what I mean. There is a difference between a passing thought and the "knowing" I experienced that morning. A miracle happened, and my life hasn't been the same since.

Because of my experience when I left the detox that morning I no longer question the power of prayer or the power of God, *as I understood Him.* I wasn't born again, and I honestly haven't attended a religious church service since I was a kid, even when mom twisted my arm. I was baptized a

Christian as a baby, but organized religion just isn't my cup of tea. You may love your religion, and I respect your right to believe whatever you believe. However, the simple truth for me today is that I love my relationship with my God and don't feel the need for a middle man on Sunday morning to mess with it. Perhaps my attitude will change, but I seem to find what I need of a spiritual nature in the meeting rooms of AA.

God removed my desire to drink, but only after I had accepted responsibility for it and then became entirely ready to let go of it. I was sick and tired of being sick and tired. My way didn't work. Since then I have gotten on my knees most mornings and asked for God to help keep me sober and to offer me some direction with the insanity of my life. To be very honest, I struggle with Step Six and being "entirely ready" to let go of my character defects. I am a very imperfect human being, and it seems relief comes only after I have struggled with a given situation and find myself in sufficient pain. It seems that only when I accept that I am powerless over the situation and become entirely ready to ask God for help, does a solution surface. But by then, I have usually had to learn a lesson or two regarding my behavior, and for that effort, I am rewarded with a large helping of humble pie.

Often my problem only requires acceptance. I have a choice between stirring myself up over a given situation, usually because of something somebody else did or was supposed to do, or accepting the fact that not everybody in the world sees situations as I do. You see if I want to be happy, joyous, and free I must accept the fact that I can't change you. If I believe you are the problem, my peace and serenity go out of the window the moment I try to manipulate, coerce, or force you to do things my way. If it didn't work with my ex-wife, employers, or the courts, why would it work in the realm of international politics and finance?

In the same manner on the international stage, we do not have to get involved in every problem that transpires; however, if our motives are free of greed and selfishness, we may wish to help when requested to do so. We can accept that others are entitled to believe what they wish. We may feel our ways are superior, but we do not have to force our beliefs on others. We come to believe in attraction rather than promotion. As individuals, by being entirely ready to have God remove *our* shortcomings, we focus on being the best individuals we can be. By adopting those qualities of living on the international scene, we can create a positive example for others to follow, rather than utilizing coercion or force as we have in the past.

Being the biggest kid on the playground doesn't necessarily make you the smartest. Imposing your will on others does not foster good relationships with the other kids. If your ego suggests a need to be viewed as the biggest and the toughest instead of the kindest and most benevolent, then perhaps there also exists an inferiority issue which should be addressed. To many in the rest of the world, we in the west simply appear to be bullies. Many of you may think being the top dog is macho or cool. But is it working? Perhaps it is time to let the rest of the kids enjoy their milk money.

Change is difficult, and letting go of our old ways isn't easy. Fear seems to be my greatest obstacle to change, and I ask my God on a frequent basis for the courage to do the right thing. For nineteen years the "right thing" has not involved drinking or jail. And it has not involved physical violence either. What I believe today is that anyone can pick up a drink or a gun. But accepting your faults and becoming entirely ready, each and every day, to become honest, loving, peaceful individuals takes great courage. And the only source for that kind of courage, the kind of courage I needed in order to change my life, had to come from a Power greater than myself. It had to come from God.

I tried everything imaginable to fill the hole inside me. In a society which embraces high-tech solutions and chatters about increased productivity, who would have ever thought that a Group Of Drunks (GOD) could provide us with the design for living that works when nothing else does. But I am living proof, and the emptiness that was once the hallmark of my existence has been filled with the love I found courtesy of the fellowship of AA and a God that I am sure the Pope would never approve of. I hope he gets over it.

Striving to live without the need to control other people and situations, while developing an attitude of trust and reliance upon God, has been a difficult, albeit amazing, experience in my life. Oh, there are moments when my old need to run the show returns, usually when I am bathing in self-will. Those moments are not as frequent, or as lengthy, before I am reminded by one of my friends in AA that my way doesn't work. Today, I try to be of service to God and to my fellow man and do what is in front of me to be done. And my good friend, Norma, has repeatedly told me that writing this book was something God gave me to do. I am never 100percent sure about these things, but I do know my heart is full these days, and if writing this can help others see the futility of killing each other, I will consider the endeavor well worthwhile. You see I believe that the people of the world, the entire world, want peace. And perhaps you just need a recipe, and the GOD I have come to know and love just happens to have given us drunks one that works.

In order to change, the thing we as practicing alcoholics needed more than anything else was humility. Our egos had to go. Our pride had to be crushed. We had to see, and accept, the truth of who we were and the reality of our actions. Is there a lesson here for all of us? Is there a lesson here for our political leadership? When most of us, regardless of religion, color, or political beliefs simply want to raise, educate, and feed our kids and live in peace, why do we have this constant insanity being forced on us? And for whose benefit? Can you accept that many of the actions taken by groups we consider to be unfriendly around the world are actions provoked by the behavior of our corporations and our governments? Are we willing to accept that a small, powerful group, motivated by greed and selfishness has brought us to this place? Are you willing to follow the money? Are you sick and tired of being sick and tired? In a world where we have the technology and the capability to create such positive change for all mankind, why does this insanity persist? And what are we going to do about it?

Can you also see we have the power to change and that we have a choice? Are you entirely ready to have God remove those character defects from within you which block the path and prevent us from living in peace? Let go of your fear. Are you entirely ready to change? Are you entirely ready to trust that voice deep down inside you? Are you entirely ready to trust God?

STEP SEVEN

Humbly asked Him to remove our shortcomings.

Focus on the Principle of Humility.

Prayer doesn't change the situation, it changes me.

—Anonymous

Humility doesn't mean you think less of yourself. It means you think of yourself less.

—Ken Blanchard

All human actions are motivated at their deepest level by two emotions—fear or love. In truth there are only two emotions—only two words in the language of the soul . . . Fear wraps our bodies in clothing, love allows us to stand naked. Fear clings to and clutches all that we have, love gives all that we have away. Fear holds close, love holds dear. Fear grasps, love lets go. Fear rankles, love soothes. Fear attacks, love amends.

—Neale Donald Walsch (*Conversations with God*)

As an alcoholic, I lived to extremes. Life seemed to be all or nothing. There were moments when I thought of myself as the ultimate authority in every situation facing mankind, and the next moment, perhaps only a few seconds later, my mind would have me convinced I was the lowest life form on the planet. Rarely, if ever, did I feel "okay" being who I was, and I thank God for the more balanced perspective which came my way as I developed a shred of humility due to my involvement with AA.

When I first heard the word humility mentioned at an AA meeting, my heart sank. I confused humility with "humiliation", and I really didn't want more of that. I had felt humiliated and inferior for much of my life, and to counter these feelings, I developed an ego which publicly projected a cocky, know-it-all persona. I lived at these two extremes on the emotional spectrum, and neither reflected who I really was.

By the time I arrived at Step Seven, I hadn't had a drink for a couple of years. Being sober and the process of discovering my character defects were providing me with an opportunity to see past my ego. I realized I had lived my entire life without the foggiest idea of who I really was. By this time, I was very aware that the answers to life's problems didn't come out of a bottle, but I was still relatively confused about a number of things. Apparently I was a long way off my path.

Steps Four and Five held me accountable for my thoughts and actions of the past. Step Six encouraged me to accept my imperfections and develop a desire to rid myself of the shortcomings, which prevented me from moving forward. And in Step Seven, I would ask God, the same God who had removed my obsession to drink, to remove from me those character defects which stood in the way of my usefulness in this world.

Humility, I would come to understand, develops in our coming to grasp the truth about ourselves. To understand and accept that I was powerless over alcohol as I had concluded in Step One had been absolutely necessary if I was going to survive. I had needed God's help in removing the obsession to drink, and Step Seven informs me that I could obtain some relief from my other character defects as well, if I were entirely ready to seek God's help. I could also quite clearly see that my character defects would drive me back to the bottle if I allowed them to persist. If I wanted the peace and serenity exhibited by the old-timers around the tables in AA, I was also obligated to accept my powerlessness over my dishonesty, selfishness, fear, resentments, intolerance, judgmentalism, and my dependence on others to feed my ego with unearned praise and exultation, all of which had been buried under years of drinking. And perhaps, more importantly, humility would teach me that the only person I could really exercise any amount of control over was me, and that if I simply kept my side of the street clean, many of the problems I had with others, would simply disappear.

During my stay in detox, I had prayed earnestly to the Power which had consistently urged the sun up over the eastern horizon every morning for eons, and my desire to drink had been taken away. Having been part of that experience why would I think for a minute that God, *as I understood Him*, would not relieve me of the other character defects which had caused problems in my life, if I were sincerely prepared to surrender them? Therefore, with as much grace and sincerity as I have been able to muster over the course of the last nineteen years, I try to ask God on a daily basis to remove from me those things which stand in the way of my usefulness to Him and my fellow man. I am grateful that He was gracious enough to remove the desire to drink almost immediately. However, He has been very reluctant to exorcise the remainder of my character defects and render me a saint. I occasionally catch myself in a lie. There are times when my ego, which seems to patiently lay in the weeds and wait, will make a grand entrance. There are times when I overreact and get angry for almost meaningless reasons. Sometimes I behave a lot like the asshole I used to be, but for the most part my life is nothing like it was. "It gets better," I was told. And it has. One day at a time life has gradually become a thing of beauty, and all I have to do is look back at the guy I was twenty years ago to appreciate, regardless of how difficult my life can be, the man I am today. And I owe all that to God, the fellowship of AA, and the Twelve Steps.

Our goal here is peace. And the basic premise of this entire exercise is simple: If you want a peaceful nation, you must be peaceful people. Can you not see that as long as corporations are allowed to exercise such a great influence over government the best interests of the people, which include any hope of peace, will never transpire? If our corporations and our governments do not feel obligated to conduct their business according to some morally acceptable values it is up to us, in our democracies, to direct our leaders toward change. However, it is easy to understand why our politicians will be reluctant to change when such a mutually beneficial financial arrangement exists between political and corporate leaders.

Due to our signing of certain trade agreements, and the process of globalization, we have lost thousands of jobs to Third World countries where some of our most highly regarded corporations utilize sweatshops. Is this acceptable? Which corporations hire death squads to intimidate or kill workers? Do they seek to overthrow democratically elected governments? Which of these corporations contribute to the campaigns of our elected officials? Who hires lobbyists with a goal of changing legislation which will have an adverse effect on people? Which of these organizations also seek to obtain government contracts? Can we hold these companies and our governments accountable?

The truth is I don't know. All I really know is that this system doesn't seem to be working very well for the average person who once believed in democracy. I don't know where the path leads for us as a society any more than I knew where the steps would take me as an individual when I made a decision to adopt them into my life nineteen years ago. I only knew I couldn't continue as I had. Something had to change, and it was me. I could no longer blame anyone else.

When there is no morally acceptable manner of conduct in government or business how do we police these scenarios? When the standards have fallen by the wayside, and anything goes, where does this all end? Without any guiding principles in our culture how does the honest businessman compete with those willing to break and/or bend the law? It is easy to recognize that we cannot force anyone to be honest or to act with integrity. But it almost seems as if a commitment to lawlessness, and a lack of sound moral values, places you on the list of upwardly mobile junior executives, and being honest, an attribute of past generations, may result in you becoming unemployed.

The Twelve Steps to Peace began with a basic concept; if enough of us 20percent, 40percent, 60percent, I don't know where the number is, adopted the principles of honesty, love, and tolerance, our world would change. If we actually placed peace ahead of greed and selfishness what would our world look like? We are what we do. By adopting these principles, our collective conscience would gradually change, and our actions, our faith, and our beliefs would be enough to bring our world to a more peaceful place. Or we can continue as we have, selling political favors as democracy goes in the toilet and killing in the name of peace, while stealing the resources of those we label as enemies in the process.

If our corporations can't make a profit without killing people, will they then go bankrupt? If our banks cannot stay in business without bailouts or stealing from their investors, will they fail? If our governments need to invade countries to control the oil industry or to be involved in the drug business, then we the people may feel the need to reconsider the role *our* governments play in our lives. Because, after all the dust settles, the government, in a democracy, works for the people. The people are not a cash cow designed to fund the endless desires of those already to wealthy to remember what it was like to live on Main Street. And it is especially troubling when the taxpayer's funds are used to finance wars and bailout Wall Street banks while we lose our homes and close our schools.

Perhaps our corporate leaders and those on Wall Street need to learn about humility.

The Step Seven Prayer from the Big Book of AA is something I try to say every morning and it reads:

> My Creator, I am now willing that you should have all of me, good and bad. I pray that You now remove from me every single defect of character which stands in the way of my usefulness to You and my fellows. Grant me strength, as I go out from here, to do Your bidding.

As you can understand if my anger, selfishness, dishonesty, and my need to control are removed, my actions will have a much better chance of having a positive impact on people whose paths I may cross today. If I can let go of my way and embrace the values offered by a loving God and the fellowship of my friends in AA, the result, while not guaranteed, has a much better chance of being peaceful.

God, *as I understand Him,* has become a great friend. He is my commander-in-chief. While there is still fear in my life, I find much of that fear is rooted in man-made propaganda and is used to control and manipulate me, which is something both my God and I abhor. By accepting my character defects as simply being a part of who I am, and then inviting God, on a daily basis, to remove those defects He chooses, I am allowed to live my life in the best manner I know how.

I am not perfect, and I may not always know what the right thing to do is. But I do know, and so does each and every one of you who has a conscience, what the wrong thing to do is. We all know taking the kickbacks, lying to our constituents, selling our vote, accepting the campaign contribution with strings attached, changing legislation which protects investors, and interfering in the affairs of a sovereign state without the endorsement of the population in that country are the wrong things to do. Perhaps, with your chest stuck out, you look into the lens of the camera and retort, "I am not a crook." And perhaps you didn't break the law, but was it the right thing to do? Were your actions something to be proud of? Or did your gut knot up just a little at the thought of it? You be the judge: Or better still, ask God.

Ask God what the right thing to do is? Instead of asking what's in it for me, ask that small voice deep inside you what's in the best interests of the most people. What good can I do in the world today? Perhaps we can adopt the right thoughts which motivate the right actions. What I do know is that, as an individual, left to my own devices, I was powerless. It was only due to a loving God that my friends in AA and I were able to find a solution to our common problem. We had to rely on God to direct our thinking and show us the right thing to do. Self-reliance had failed us. We needed a new direction, and people continue to arrive at the door of AA seeking the new way of life offered by the Twelve Steps, for no other reason than these steps work where nothing else could.

STEP EIGHT

**Made a list of all persons we had harmed, and
became willing to make amends to them all.**

Focus on the Principle of Willingness.

From the perspective of Love and Spirit, forgiveness is the
willingness to let go of the hurtful past. It is the decision to no
longer suffer, to heal your heart and soul. It is the choice to no
longer find value in hatred or anger. And it is letting go of the
desire to hurt others or ourselves because of something that is
already in the past. It is the willingness to open our eyes to the
light in other people rather than to judge or condemn them.
—Gerald G. Jampolsky (*Forgiveness*)

While Steps Five through Seven help us resolve issues which stem from
our character defects as noted in Step Four, Steps Eight and Nine focus
on rebuilding the relationships that have been damaged as a result of our
behavior.

How can we rebuild relationships with those who have been harmed
by our actions if we are not honest and willing to accept responsibility
for those actions? It is indeed a humbling process. Writing a list was easy.
Developing the willingness to make amends, however, requires a much
more committed approach.

Who I had harmed had been clearly revealed to me in Step Four, but
I also knew who I had harmed at a deeper level; I knew it in my gut.
I knew which relationships had been damaged as a result of my selfish,
self-centered behavior. I knew who I had lied to and who I had cheated.
I knew which employers had not received their money's worth. I knew

whose trust had been violated in my personal relationships. I knew who I did not wish to encounter as I walked down the street.

My parents had done everything they could to help me, and I had let them down. I had borrowed money and not repaid it, and I had caused them no end of worries as they had watched my life spin out of control. My children, who I had abandoned in an effort to selfishly separate myself from the pain of the custody situation, had to go on my list. There were some friends, employers, and some business associates who had to go on my list. The simple fact is I had acted irresponsibly and whether my actions had been intentional, or simply the fallout of alcoholic negligence, was not the issue. I could not rationalize my behavior, blame someone else, or find a way to suggest they deserved what they got. The truth was my actions had harmed others, and I had to acknowledge my behavior, and amends, financial or otherwise, had to be made.

In discussions with people in AA, an interesting perspective arose regarding the relationship we all have with ourselves. Did I put my own name on that list? My past behavior most certainly had a negative impact on my life. Some suggested it was a selfish act to place our own name on that list. Others, however, felt an important aspect of healing was our ability to understand and acknowledge the damage we had done to ourselves. I believe it is truly fortunate I had not been able to treat another human being in the same manner I had treated myself and, when viewed in the perspective, I did deserve to be on that list. What I know today is that what I needed was a sincere willingness to forgive myself. After all, wasn't this entire exercise about my happiness, peace, and serenity? Wasn't this about my becoming a better human being? Had I not wanted to feel better about myself why would I have ever bothered to get sober? In fact, and this took some time, but didn't I deserve to be treated much better than I had treated myself? And today I subscribe to the old adage that you can't love anyone until you can love yourself. My drinking life had been a long, slow downward spiral, and, I would learn, the healing process would be much the same way, only in the other direction. There were no quick fixes.

Another point of view on this issue is today I believe that when I harm you, I harm myself. Something deep inside me is damaged when I act in a manner harmful to another human being. How can a negative action directed toward another ever create a positive result in me? How can I swindle you and go home and teach my children about honesty and integrity? And it is for this reason that the steps of AA focus on changing my behavior, not yours. It is much easier to stay sober, and therefore, healthy and happy, when my actions promote positive, rather than negative, relations with my fellow man.

Initially the idea of approaching those who had been negatively impacted by my behavior seemed to somehow acknowledge that, while I may have been wrong, my amend would make the other person "right". Once again I began to rationalize and my desire to blame rose to the surface. My old thought process, which I could slip back into in the wink of an eye, suggested I didn't have to make amends, especially to those who had also harmed me. Occasionally, I even tried to convince myself they actually owed me amends. For example, if my boss hadn't been such an ass, I wouldn't have missed so much work, or if my ex-wife hadn't been so difficult, you get the picture. Again the guys in AA pointed me in the right direction. "You don't have any control over other people," my sponsor explained, "Whatever your boss or your ex-wife did is not what we are talking about here. This is about what 'you' did. The goal here is to clean up your side of the street and accept responsibility for your actions, regardless of what others may have done to you." I didn't like it. Just the thought of standing in front of some of the people on my list was humbling and made me feel vulnerable.

But by this juncture, I had come to realize that my discomfort came largely from the deflation of my ego. I understood the merit of the step, and I also understood that I was doing these steps because it was in my best interest to do them. I wasn't doing these steps for the benefit of an old boss or my ex-wife. This entire process was about changing my life for the better, and in order to change, my ego had to go. It was that simple. I was letting go of my old life, which was no longer serving my needs, and my new life would begin from a place where those close to me would be aware that I was at least attempting to do the right thing. My willingness to change and become a better friend, father, son, employee, and in fact, a better member of society would be exemplified by my willingness to make amends to those I had harmed in my past.

The idea of facing those I had mistreated, regardless of what they had done to me, and accept responsibility for my actions wasn't appealing. But I paused and looked back at the work I had accomplished so far and felt good about my progress. For years I had felt hopeless, but, as a result of these steps, I now had some hope. The fear I had felt every time I had approached a new step had somehow been transformed into a faith and a belief in the "wholeness" of my new life. Originally I had not wanted to do any of the things suggested by the people in AA and was motivated to move forward only because I knew going back to my old ways simply wasn't the answer. I wasn't really willing to make amends to anyone, but I certainly wasn't willing to give up on what appeared to working in my life. So I wrote my list and worked at developing the willingness to make the necessary amends.

What I have learned as a result of my doing these steps, and from listening to others suffering from addictions, is that many of our problems stemmed from the fact that we had to have our way. Our selfishness dictated that we had to be in control. What we perceived as being requests consistently appeared to others, as demands. My ego-driven desire to control others had created many of the problems I now felt compelled to make amends for.

When we finally hit the end of our rope, regardless of how hard we try to get the world to behave, we discover that self-reliance has failed us. It is then, and only then, that we discover the only real and ultimate authority we can rely on is the Power of the universe, which I choose to call God. And in Step Eight, we ask ourselves if we can let go of our childish need to run the show and develop the willingness to do the right thing for those we share the world with and, ultimately, ourselves.

It seemed the more research I did in writing this book, a similar, consistent pattern, and one I was all too familiar with, began to appear. How many of today's problems on the international political stage are rooted in actions of the past where one country tried to control the actions of another? We wish to look at our respective countries and corporations and ask how often our actions had a negative impact on those of other nations. How often, with little concern for the wants and needs of others, have our governments and corporations selfishly coerced and manipulated the governments of other sovereign nations? And how often, when coercion wasn't enough, had we then brought out the weapons! Haven't we in the west tried to control the wealth of the world as if it were simply ours for the taking? How would we feel if the shoe was on the other foot? Do we not owe millions of people around the world some kind of an amend? If our goal is to live in peace should we not lead in that direction? Therefore, doesn't developing the willingness to make amends illustrate our willingness to change and to live in peace?

But then again what good is it to have the most sophisticated weapons systems in the world if we let them rust away? There are those who insist the relationships forged between defense contractors and politicians have to be maintained; there was simply too much money at stake. We need war.

Our economy needs war. And isn't the economy much more important than the lives of those we have labeled as being Communists, terrorists, and anti-American? Isn't the money more important than peace? Doesn't our entire system hinge on having an enemy?

Rarely did we pick a fight with someone who could fight back. That would be too risky. Instead we focused on the small and the weak, preferably those with resources we could exploit. And in the course of the last seventy-five years, there have been dozens of countries, who were incapable of hurting the west in any way, who have felt the wrath of our armies. The proud and the brave out on the world's playgrounds, gathering up the milk money of the scared and innocent and returning home heroes.

So now what? Where do we go from here? Am I a patriot for seeking the truth and asking these questions? Or is this an act of treason? Am I inciting anarchy? Or am I encouraging you to bravely step forward and reclaim your power as a participant in the democracy your forefathers believed in?

As individuals, through social networking, we can tell the people of the world we want peace. We can honestly state we did not know the truth or the magnitude of the government's actions. While ignorance is no excuse, we are now willing to see the errors of our past. We are now willing to make amends and embrace peace. We can ask our politicians and the CEO's if they wish to be held accountable and if they are willing to make amends? Are they willing to prepare a list of those people in the world, from Afghanistan to Zambia, of the damage done, of those we have killed, coerced, and manipulated to satisfy our greed and insatiable need to control?

And you, the citizens, will you find the willingness to stop listening to your elected officials, and instead watch what they do? Are you willing to search the internet for a more balanced perspective of the truth? Are you willing to follow the money? Are you willing to ask for a constitutional amendment banning lobbyists and corporate campaign contributions? Are you willing to make the actions of the CIA much more transparent? Are you willing to grasp the truth that the vast majority of the world wants peace? Can you understand why many around the world view America as the terrorist threat and that there is, at the very least, a substantial amount of evidence to support their case? Are you willing to see the government has little interest in peace and that we do create enemies so there is someone to buy our bombs? Are you willing as a culture to embrace the concepts of love, honesty, tolerance, and peace so that our world can thrive rather than struggle under the burden of war and corporate corruption?

Confused! Is it because the lies and deceit, the propaganda, is so overwhelming you have no idea what to believe about anything anymore. Like a drunk on a bender trying to cover his tracks regarding his recent whereabouts, have we become lost in our own story? The insanity of our world can be overwhelming.

How do we extricate ourselves from this terrible mess we have placed ourselves in? The beauty of the manner of living offered by the Twelve Steps lies in the simplicity. To live honestly and with integrity is simple. The chaos is created in the web of lies and deceit spun to rationalize and justify the insane behavior. The lies surrounding Iraq's nuclear weapons and weapons of mass destruction are excellent examples of these lies. And a similar story is being played out as the war drums beat regarding Iran. Can you imagine what would have transpired had the leadership of the last seventy-five years been honest and acted with integrity? Do we continue to lie and deceive to cover our past deeds, or is it time to change? And can you see that the only way this will ever change is through the will of the people and their willingness to have their democracy back?

Norway, Sweden, Denmark, and Germany all have high standards of living without the need to go to war. Why is that? Are we addicted to war? Are we addicted to greed? Can we continue as we have. or are you willing to let go? Is war working? Are you willing to shut off the television and ask that little voice deep inside you if killing anyone is ever really going to help the world be a better place for your grandchildren? If killing is your answer, are you willing to live with the consequences?

This step does not discriminate. It asks us to make a list of <u>all</u> the persons we had harmed and become willing to make amends to them all! When we look at the wreckage of our past, it will take a major act of courage to find the willingness for us to set things straight with the people of the world. But our lies and deceit have painted us into a corner. We are not trusted even by those we call friends and many pay us homage solely through the threat of economic losses. When our politicians lie about the obvious they, like the boy who cried wolf, lose any integrity they may have ever had. And more people die.

One of my favorite analogies is when I consider the entire world being one human body with each of the seven billion people on this planet representing a single cell. The body consumes food, minerals, and water in order to survive and maintain its health. But what would happen if one group of cells insisted they deserve a vast majority of the daily nourishment? When each cell depends on a working relationship with the cell next to it in order to survive, does it make any sense to see the cell next door damaged? Can we not see that, despite our differences, all these cells are necessary in order to be healthy and content? Can we not see that promoting good health for the heart is as important as having healthy kidneys? Do the cells of the body not aid each other and work together when disease strikes? Can we see that the cooperative relationship between these cells is vital if the body is to survive?

Perhaps, this analogy may be misunderstood. Perhaps, some would say we are one body, but this group over here is a cancer because it does not think and function as I do. It is different and must be removed for the body to prosper. And we label these cells as being bad and call them Muslim, or black, or communist, and we do our utmost to steal their nourishment because they are not like us and, therefore, do not deserve to be nourished as the rest of us. The cells begin to fight each other and, as a result, part of the body begins to die, while one part becomes stronger. As the strength of one part increases, it takes more and more of the body's nourishment justifying its actions as being "right" and "good" as the rest of our body becomes hungry, sick, and begins to fail.

Is there really a cancer, or could it be just a story we have been told by the one group of cells which believes it is superior to the others? Can we not see that it is our thinking that must change and realize that the body will function at a much higher level if the cells work together and nourish each other?

The logic used to justify war is not much different than the logic used by alcoholics to justify spending the rent money at the local bar. For those of you who remember the television series "Cheers" you will also remember postal worker Cliff Claven, who not only carried the mail, but was the world's foremost authority on practically everything. Cliff, in a discussion with Norm, rationalizes the benefits of drinking by explaining his "Buffalo Theory":

> "Well, you see, Norm, it's like this. A herd of buffalo can only move as fast as the slowest buffalo. And when the herd is hunted, it's the slowest and weakest ones at the back that are killed first. This natural selection is good for the herd as a whole, because the general speed and health of the whole group keeps improving by the regular killing of the weakest members.
>
> In much the same way, the human brain can only operate as fast as the slowest brain cells. Now, as we know, excessive intake of

alcohol kills brain cells. But naturally, it attacks the slowest and weakest brain cells first. In this way, regular consumption of beer eliminates the weaker brain cells, making the brain a faster and more efficient machine.

And that, Norm, is why you always feel smarter after a few beers."

Cliff's explanation is hilarious, but isn't that the logic at work in our world? Why are we more than willing to believe our leaders as they attempt to justify doing the same thing we have proven a thousand times over does not work! Why? Can we not become willing to set aside the greedy and selfish motives we are being sold and try a different tack? If our thought process allows us to justify the killing of a few here and a few there, where does this end? This body, this planet, is our home. It is all we have. We are all so amazingly similar, and yet isn't the fact that we have differences a magnificent thing? Acknowledge our similarities and embrace our differences. How boring would this world be if we were all the same? Why can't we learn from each other and be grateful for the differences and the lessons those differences provide?

As I have written these pages, I have travelled. Uruguay, Brazil, Columbia, Mexico, Costa Rica, California, Georgia, Cuba, Cayman Islands, and Canada have played host this past year as I have spread this ink around the page. The travel has been spectacular, and the people I have met, amazing. But much of the writing, especially the moral inventory of Step Four, has been a depressing process. It is not easy to look at who we have become as a society in much the same fashion as it was not easy to see what I had become as an alcoholic. In fact, it took me a long time to write Step Four because I could not sit with the emotions for more than a couple of days at a time. It was simply too painful, and as Step Four turned into months, my depression grew.

But the beauty of the steps has unfolded. I finished Four and spent ten days with the love of my life, my granddaughter, in Cuba. We escaped the tourist spots opting for the beauty and peacefulness of Cienfuegoes. We had a great time, and my mood lightened. I returned to my writing, and as I began to work on the remaining steps, my depression began to lift. And I was once again reminded that these steps work. I called my mother one night, and the little voice inside me suggested I come home. I didn't know why it was time to head home, but I am well past questioning these things, and a few days later I was on a plane.

Once again I am surrounded by family. My mother, son, daughter, and granddaughter are here. Also here is my AA family, those amazing individuals, who helped me alleviate the anger and the loneliness I once carried and saved my sorry ass when I couldn't see the truth of who I was. And I suddenly realize why that little voice suggested I come home. My life, my writing, has come full circle. It began by going out into the world to learn what I needed to learn: my truth about the world and the truth about me. I have written the dark side of what I have learned in Step Four, and now I will finish this book here, surrounded by my friends and family, because I have just been shown how this thing ends. It ends with love.

I have a choice. Am I willing to make amends and repair the relationships I damaged due to my reckless, selfish, insane behavior? You see, I have never, ever really known what was good for me. But God and my friends at AA did. Love is the ultimate outcome of these steps, and John Lennon was right about that—it is all we really need.

STEP NINE

**Made direct amends to such people wherever possible,
except when to do so would injure them or others.**

Focus on the Principle of Forgiveness.

We are there to sweep off our side of the street, realizing that
nothing worth while can be accomplished until we do so, never
trying to tell him what he should do. His faults are not discussed.
We stick to our own.

—Big Book of AA

I am now convinced that to be truly happy and peaceful, we
must learn the value of forgiving and loving ourselves and
others. Happiness and peace come about when we cease to look
for someone else or something else to blame when things go
wrong in our lives. Blaming cannot bring us the happiness we
desire, nor can revenge and punishment. Only forgiveness can
provide what we seek. We, therefore, must be the ones to stop
recycling the anger, hurt, bitterness, and pain of both inside and
outside wars.

—Gerald G. Jampolsky M. D. (*Forgiveness*)

By the time I was five years sober, I thought I had a pretty good handle on
life. I had worked through the steps and was relatively content in my sobriety.
My life had developed into a rather interesting journey. While things were far
from perfect, they were so much better than anything I had ever known. I had
also acquired a sailboat and discovered that sailing was an interesting analogy
for my new life. I could not control the wind; all I could do was adjust my

sails. The spiritual side of my life, which had been nonexistent when I was drinking, had developed, and I felt like I was making some progress.

On Sunday mornings, there was an AA meeting on the beach on the other side of the sound, and my normal mode of transport to that meeting was to sail. I was in the process of making amends to those I had placed on my Step Eight list when my son Craig, who would have been around twenty-years-old at the time, decided to come for a Sunday morning sail with me. I was grateful for his company, and it was another beautiful Caribbean morning as Craig and I pulled away from the dock.

Craig has always been quiet and a thinker. He is one of those guys who, when he does say something, tends to be either very profound or totally off-the-wall hilarious. His smile melts people's hearts, and I have yet to meet anyone who doesn't like him. There hasn't been a second in my life when I haven't been proud to be his father, but I know it would be asking too much to expect him to feel the same way.

I don't know what opened Craig up that morning, but, for the first time in his life he talked about what it was like for him growing up. The details he shared with me were a snapshot of what it was like for him as a twelve-year-old growing up. He told me of a particular night when he was in his bedroom trying to sleep as his mother sat upstairs sipping on a cocktail watching television. Around midnight his step-father came home drunk, and a loud, angry, alcohol-induced argument ensued between them. Craig told me that scenario happened frequently, and then he looked at me and said, "Mom was drunk, Joe was drunk, and I had no idea where you even were."

My eyes filled with tears and my heart hurt, and I will never forget the look on his face. This isn't about judging his mother or step-father. This is, however, about looking at the world through the eyes of my son, someone I love dearly, and seeing my part in his anguish. It is about looking at what is truly important. What tore my heart was Craig's feeling of being abandoned. I wasn't there when he needed me. I had turned my back on my children and had crawled into a bottle. What kind of example had I set?

By this time, I had worked through most of these steps and believed I was doing a good job of accepting responsibility for the wrongs I had committed. I was able to intellectually address the events of the past, but that morning I was forced to feel the impact of my selfish behavior from the perspective of those I had harmed. Up until that point, my recovery had been focused on what I thought I had done, but Craig had given me a great gift. He had given me his perspective, his truth, and as painful as it was, I listened. What I began to see was that the consequences of my behavior and my absence had much greater impact than I had cared to admit. Today I am grateful for Craig's courage and willingness to tell me his story. I am also grateful for the changes in my life which provided me with the willingness to listen and embrace both his pain and mine.

My son and daughter were alive, and I knew that there were children all over the world who had suffered greater loss than they had, but the fact still remained that there was never a need for them to be hurt in this manner. Craig's pain, in part, was due to my selfish behavior, and I had to somehow make amends for that behavior. These were the people I professed to love, and yet I had failed so miserably in being the father I had really wanted to be. Thank God history does not have to repeat itself.

Making amends begins with me recognizing that I cannot change the past. But I can accept responsibility for my actions and commit to those I have harmed, and to myself, a sincere desire to change for the better. The future can be different, and I hope since that beautiful day on the water, I have provided my son with a much better example than the one I had provided him with for the years of his youth. This doesn't make me a saint, and I know he will smile when he reads this because we don't have what most would consider a typical father-son relationship. It is much better than that.

My daughter Sherry wrestled with life for a long time and has emerged from the rocky past as one of the hardest working people I have ever known. She is an excellent mother, and she and my granddaughter are inseparable. She has never once criticized me for disappearing or for my lost decade, but I know it had an impact on her. She has valiantly worked through a mountain of life's problems and has raised my granddaughter while going to university, graduating with excellent grades and a degree in International Studies. Sherry also has the great ability to live her life while consistently being able to take into account the feelings of others. I trust her thought process and often turn to her for advice. And then there was the night when I was engaged in a minor disagreement with Sherry, and Craig settled the issue for us when he stated, simply and accurately, "Forget it, Dad. She's smarter than both of us." It took me less than a second to realize he was right, and I shut my pie-hole.

I have learned so much about making amends and the process of forgiveness from my children. Tears well up as I write this because I most certainly don't know what I did to deserve their forgiveness and their love. I am the luckiest man alive to have them in my life, and all I really had to do to repair the damage done was to stop doing what I was doing, acknowledge my mistakes, and begin to at least try and be the father I had never been. And years later, it is an amazing thing to look back and see the changes in so many lives as a result of my simply doing the right thing for myself. The changes in my life and the willingness to make amends and forgive others have had such a positive impact on the lives of many, but especially my own. I am reminded that Step Nine may appear as if I am somehow apologizing and humbling myself for the benefit of others, but nothing could be further from the truth. It is a necessary step in the process of my healing and becoming the best person I can be.

The Big Book of AA tells the following story of a businessman who was trying to live his life according to these steps, but was struggling with Step Nine:

> While drinking, he accepted a sum of money from a bitterly hated business rival, giving him no receipt for it. He subsequently denied having received the money and used the incident as a basis for discrediting the man. He thus used his own wrong-doing as a means of destroying the reputation of another. In fact, his rival was ruined.
>
> He felt that he had done a wrong he could not possibly make right. If he opened that old affair, he was afraid it would destroy the reputation of his partner, disgrace his family and take away his means of livelihood. What right had he to involve those dependent upon him? How could he possibly make a public statement exonerating his rival?
>
> After consulting with his wife and his partner he came to the conclusion that it was better to take those risks than to stand before his Creator guilty of such ruinous slander. He saw that he had to place the outcome in God's hands or he would soon start drinking again, and all would be lost anyhow. He attended church for the first time in many years. After the sermon, he quietly got up and made an explanation. His action met widespread approval, and today he is one of the most trusted citizens of his town.

I read that story many years ago, and it has fueled a fantasy I have carried from my earliest thoughts regarding *Peace Anonymous.* This dream of mine had the president of the United States speaking to the General Assembly at the United Nations. The speech was being broadcast all over the world on television and the internet. In my fantasy, I saw the president standing at the podium and telling the truth about America's past actions around the world. He admitted to America's involvement in overthrowing legitimate governments, economic manipulation which had impoverished millions, and to the senseless deaths of millions more. And then he apologized for the actions of the government and promised to do everything in his power to help the people who had been hurt as a result of those actions. In the days to come, one by one the leaders of the rest of the world followed suit and stepped forward, accepting responsibility for the actions their governments had taken as a result of their addictions to greed, power, and control. The wave continued as captains of industry and banking institutions began to publicly accept responsibility for wrongs they had committed as the concept of honesty and transparency became the order of the day in countries all around the world.

Okay, enough already! If there is one thing I have learned it's that if you wish to snap yourself out of a positive, albeit, delusional fantasy regarding politicians who tell the truth, all you have to do is turn on CNN and let reality sink back in.

So maybe the fantasy is a bit over the top. Would we settle for addressing the world on a State of the Union and having the president tell the American people and the world, rather than blaming everybody else, that we have been responsible for at least some of the bloodshed in this world? Would acknowledging past actions, apologizing, and committing to a process which encourages the United Nations to take a much more active role in ending war be an acceptable start? Could our leaders be honest enough to tell us why so many of the covert actions of the CIA just coincidentally happened to be extremely profitable for American corporations, while being extremely oppressive to local populations in so many countries around the world? Could we begin to insure that people of the Third World maintained some control over their own resources, and that the people of their respective countries, not just the hand-picked leadership which kowtows to American corporate interests, share in the wealth of their nations? Could we at least be told the truth about our real motives for war and, subsequently, shrink the budget by downsizing the propaganda division? Could the president step forward and say, "Look,

Iran has been angry with us ever since we overthrew their democratically elected government in 1953 so we could steal their oil. It's understandable they don't trust us and we want to know what we can do to make the situation right."

But the truth, which would add such a different perspective to the story, is rarely, if ever, mentioned. How much money is spent in any given year protecting mankind from mankind when honesty from our leadership, rather than the spin the public gets, would resolve, or possibly prevent many of the problems from ever developing? What would happen if our leadership let go of the selfish, hidden agenda when heading into war? Would we ever have invaded Iraq if they had no oil? Would Israel build fences if they really wanted peace with the Palestinians? What would happen if we simply acknowledged our transgressions and put our weapons down? Are our egos so large we can never be wrong? Rarely do we ever hear a politician or a corporate leader accept responsibility for making a mistake or apologize to anyone? Can't we strip away this veneer of never being wrong? Can we accept our humanness, our imperfection? Are we able to find the courage to make amends and seek forgiveness?

In the chapter of the Big Book of AA dealing with Step Nine lies what is known as "The Promises":

> If we are painstaking about this phase of our development, we will be amazed before we are half way through. We are going to know a new freedom and a new happiness. We will not regret the past nor wish to shut the door on it. We will comprehend the word serenity and we will know peace. No matter how far down the scale we have gone, we will see how our experience can benefit others. That feeling of uselessness and self-pity will disappear. We will lose interest in selfish things and gain interest in our fellows. Self-seeking will slip away. Our whole attitude and outlook upon life will change. Fear of people and of economic insecurity will leave us. We will intuitively know how to handle situations which used to baffle us. We will suddenly realize that God is doing for us what we could not do for ourselves.

> Are these extravagant promises? We think not. They are being fulfilled among us—sometimes quickly, sometimes slowly. They will always materialize if we work for them.

By the time we reach Step Nine and *The Promises,* most of us have been in recovery and sober for a reasonable period of time. Alcohol, therefore, is no longer a factor in our lives, and this step is not concerned with drinking. It is, however, concerned with changing how we think, rebuilding the relationships which we have damaged due to our selfish behavior, and the development of sound principles such as honesty, integrity, and love for our fellow man.

By committing to this manner of living, we discover that the steps do change our lives and that *The Promises* are, in fact, promises and "will always materialize if we work for them." Living my life according to the steps has changed how I interact in the world, and *The Promises* have come true in my life and in the lives of millions of others. Today, I do "comprehend the word serenity and I do know peace."

It was only when I was ready to change, when I'd had enough, when I realized that I was the "thing" standing in the way of my own happiness, that God heard me. "God is concerned with us humans when we want Him enough," Bill Wilson has so rightly taught us. Do you really want peace? Are willing go to any length to get it? Are you willing to embrace those whom you have harmed in the past in an honest and sincere desire to have a different world in the future? Are you willing to listen to that little voice, the Collective Conscience, the Great Creator, the Universe, God—whatever you wish to call your Higher Power, and do the right thing? Can you see the futility of your self-will? Can you see how our selfishness, dishonesty, and greed have brought us to this point? Can you see that the harder we try as individuals, or as nations, to control the world, it is going to lead us right back to this point? Can you see there is only one way to get off this merry-go-round?

Go ahead, STEP off.

STEP TEN

Continued to take personal inventory and when we were wrong promptly admitted it.

Focus on the Principle of Maintenance.

Late one night, bombs fell on the village of Kama Ado, a tiny, isolated hamlet of mud houses. I interviewed people who were hauled from the wreckage. I wrote a story about it. I fell asleep.

By morning, my story wasn't the same. Instead of leading with the news of the crushed village, the top story had Pentagon officials denying reports of the bombing. The first voice in the article was no longer that of an Afghan victim. Instead, it was a Pentagon official who said, "This is a false story."

Defense Secretary Donald Rumsfeld said the same: "If we cannot know for certain how many people were killed in lower Manhattan, where we have full access to the site, thousands of reporters, investigators, rescue workers combing the wreckage, and no enemy propaganda to confuse the situation, one ought to be sensitive to how difficult it is to know with certainty, in real time, what may have happened in any given situation in Afghanistan, where we lack access and we're dealing with world class liars."

I read it once. I read it twice. Were we to believe the village had spontaneously collapsed while U.S. warplanes circled overhead?

Every man in this village is a liar.
—Megan K. Stack (*Every Man in This Village is a Liar*)

This step is as obvious as things can possibly get; when we screw up we admit it. We scrutinize our own behavior and accept responsibility for our actions. We don't lie or blame others. We all make mistakes and recognize that mistakes are simply part of being human. Step Ten provides me with an opportunity to correct my many mistakes as I go about living my life. In fact Step Ten allows us to go out into the world and take risks with the knowledge that, if I am honest, sincere, and willing to accept responsibility for those times when I do step on the toes of others, I will be forgiven.

Despite my desire to live my life on spiritual terms for the past couple of decades, I am still capable of doing great wrong. My experience tells me that much of the trouble in my life came as a result of my attempts to further complicate those situations where I had made mistakes by lying or blaming others. What I have learned is this: If I am acting honestly and with integrity the times when I hurt others will be greatly diminished. And for those occasions when my actions still have a negative impact on others the situation will be much more tenable if I accept responsibility for my part in the problem. If the other parties involved have also acted badly and do not wish to accept responsibility for their part that is entirely up to them. I have no control over their behavior. But experience has taught me that when I approach others with an honest and open attitude very often they will respond in kind.

There may be times when we are not at fault and did no wrong but recognize the pain of others in a given situation. For example, a good friend and fellow member of AA, let's call him Paul, was knocked off his motorcycle by a teenage girl who had just received her driver's license when she rolled through a stop sign. Paul was seriously injured, but during his hospital stay, his thoughts turned to the well-being of the girl who had hit him. He realized she must be carrying tremendous pain and guilt as a result of the accident, a burden she would no doubt carry for the rest of her life. Paul had to accept that the outcome of the accident could not be undone and was able to contact the girl who came to the hospital where Paul forgave her.

Today, Paul is a paraplegic. His life has not been easy, and he continues to deal with significant physical pain, despite the many years since the accident. But he is also incredibly grateful for the moment when he was able to forgive the girl and release her from the pain of the incident. While his body may be confined to a wheelchair, his soul isn't confined in the least. I really believe Paul made peace with the situation and realized there was nothing to be gained by seeing the girl live her entire life scarred by a single moment in time. At first glance, it appears Paul gave the girl a great gift, which he did. But he also did much to free himself of any resentments or feelings of ill will many of us would have carried for years, and possibly forever. In his wisdom, Paul understood it was also in his best interests if he could free himself of the anger, self-pity, and bitterness. He achieved this by forgiving the girl. As a result, his forgiveness has allowed him to maintain his sobriety and his peace of mind at a much higher level.

For much of my life, I simply didn't care about anyone or anything, and my actions were motivated by selfish, alcoholic thinking. When I sobered up and began to look at my thought process, I can tell you it was a long time before I knew what the right thing to do was in a number of circumstances. I didn't know where I wanted to work, what work I really wanted to do, who to date, or if I should date anyone at all. It was confusing, but it seemed, given a set of circumstances, and a bit of thought, I could usually determine what the wrong thing to do was. It felt like I was learning to live life going backwards, but given enough time and enough lessons, and enough help, I was able to turn things around to where life began to make sense. This shift was largely due to listening to others, working through the steps, and learning to trust my God.

By the time we get to Step Ten, we are witnessing a change in our attitude. Our selfishness and self-centeredness is being replaced by a sincere desire to be of service to God and to our fellow man. We want to do the right thing for others because we have learned that in doing so, we are ultimately doing the right thing for ourselves.

It isn't difficult to know when I have stepped out of line. My gut is often the first indicator and when that fails, people are usually kind enough to inform me I am behaving like an ass, if I am willing to listen. And when I do monitor my thought process and catch myself slipping into negativity what usually surfaces as the root cause is fear about something from my past or something in my future. In AA, we are taught to live and solve our problems by living "one day at a time." I, like my friend Paul, can't change anything in the past. I cannot "un-build" a raft. Not even God can change yesterday. But I can learn to forgive others and, in the process, I can learn to forgive myself.

In the preceding steps, we have dealt with our past and have worked at repairing damaged relationships with those we have harmed. In our efforts to insure a bright future, we must live well in the now. In Step Ten our goal is to resolve any issues as soon as possible before they can develop into long-standing resentments, which will lead to future problems of greater consequence. We wish to nip things in the bud and honestly deal with problems as they arise.

If you look at the large picture what would our world look like if every American would have accepted that slavery was detrimental to our society in the moment instead of waiting 125 years to abolish it? But the lessons didn't stop there. It has been over hundred years since the Civil War, and there still exists a significant amount of tension between the white and Afro-American community. Does the problem not exist in how we think?

During the nineteenth century in Canada, the government established Indian residential schools, primarily operated by religious organizations, and made it mandatory for Aboriginal children to attend. The stories of physical and sexual abuse these children were subjected to in an effort to "civilize" them are unparalleled. Today, the First Nations people in Canada still suffer from the effects of this abuse which is reflected in drug and alcohol abuse and a significant lack of self-esteem.

Can you see the common thread here? Can you see that our need to dominate and control others not only damages those we desire to control, but also consistently causes problems for ourselves and our entire society? One does not have to travel to Guatemala, Vietnam, or Iraq to see the impact of our thought process. We only have to look in our respective backyards to see the damage our thought process has caused. We are what we do.

Perhaps you believe our problems in the Middle East are all the fault of the citizens in those countries. Please explain how Iran could possibly be held responsible for the CIA's operation, which overthrew Iran's democratically elected government in 1953. Perhaps Britain and the USA should publically admit they were wrong and make amends. Perhaps that would go a long way to resolving the problems we face today.

Perhaps, the people of Chile should apologize for electing the wrong president in their democratic elections of 1973. Perhaps, Nixon and Kissinger had a much better idea of what was in the best interests of the people in Chile, who went to the polls exercising their democratic right. And because of their folly the citizens of Chile deserved a dictator like Pinochet, who subsequently murdered thousands. Or, perhaps the world would we be better served if the American government were to accept responsibility for their actions and apologize to the people of Chile.

And what of Honduras, Nicaragua, Panamá, Ecuador, Angola, Afganistán, The Congo, etc., etc., etc.? Are we leading the world, or are we taking it hostage? Do we wish to establish friendly, positive relationships with our global neighbors, or do we think we have done our part by controlling their economies and providing them with a few thousand sweat-shop jobs? Can you not see where our economic and military attempts at controlling the world have led us?

The land of opportunity still exists, and the governments and corporations have provided an excellent example of exactly what it takes to be successful. If you are willing to lie, cheat, and steal perhaps you can be monetarily successful. If you are willing to kill or sell drugs you will no doubt be able to get the upper hand on your competition. If you are willing to set aside your moral compass and do anything imaginable to acquire wealth, then I am sure you will succeed, and I wish you happiness beyond your wildest dreams. But what happens to your soul and the collective conscience of our society? You cannot build a wall and live on the other side of it.

A few days ago, an American army staff-sergeant walked into a couple of Afghan homes and killed sixteen people, many of whom were women and children. The event was immediately condemned by leaders from all over the world, as well it should be. But what happens when it is the politicians who make the mistake by going to war in the first place? Where are the admissions of wrong-doing then? It should also be noted that while many around the world may deplore the actions America takes on the international stage, they are reluctant to speak out due to the economic repercussions of speaking out. They live in fear, and I ask how can you possibly be free if you are afraid?

It is clear that we have no control over what another individual does, but, if I remember correctly, we, as citizens, do have some control over the actions of our government. We do, after all, live in a democracy, and when our government is involved in supporting the selfish endeavors of a few individuals who place personal gain ahead of the best interests of the people, we are obligated to courageously take a stand.

Are we willing to admit we have been wrong? Do we have that kind of courage and that kind of humility? Can we find that kind of love for our planet and for those who inhabit it? Admitting we are wrong and trying to do the right thing, as opposed to the most profitable thing, may be a sign of our willingness to grow and change.

Must our lives be wrapped in war and fear? Is that working? Do we have the courage to love? Ghandi said, "A coward is incapable of exhibiting love; it is the prerogative of the brave." Perhaps it is time we changed and ventured down the path or patience, tolerance, and love? Are you that brave?

Admitting we are wrong doesn't make us weak, it makes us human. Can we admit where we have been wrong regarding our environment and our treatment of others? Can we see the selfishness in our approach to dominating the people and the resources of the world? Can we see that we possess so much of the technology to solve over-population, world hunger, and environmental issues, and the only thing we lack is the will and the courage to do the right thing.

Perhaps our greatest wrong is the pervasive need of a few very wealthy individuals who have somehow concluded that their wealth entitles them the right to control the functions of government in their best interests, as opposed to the best interests of the people. They somehow believe the "Golden Rule" which suggests those with the gold, rule. I would suggest that our nations are populated by people who only a few generations ago left their homes in Europe and crossed the Atlantic seeking to escape that same kind of thinking. Perhaps it is time for our elected officials to set aside personal gain and develop the courage to admit they are wrong in catering to the needs of corporate leaders, as opposed to the people. Perhaps those in Washington and on Wall Street need to understand that government's major priority is to place the interests of the people all over the world, ahead of the financial interests of a few. And perhaps what the people of the world need to understand is that this will not happen unless they are willing to seek those changes.

Perhaps it is time for every man and woman to find the courage to admit where we have been wrong. We have a choice. We can continue in the same manner as we have, or we can change. What is the right thing to do? You have a choice. Search your heart and soul. Deep down inside you know the answer.

Step Eleven

Sought through prayer and meditation to improve our conscious contact with God as we understood Him, praying only for knowledge of His will for us and for the Power to carry that out.

Focus on the Principle of Gratitude.

Military cemeteries around the world are packed with brain-washed, dead soldiers who were convinced God was on their side.
—George Carlin

The Bike Ride

At first I saw God as an observer, like my judge, keeping track of things I did wrong. This way, God would know whether I merited heaven or hell when I died. He was always out there, sort of like the President. I recognized His picture when I saw it, but I didn't really know Him at all.

But later on, when I recognized my Higher Power better, it seemed as though life was rather like a bike ride, on a tandem bike, and I noticed God was in the back helping me pedal.

I don't know when it was that He suggested we change places, but life has not been the same since . . . life with my Higher Power, that is, making life much more exciting.

When I had control, I knew the way. It was rather boring but predictable. It was always the shortest distance between the points.

But when He took the lead, He knew delightful cuts, up mountains, and through rocky places and at breakneck speeds; it was all I could do to hang on! Even though it looked like madness, He kept saying, "Pedal, pedal!"

I worried and became anxious, asking, "Where are you taking me?" He just laughed and didn't answer, and I found myself starting to trust. I soon forgot my boring life and entered into the adventure, and when I'd say, "I'm scared," He'd lean back and touch my hand.

He took me to places with gifts that I needed; gifts of healing, acceptance and joy. They gave me their gifts to take on my journey. Our journey, that is, God's and mine.

And we were off again. He said, "Give the gifts away, they're extra baggage, too much weight." So I did, to the people we met, and I found that in giving I received, and still our burden was light.

I did not trust Him at first, in control of my life. I thought He'd wreck it. But He knew bike secrets, knew how to make it bend to take sharp corners, jump to clear places filled with rocks, fly to shorten scary passages.

And I am learning to shut up and pedal in the strangest places, and I'm beginning to enjoy the view and the cool breeze on my face with my delightful constant companion, my Higher Power.

And when I'm sure I can't go on anymore, He just smiles and says, "Pedal . . ."

—Author Unknown

There is a faith and a trust that lives in AA, which may be unlike anything else in this world. You may get it when you go to church and listen to the preacher tell you about God. But I get it when I go to a meeting of AA and listen to a GOD (a Group Of Drunks) tell me about the hell they went through and the Power they found in order to escape that hell. And that faith and trust—that "Power"—is a feeling I have found at every meeting of AA I have ever attended.

The reality is that this Power could only be discovered when we surrendered. It was only when we stopped fighting and realized, that left to our own devices, we could never resolve the dilemma which had led to our demise. We needed a spiritual solution to our spiritual malady. And it was only when we finally surrendered were we able to develop the kind of willingness necessary to let God into our lives. It was only when our egos were crushed, and we realized we had nowhere else to turn and accepted we were powerless and incapable of managing our own lives, did we turn to God. And it was only in this final act of desperation that we were provided with the Power which saved our lives.

Many of us came to the doors of AA only as a last resort. And, at first glance, many of us were not pleased to hear our problem was of a spiritual nature, and the help we so desperately needed could only come from God. Many of us turned away, unable to let go of our self-centeredness and our egos. And, had I not wanted to be the world's greatest grandpa, I may have gone with them and died a solitary, alcoholic death. God, however, had other ideas, and eight months after my last drunk my angel arrived—and I wept. It had been a year of miracles.

Alcoholism, I believe, is a spiritual disease, and recovery can only be achieved on a spiritual basis. It is said that addiction is the only disease we as humans may encounter where we can be healthier and better people in recovery than we were prior to the onset of our disease. And I couldn't agree more. The changes in my life as a result of my reliance on the steps and God, *as I understand Him*, have had a very positive impact on my life. And the good news is I am not alone. There are millions who feel the same way I do.

When I began writing this book, I knew it would be difficult to express the God concept in a manner appealing to all pallets, all religions, which is exactly why it is so important for you to discover your own concept of God. Throughout these pages, I have attempted to write from a politically correct perspective, while remaining true to my experience. However, I keep feeling that I am coming across as a religious zealot when nothing could be further from the truth. This is by no means an apology for my beliefs and yet, at the same time, I have no desire to be disrespectful of anyone's faith. In Step Eleven, there will be more discussion regarding God and the simple fact of the matter is I have come to have a deep, profoundly loving, and insanely humorous relationship with this power I call God.

In fact, God, *as I understand Him,* is nothing like the God I was introduced to in church as a child. Today, I have no fear of being punished and burning in hell for eternity. The one truly beautiful thing about the Twelve Steps is that I am encouraged to develop a personal relationship with this Power. I have heard people describe AA as a cult, and I laugh because, if that were the case, they have failed miserably. I have never been told what to believe other than the obvious fact that left to my own devices, I am powerless over alcohol. I am free from any or all religious and social pressures to believe whatever I wish. What I believe today is that we are mind, body, and soul, and, as a result, God lives in all of us. The Big Book states:

> We finally saw that faith in some kind of God was a part of
> our make-up, just as much as the feeling we have for a friend.

> Sometimes we had to search fearlessly, but He was there. He was as much a fact as we were. We found the Great Reality deep down within us. In the last analysis it is only there that He may be found. It was so with us.

Our collective conscience in AA stems from each of us searching our souls regarding the decisions we make which will have an impact on us all. Our lives and our futures depend upon this inner searching and our individual relationships with our individual Gods. I am so grateful there is no major television network with a number of extremely attractive individuals being paid a fortune to tell me on a daily basis what I need to believe in order to be a good member of AA. I am so grateful to everyone in AA who simply encouraged me to find a God *of my understanding*.

You see it is my responsibility to cultivate this relationship with God. It is up to me to search my soul in order to determine which direction is best for me to travel in. I listen to others, primarily those in AA, and I know today these people have only my best interests at heart. They have no other vested interest and realize that happy, contented, peaceful individuals make up a happy, contented, and peaceful world. A world completely different and far removed from the world of their drinking days.

The people in AA seem to understand that we must learn to trust ourselves, and we do that by discovering "the Great Reality deep down within us." It seems that we have abdicated our responsibility to ourselves, our children, and each other. We are being told by others what to think and what to believe. We are told "you are either with us or against us" with the underlying message being that it is unpatriotic to have a different opinion, to think for yourself, or search the Great Reality deep within you as you search for a better way. When in reality, the knowledge of His will for me means I can learn to think for myself and trust that little voice within me.

Like an alcoholic who pulls his friends and family into the vortex of his insanity created by his need to drink we, as a society, have been pulled into this insanity created by the captains of industry as they pummel the world, our world, demanding more and more of everything. We are taught to hate and fear and wage war on other innocent people in order for the few to profit and control. Is this what you want? Is this what God wants? Is this God's plan, or was this plan drawn up by generals on a battlefield, or by corporate executives in the boardrooms of major oil companies?

I have come to know only a little about my God through hours of reading and meditating. The greatest lessons have come from a GOD

(Group Of Drunks) and the view from the backseat as I have pedaled through life over the course of the last nineteen years.

While you may subscribe to a particular religious faith, I can't decide if I like them, or dislike them all, equally. Like people, nations, and cars, religions are neither all good nor all bad. There is much to learn from all of them, and I have stolen bits and pieces from many of them in coming to believe in a God *of my understanding*. The little voice inside me is content with my beliefs today, and I realize I am not finished learning. And, because I am still breathing, I assume He is not yet finished with me, and for that, I am most grateful.

There are seven billion people on this planet. And at the root of *Peace Anonymous* lies the belief that a vast majority of the people in this world want peace. It is a simple question to ask yourself and each other; "Do you want peace?" and, of course, the answer is a resounding, "Yes!" And it does not matter whether you are in Los Angeles, London, Moscow, Jerusalem, or Kabul rarely will you meet anyone who chooses war. So why do we even have war when it seems to have developed such a bad reputation? More and more it seems people are losing interest in war. They say it makes survival difficult and unsettling. I've actually encountered people who would rather go to the beach for the weekend than spend it killing poor innocent people in Afghanistan. I know you find that hard to believe. But regardless of my daft sense of humor what I find most difficult to believe is that we have arrived at this stage, and after all we've been through, there is still hope; we haven't managed to entirely fuck this thing up yet. God, our collective conscience, Higher Power, Master of the Universe keeps giving us chances to fix this thing. We keep waking up, albeit with ever worsening hangovers, to the realization that perhaps there is a better way, and it is either fear or common sense which keeps us from going down the road to complete destruction. And I ask you how long are you willing to live in the problem rather than the solution?

Listen to that voice inside you. Look around you, and see all the people who would gladly embrace peace. Do we listen do them? Do we listen to God? Do we do the right thing, or do we continue to follow the same people who have only one agenda: More wealth and more war? Do we sacrifice our planet, our future, our children's future so a few people can accumulate more wealth?

Control by those who have the wealth and the biggest guns seems to be the order of the day. We are told the Israelis believe, there will be peace if the Palestinians and the rest of the Arab world accept life on their terms.

We are told that there will be peace, when we can stop the terrorists. We are told our society will be better off, when we build a wall to keep the Mexicans out. We are told we should be afraid of people who are black. Everybody has their own agenda, and we find in every coffee shop around the world the same discussions: Black versus white, communist versus capitalist, rich versus poor. And I shake my head because when asked as individuals, we find that we all want the same thing: Peace! Every mother in the world wants simply to be able to feed and educate her children. There is nothing complicated about this unless, of course, you believe you need to control the world's population in order to control the world's wealth.

There are a lot of people around the tables at AA meetings I would have never associated with prior to my joining AA. We are a strange, motley crew from every religion and every walk of life, who normally would never have mixed. But we have found a way to live together in love and tolerance, and what I hear is God saying, "You drunks are my example to the world. After all if you guys can learn to live in peace, anyone can."

If man's thought process has brought us to where we are today, can we rely on that same thought process to lead us to peace? If it takes a different thought process to solve the problem than it took to cause the problem, where do we turn? It is unfortunate for you, but the beautiful thing about my life as an alcoholic is that I had run out of choices: I either turned to God, or my life was over. Simple!

Don't you find it amusing that it is only when we have really screwed up and find ourselves in desperate situations, do we pray to God? When we want our team to win we pray to God. When we score that touchdown we pray to God. We never ask the president or the governor to save us when we are in trouble or to help us win the big game. But when it comes to making decisions about war, and who lives or dies, we leave that up to the politicians. When the president, the commander in chief, wants us to pick up a rifle and kill people we do it, but the people who have claimed God told them to kill someone, we send to an institution for life. Being rational people, we don't believe God would ever tell anyone to inflict pain another human being; we leave that messy ordeal up to our elected officials, who by the way, arrived in office with their campaigns funded by our corporate elite.

We believe man was created in the likeness of God, but, according to our elected representatives, some men simply deserve to live, and it is necessary for some to die. Well I am sorry to tell you that, as a result of these steps, my God has brought peace into my life; something the president wouldn't or couldn't do. And today, given a choice between listening to my God or the president, I am going to choose my God every time.

Deep down inside we all know what the right thing to do is. We have watched our armies, which are funded by the taxpayers involving themselves in wars where a handful of corporations share the spoils. The directors of these companies then lament about inefficient governments being involved in the business sector. They want government out of business and government organizations privatized. Privatization will be more efficient we are told, and we will soon be living in a world owned and controlled by a board of directors who are running our country in their own best interests. Where will democracy be then? Laws are changed now which benefit the corporate world at the expense of the people, so I ask you to imagine what it will be like if corporations are granted an even larger share of the power and control?

Rather than forcing government out of the business sector would it not be more prudent to ask the corporations to bow out of government? Rather than getting the government out of business, perhaps we should get business out of government? After all, government in a democracy is supposed to represent the people, isn't it? Maybe I am wrong here, but as I understand the situation, it seems that corporations fund candidates who run government with your, the taxpayer's, money. Don't you think it would be a better idea if the candidates were not allowed to be influenced by corporations? Don't you think it violates every conceivable notion of fairness? Don't you think it is a major conflict of interest?

We have watched corporations and government together at work. We have witnessed Iraq and Afghanistan. We know about Columbia, Guatemala, and Honduras. And we now know how the game is played. Can we continue? Is this what we want? Or do we want to live in peace with our global neighbors?

What does God want? Be still. Ask Him. Listen carefully to your heart. Does He really want us to kill each other?

We have all heard that the Mayan calendar ends in 2012. Some believe there is a massive spiritual shift taking place? Perhaps it is the end of the world. Or perhaps it is the end of the world as we know it. Perhaps we can change the direction we have been heading in for a long time now. Perhaps we can begin to place the well-being of the immigrant from Yemen who sits on the subway next to us ahead of our own. Perhaps we can stop listening to the media as they hammer us with fear-based advertising in an attempt to sell us more things we really don't need, including wars. Perhaps the people of the world will embrace a willingness to forgive each other and come to realize how much we really have in common with each other and that we in the west are no different than those in Syria, Indonesia, and Russia.

Perhaps we will see the truth, a truth that I have been very fortunate to occasionally glimpse. And I have often wondered how I ended up with the job of writing this book. *The Bike Ride* exemplifies my life since I joined AA almost nineteen years ago. I was scared at first and most certainly did not want to let go of the control in my life. There were countless attempts at letting go and countless times when I would attempt to reassert my need to control and try to get on the front seat of the bike. Learning to trust God was not a smooth transition, but my attempts at being in control usually ended in misery. I began with training wheels, and the people in AA helped steady the bike as I climbed on into the backseat; I did my best to stop giving directions to God. Since then, He has taken me all over the world. But it was only after I left Iraq and was sitting in a café in Atlanta with my dear friend, Anita, watching the crowds riot in Cairo on television, did I realize what my journey was all about. The little voice spoke, and by this time, I knew not to ignore it. Writing this book has been part of my bike ride. I have tried to walk away, but God wouldn't have it. I tried to avoid it, but would somehow always get pulled back to it. I applied for jobs that I was more than qualified for, and finally today, as I put the finishing touches on this book, did I finally get a response from a perspective employer. I am not the one steering this bike. I am not the One in control here. And the more I accept that fact, the happier I am. The more committed I am to living in peace, God's peace, the happier I am.

If we are to thrive, or possibly even survive as a species, we must learn to live together in peace. There is no other way, and the steps are designed to help us let go of our fear and resolve the flaws in our nature which have blocked the path to peace. We must stop this idea that because we are white or wealthy, we are somehow superior. That attitude has to be smashed.

There is nothing I am more grateful for today than the steps and the fellowship of AA. The people in AA gave me the chance to rebuild my relationship with my children and have given me the chance to become the world's greatest grandfather. (You are entitled to your opinion.) Without AA, I would have never had the opportunity to travel the world and experience one-tenth of what I have witnessed. Today, I have friends in every corner of the world. The promises in Step Nine have become part of my life. I do not regret the past as my story has helped others come to terms with the problems in their lives while providing me with some incredibly valuable lessons. And I am deeply grateful that I have a choice and that I no longer have to live with the insanity of alcohol.

But more than anything, AA gave me the opportunity to develop a relationship with a God that has become a great friend with a tremendous sense of humor. There are several stories which have come about as a result of this relationship with my God. There was the time I had to be at work forty miles out of town by Monday morning, and I needed to buy a vehicle. It was Saturday afternoon and didn't know what to do or where to go in search of a vehicle; I only knew I had very little time to spend looking for one. I had borrowed my son's truck and was searching for a vehicle to purchase but was bewildered as to where to begin with such a tight time frame. As I sat at a red light, I looked up and said, "You know I need a vehicle." Within seconds, before the light could change, an old Buick pulled up beside me with an orange "For Sale" sign in the window. I laughed, looked up, and said, "Okay." A half block later, I had the driver of the Buick pull over, and we made the deal on the side of the street. It has been over eight years since I bought God's car, and it continues to run like a Swiss watch.

The Bike Ride story at the beginning of this chapter is another example of how this relationship with my God has come to be. I was reluctant to tell it here because you might think the turnip truck needs to be summoned, but I asked several of my friends in AA who know the story, and they suggested I go ahead and tell it. My God has a tremendous sense of humor:

Shortly after joining AA, my mother sent me a copy of one of the first "*Chicken Soup for the Soul*" books, and in it I read *The Bike Ride.* I loved the simplicity of the story and the idea of getting on the backseat and pedaling, while relying on God to provide the direction, seemed like a very appropriate thing for a newly recovering alcoholic to do. I liked the story so much that over the course of the next two or three years I read it almost every day.

Then in 1995, my dad had a major stroke. He had been a very vibrant man, and suddenly he was functioning, both mentally and physically, at 20percent of his former self. The doctors did what they could, but the fact we were forced to accept was that he would never recover and advised us to place him in a home. For nearly two years, my father walked the halls of that home, knowing something terribly wrong had happened, but was incapable of understanding the nature of his situation. And it tore our hearts out to see him like this.

I had continued to read *The Bike Ride*, when early one morning the phone rang. The woman on the other end of the phone identified herself as a nurse at my father's nursing home. As she spoke, a vision of incredible clarity slowly passed through my mind. In slow motion, a bicycle built for two crossed through my mind, and my dad was sitting on the backseat, looking directly at me and smiling from ear to ear. I didn't hear anything the nurse said, but I knew exactly what was happening. I picked up my mother, and we met the ambulance at the hospital. My father passed away a few hours later.

At that time, my siblings were scattered all over the world, and I had a non-refundable ticket to go to the Caribbean. But I couldn't get on the plane. The little voice inside me wouldn't let me. Had I left, my mother would have been home alone to deal with my father's passing, and I am so grateful for the opportunity to have been there with her and for her.

Now you may consider this story in itself interesting and touching. But the funniest thing about all of it is that while my father sat on the backseat of that bike grinning from ear to ear, the guy on the front steering that bike was George Carlin.

Please do not misunderstand. I am not suggesting that George Carlin is God, but then who really knows anything for sure. Today, when I think of God, *as I understand Him,* I see George. I not only see the image, but I see the rigorous honesty and the humor. And whether you liked George or not, I wonder what a beautiful world it would be if our leaders would speak in terms as honestly, clearly, and as concisely as George did. You have to admit there was little ambiguous in anything he had to say. And I clearly see how we, all of us, can take life much too seriously, and George reminds me that this is supposed to be fun. We are supposed to enjoy this life, unless, of course, you are one of those who believe God wants us to somehow suffer through some kind of painful, sterile existence. And if you are, I remind you that you are entitled to suffer all you wish. I suffered enough when I was drinking, and I thank George those days are over.

And so you see we learn to laugh at life. We are supposed to enjoy this ride, this life we have been given. We are not supposed to spend it dodging bombs and being taken advantage of by others who have usurped the power of the state. God didn't bring me, or you, this far to drop us. He wants us to be happy, joyous, and free.

Ask yourself what direction have we been going in the last few decades? Is there a selfish, egotistical addiction to power, greed, and war which is at play here? And do we not support this behavior by ignoring it and/or looking the other way? Dante said, "The hottest place in Hell is reserved for those who in time of crisis remain neutral." Can we continue to live in this denial? In the course of the last few decades, have our problems improved or gotten worse? Can we continue to believe that our leaders in the west are doing what is in our best interests? Is it realistic to expect these problems to solve themselves, or do we have to expose these things to the light of day in an effort to change?

I was once told that alcoholism was the 2 × 4 that God used to get my attention. You may scoff at the idea of prayer and meditation, and I understand because there was a time had you suggested I embrace the idea of turning my life over to the care of God, I would have written you off as a lunatic. Believe what you will. But I believe today that millions of people have changed their lives by finding a Power, a God that works in their lives. And God doesn't care if they're Muslim, Buddhist, or Christian. God doesn't care what color they are or where they came from. He was simply there when those of us who needed His help wanted Him badly enough.

At the beginning of this book, I suggested that perhaps the only thing capable of changing this world was the will of the people with the help of God, *as you understand Him.* I know from experience that the only time many of us seek, and ultimately find God, is when we have exhausted every other conceivable notion. My question to you is how long do we have? Are we there yet?

Step Twelve

Having had a spiritual awakening as the result of these steps, we tried to carry this message to those seeking peace, and to practice these principles in all of our affairs.

Focus on the Principle of Service.

Never doubt that a small group of thoughtful, committed citizens can change the world. Indeed, it is the only thing that ever has.
—Margaret Mead

Arriving at Step Twelve meant I had experienced a few significant lessons and had witnessed some major changes. I clearly remember sitting in an AA meeting one night as I neared my third anniversary of sobriety when I was hit with a thought-provoking question: given the opportunity to be released from the disease of alcoholism, and the ability to safely leave the fellowship of AA and walk into a bar with the knowledge that there would never, ever, be any negative repercussions as a result of my drinking, would I want that? Would I, after three years of being sober, want to walk away from the manner of living I had been granted as a result of the steps and the fellowship of AA?

I pondered that question for only a few seconds, but the answer didn't take long to arrive. While society views alcoholism in a very negative light, which, to a degree is understandable, most of us, who are fortunate enough to have had our lives changed by the steps and the fellowship of AA, would hang on to our new manner of living with a grip even stronger than the grip with which we had used to hang onto the bottle during our drinking days. Today, I can't imagine living any other way. Why would I want to? And I know what I have experienced is a dramatic change, an awakening, as a result of these steps. I love being a recovering alcoholic. I love my life today, and there is nothing about that I would wish to change.

Perhaps the greatest reason why some alcoholics never quit drinking, why they can't see the devastation their problem is causing, is simple; it is simply too painful to look at ourselves. It is the pain of seeing the truth that keeps us drinking. As a result, many of us die before we can find the courage to do the work that gets us, and keeps us, sober. We begin to do that work when we commit to doing the steps. And, as we do the work, a change gradually takes place in our lives. We develop a personal relationship with a God *of our understanding*, and we find peace, as a result of these steps.

Alcoholics tend to be sensitive people, and I was no different. Subsequently, I suffered from feelings of inadequacy. Emotional pain of any kind was difficult, and the death of my sister became a weight I struggled with. Due to this sensitivity, I would blow the smallest emotional issue out of proportion, especially if I could somehow use it to control or manipulate others. And then along came alcohol which numbed me and protected me from feeling pain. So rather than deal with any problems of an emotional nature, I drank. In alcohol I thought I'd found a solution, but the reality was my problems didn't go away and simply piled up in my life until I could find no way to escape them. By the time I sobered up, I had numerous difficult issues waiting to be resolved.

When I look at our world today, I wonder why we have a mountain of unresolved problems when we have all the technical and intellectual capabilities to solve them. And I realize it comes down to having the will to resolve them. I couldn't, or wouldn't, deal with alcoholism until the pain of not dealing with it became too great. Dealing with our issues, whether they be financial, environmental, issues surrounding peace, or sobering up requires our making the conscious choice to actually solve those problems. Slipping into denial and pretending those issues do not exist resolves nothing. Is it time to face our pain? Is the party over, or can we continue to keep fooling ourselves?

I suspect our leaders, both political and those in the business world with close ties in government have been drunk on greed and power, while the problems have piled up. Of course, the dilemma isn't as great for them, because they are in control and have the power to insure their future is bright, largely at the expense of the rest of us. We only have to look at the recent bank bailout fiasco to realize there is a different set of rules for the privileged few. But even Rome wasn't too big to fail.

So what can we do?

Homework! And there is lots of it if you wish to do it. You can begin by forgiving our leaders of the past as there is nothing to gain by venturing into this maze full of anger and resentments over past deeds. However, I strongly suggest we learn from their mistakes by understanding exactly how we arrived in these circumstances so we do not make the same mistakes again. You can develop a clear understanding that war is typically an exercise in economics, which makes a few people extremely wealthy, at the expense of others. And you can learn about other cultures, and perhaps you will see that we are very often the aggressors, and much of the violent reaction of others is simply due to the fear they feel as a result of our behavior. Ultimately, you can learn to listen to your heart and develop a relationship with a God who wants us to live a peaceful existence and be happy, joyous, and free.

If you so desire, in an effort to carry this message of peace, you can start a Peace Anonymous group in your neighborhood (there will be more about that in the last chapter), and you will discover you are not alone. After all, the primary purpose of the members in AA is to carry the message of recovery to the alcoholic who still suffers. We find that in helping each other we ultimately help ourselves, and there is nothing more comforting than to hear the words, "I know how you feel," coming from another human being. The helplessness we all feel can and will change when you discover that together you can make the changes we all so desperately need.

Today, I look back at my old life and laugh at myself. I did everything I could to avoid coming to AA and learning these steps. What a fool I was. This has been the most incredible, amazing, ride of my life for no other reason than it is "my life"—the life I tried to destroy by drinking it away. I am alive, and even the unpleasant events of my past have provided me with an education that I am grateful for. If you are going through hell, keep going, and try to remember "This Too Shall Pass" because nothing goes in a straight line forever. Change is inevitable, but we can make choices and move in directions which, at the very least, provide us with the opportunity to have a positive outcome, as a result of those changes. We cannot change the wind, but we can adjust our sails.

The world looks much different if I view it as an alcoholic who needs to learn, rather than a CEO who demands a profit from it. Once I was able to honestly look at my life, I was able to step past my fear and deal with my alcoholism. Once I was able to let go of the thought process

I had been indoctrinated with, and step past the illusion of fear, I was able to enjoy my trips to the Middle East and elsewhere. And I have begun to identify with people from all over the world in much the same way as I have learned to identify with recovering alcoholics. Whether we suffer from alcoholism, or simply the condition of being human, we realize we are all so much alike. I am amazed at how much in common I have with all people, and how much I love and respect the people in Afghanistan, Iraq, Columbia, and Cambodia. I have come to see their goodness, and I know they have children and grandchildren they love and want to feed, clothe, and shelter as a result of that goodness. Just like me.

In carrying this message to those seeking peace, I am reminded of how AA began with one alcoholic talking to another. When Bill Wilson and Dr. Bob Smith discovered that by honestly sharing their innermost thoughts and feelings they could help each other overcome their problems. Alone they were helpless, but together they went on to form Alcoholics Anonymous which has saved the lives of millions of people around the world, one alcoholic at a time. Bill and Bob discovered they had a choice. They discovered a way to change how they thought about picking up a drink. And if they can change and make different choices, why can't you? Why can't we all?

Can we not spread the word of peace in the same manner? As an alcoholic discovers the insanity of their drinking, can we not see the insanity of war? Can we not see how our actions and the actions of our respective governments and corporations have led us to this point? Can we not see how our greed and our need to control foreign governments only create hostility and resentment in our neighbors? Can we not see that as long as corporations are allowed to purchase government support through lobbyists and campaign contributions what is in the best interests of the people all over the world will never be addressed?

In *Confession of an Economic Hit Man*, John Perkins sums it up:

> I am certain that when enough of us become aware of how we are being exploited by the economic engine that creates an insatiable appetite for the world's resources, and results in systems that foster slavery, we will no longer tolerate it. We will commit ourselves to navigating a course toward compassion, democracy and social justice for all.

Admitting to a problem is the first step toward finding a solution. Confessing a sin is the beginning of redemption. Let this book, then, be the start of our salvation. Let it inspire us to new levels of dedication and drive us to realize our dream of balanced and honorable societies.

The only thing that is capable of changing the direction in which we are heading is the will of the people. We have a choice. You can listen to the voice of God, the voice of love, or we can continue to deny the truth, be mired in fear, and avoid change. It is up to you. Each and every one of you has that choice, and you can make a difference. In fact, you're the only thing that can.

The steps are about change, and Step Twelve specifically is about service. And service is about doing the right thing for others. We are what we do. There is fear in change, but there is much more fear in not changing. The day I did my Step Five with my friend the priest, he gave me the following words which were written by Nelson Mandela. These words seem even more appropriate when you consider Mandela was instrumental in changing the government of South Africa and ending apartheid in a nation where segregation and discrimination were entrenched in their system of government. I invite you to consider Mandela's words. I invite you to contemplate change. I invite you to carry the message of a peaceful world, achieved, one person at a time:

> Our deepest fear is not that we are inadequate.
> Our deepest fear is that we are powerful beyond all measure.
> It is our Light, not our Darkness, that most frightens us.
> We ask ourselves, "Who am I to be brilliant, gorgeous, talented, fabulous?"
> Actually, who are you NOT to be?
> You are a child of God. Your playing small does not serve the world.
> There is nothing enlightened about shrinking, so that other people won't feel insecure around you.
> We were born to manifest the glory of God that is within us.
> It is not in just some of us; it is in everyone.

And as we let our own light shine, we unconsciously give other people permission to do the same.
As we are liberated from our own fear, our presence automatically liberates others.

You have a choice. Does your God want you to be happy, joyous, and free? Does your God embrace love, honesty, and tolerance? If not, you may want to find a different God. You do have a choice.

Peace Anonymous

What good can I do in the world today?

Based on the Big Principle of Love

The United-States spends $87 billion conducting a war in Iraq while the United Nations estimates that for less than half that amount we could provide clean water, adequate diets, sanitation services and basic education to every person on the planet. And we wonder why terrorists attack us?
— John Perkins (*Confessions of an Economic Hit Man*)

America may be the most confusing country on the planet. Issues such as abortion we are told are debated on the basis of morality, while those same legislators who wish to ban abortion and take away a woman's right to choose subsequently refuse to adequately fund child care, schools, or support programs for single mothers? Those who criticize human rights issues in places such as North Korea and China defend torture in Guantanamo Bay. How can our elected officials debate acts of terrorism, while they and their distinguished counterparts in previous administrations have knowingly endorsed the overthrowing of democratically elected governments and the killing of thousands of innocent people in profit motivated military actions? Sorry, I don't understand.

There are those who would have you believe our political and economic problems are the fault of members of the teacher's union, welfare recipients, migrant Mexican farm labor, Afro-American gang bangers, godless liberals, radical terrorists, and communist activists who scratch out a meager living working on huge corporate farms in Central and South America. Rarely will anyone step forward and suggest that perhaps we might be well served to observe what our actions have contributed to the problems of the world. Is it possible the source of our problems regarding a peaceful world rest, at least in part, with the greed of our corporations, banks, defense contractors, and their subsequent collusion with our government?

We have been sold an illusion regarding our moral correctness and values. We, the people, are told our governments and our military are out in the world doing good deeds and upholding the values of freedom and democracy. We are told there would be peace if the world would only submit to our virtues, our values, and our system. The system, however, is designed and operated by those who receive the greatest economic profit, and they would much rather see the finger pointed at those who are incapable of fighting back as their nations are looted. And the real perpetrators rationalize and justify their actions. They lie to the people. They lie to each other. And, I sense, as they fill their pockets, they have ultimately come to believe their own lies. It most certainly sounds like alcoholic trying to justify and rationalize the insanity of a long spree. Thank God, there is a solution.

Why is it so difficult to look at ourselves? The truth, and we all know it, is that power corrupts; Absolute power corrupts absolutely. The corporate elite, which has over the course of several decades destroyed democracies in numerous countries around the world, and has had a hand in the deaths of millions of people, wants to run your governments too! What do we do? Where do we turn?

A short time ago, I was attending an AA meeting in Mexico when a young man, who had done tours to Iraq and Afghanistan, told the group he had just been discharged from the Marines, and this was his first AA meeting. First meetings are, for all the obvious reasons, significant turning points in people's lives. It is never easy to come to the realization that we are powerless and become willing to admit our way does not work. As tears ran down his cheeks, the young man told the group how his drinking had slid out of control. As he shared his story, he told us while in boot camp he had been instructed that, "His hate would become his greatest weapon." The stranger sitting next to him, an older woman, reached over and took his hand and said, "You can let go of your hate here. Love is our greatest weapon."

What kind of world do you want? Do you want to be governed by defense contractors, pharmaceutical corporations, and financial institutions, or do you want a democracy? Do you want schools for our children or do you want huge defense budgets and a CIA, which insures there will always be enemies to buy our bombs? Do you want fear and distrust around the world or do you want positive, constructive relationships with our international neighbors? Do you want a world of war, or do you want to live in peace? You have a choice, but you better act fast because there is no guarantee this window of opportunity will be there for much longer.

Will the world continue to look to governments in the west for leadership? If so, will that leadership role be based on fear of military might and economic coercion, or will it be based on honesty, mutual respect, and a shared set of values? Will the course we plot be rooted in attraction, or promotion? We were given the ability to choose, and we can choose love, or we can choose hate. We can choose peace or we can choose war. We can choose democracy or we can choose to have a small group of wealthy individuals buy political favor and manipulate the system in their own selfish interest. It is up to you. Regardless of how powerless you may feel, you do have a choice.

We live in a world surrounded by strangers. Many of us suffer from great loneliness and yet we don't even know the people who live next door. One of the greatest by-products we discover within the fellowship of AA is our sense of community. Many of us live with an egotistical perspective that we are somehow self-made, but that lonely point-of-view falls by the wayside when we come to realize we really do belong to each other. It doesn't seem to matter whether I go to a meeting around the corner, or around the world, there is a sense of belonging, a sense of community, which seems to be consistently present in the fellowship of AA. We are our brother's keeper; we wouldn't want it any other way.

There may be those of you who wish to start Peace Anonymous groups within your communities. If you follow that course I would encourage you to make a special effort to involve our veterans who are returning home after active duty. The steps may be of significant benefit to them in coming to terms with the events of their deployment, and their stories may provide the rest of us with a valuable learning experience. In addition, our veterans need to know they have our gratitude and appreciation for their efforts, and we cannot hold them responsible for the political and economic goals of the political decision makers. They must know we wholeheartedly support the troops despite having serious concerns regarding the motives our elected representatives may have had for engaging in these wars in the first place.

For three million recovering alcoholics, almost every meeting begins with the group reading the first few paragraphs from the chapter in the *Big Book* entitled *How It Works*, followed by the steps. For those of you who wish to establish Peace Anonymous groups, *How It Works* and the steps have been adapted and included if you wish to incorporate them into your meeting process:

> Rarely have we seen a person fail who has thoroughly followed our path. Those who do not recover are people who cannot or will not completely give themselves to this simple program, usually men and women who are constitutionally incapable of being honest with themselves. They are not at fault; they seem to have been born that way. They are naturally incapable of grasping and developing a manner of living which demands rigorous honesty. Their chances are less than average. There are those, too, who suffer from grave emotional and mental disorders, but many of them do recover if they have the capacity to be honest.
>
> If you have decided you want what we have, and are willing to go to any length to get it—then you are ready to take certain steps.
>
> At some of these we balked. We thought we could find an easier, softer way. But we could not. With all earnestness at our command, we beg of you to be fearless and thorough from the very start. Some of us have tried to hold on to our old ideas and the result was nil until we let go absolutely.
>
> Remember that we deal with war—cunning, baffling, powerful! Without help it is too much for us. But there is one who has all power—that one is God. May you find Him now!
>
> Half measures availed us nothing. We stood at the turning point. We asked His protection and care with complete abandon.
>
> Here are the steps we took, which are suggested as a program of recovery:
>
> 1. We admitted we were powerless over war and violence and that our world had become unmanageable.
> 2. Came to believe that a Power greater than ourselves could restore us to sanity.

3. Made a decision to turn our will and our lives over to the care of God *as we understand Him.*

4. Made a searching and fearless moral inventory of ourselves, our communities and our nations.

5. Admitted to God, to ourselves, and to another human being the exact nature of our wrongs.

6. Were entirely ready to have God remove all these defects of character.

7. Humbly asked Him to remove our shortcomings.

8. Made a list of all persons we had had harmed, and became willing to make amends to them all.

9. Made direct amends to such people wherever possible, except when to do so would injure them or others.

10. Continued to take personal inventory and when we were wrong promptly admitted it.

11. Sought through prayer and meditation to improve our conscious contact with God as we understood Him, praying only for knowledge of His will for us and for the Power to carry that out.

12. Having had a spiritual awakening as the result of these steps, we tried to carry this message to those seeking peace, and to practice these principles in all of our affairs.

When I was drinking, I was confined to a world of insanity. Once I arrived at the doors of AA the words "Rarely have we seen a person fail who has thoroughly followed our path," terrified me. It sounded like a cult, and I felt like I was being programed. Today I love those words and believe the path referred to is the path to freedom.

There is absolutely nothing wrong with drinking alcohol. A lot of people have a great time going out on the town and having a few drinks. However, if it causes you to beat your wife, kill people in car accidents, destroy relationships, lose your job, and destroy your health you might consider asking yourself if this behavior is acceptable. Is this what you want? Or have you crossed the line?

There is nothing wrong with capitalism. It is the system that has formed the foundation for the greatest societies ever known to mankind to grow and prosper. Capitalism is a good thing, but when the competitive edge falls to those who are willing to kill, overthrow governments, and control the distribution of deadly drugs have we crossed the line?

Democracy and government by the people for the people is without question the finest system of government in the world. However, when special interests groups are allowed to purchase favoritism and persuade governments to act in a manner which is not in the best interests of the people, is that still democracy? Or has that crossed the line?

Is war for profit a good thing? Or is that crossing the line?

Is it an acceptable practice for our publicly funded government agencies to be covertly involved in disrupting foreign governments with a goal of controlling their economies and their resources? Or has that crossed the line?

Writing a book about peace is meaningless if people don't want peace. You can know and believe we have a problem, and still choose to do nothing about it. We can live in our denial, look the other way, and the best case scenario is nothing changes. The worst case scenario is that things can get worse, much worse.

We may not always know what the right thing to do is, but deep down inside us we do know what doesn't work. We all know that killing for peace makes as much sense as fucking for chastity. I couldn't drink myself sober; believe me I tried. But my way didn't work; however, the God idea did.

My good friend, Norma, made a point when she said, "We need to focus on the solution so we're not repeating the same nightmare every day." And the solution for us alcoholics was to admit our actions were selfish, insane, and detrimental to our well-being and the well-being of those we loved. And is war not every bit as selfish, insane, and detrimental to our future and the future of the planet?

Is telling the truth an act of patriotism or an act of treason? Is your country best served by the truth or by believing the lies and the deceit? Does embracing the truth make you a communist? Or a terrorist? Or a threat to society? Or a godless liberal? "Many of them do recover if they have the capacity to be honest," the Big Book tells us. And I know of three million people who have changed their lives by becoming honest and seeking the truth about who, and what, they had become. Hope can only be found in the truth. Is there hope for us? Can we change? Do we have another choice? Rarely have we seen a person fail who has thoroughly followed our path.

We are what we do. You have that choice. Nobody, not the president, not even God, can do it for you. But you will discover you are not alone, and that God, and perhaps even the president, will be there if you want to change the direction we are heading, providing your motives are right.

This manner of living is simple, but it is not easy. The gifts I have received as a result of the Twelve Steps and the fellowship of AA can never be measured. When I came through the doors of AA, I was mentally, emotionally, and spiritually bankrupt. Today, I have a life beyond my wildest dreams. I have a beautiful relationship with God today. I am at peace with myself. And I am extremely grateful to be the world's greatest grandpa.

Many people die from the disease of alcoholism, and I do not understand why I was so fortunate to be given this gift. But I am grateful. I, who had no concept of a spiritual life, know that all will be just fine in my world if I don't try to exercise control over others and live according to sound principles. Today, my job is simple. All I have to do is the next right thing and pedal, as long as I remember I get the backseat. (Do you have any idea how much fun it is to have George Carlin up front. Why wait for the Rapture?)

Today, I am not afraid of burning in hell. Nor do I believe my God would ever banish a sixteen-year-old girl to hell for aborting a baby she doesn't believe she is capable of taking care of. My God is much more forgiving than that. However, I wouldn't want to try and get His seal of approval for orchestrating the mess in Iraq, the coup in Chile, or the rip-off on Wall Street. I think my God and George Carlin are pretty much on the same page there.

The basic text of the Big Book ends on page 164, and we commonly read the last three paragraphs of that text at the end of every meeting at my home group. I can't think of any words that are more appropriate to leave you with in your search for peace:

> Our book is meant to suggestive only. We realize we know only a little. God will constantly disclose more to you and to us. Ask Him in your morning meditation what you can do each day for the man who is still sick. The answers will come, if your own house is in order. But obviously you cannot transmit something you haven't got. See to it that your relationship with Him is right, and great events will come to pass for you and countless others. This is the Great Fact for us.
>
> Abandon yourself to God as you understand God. Admit your faults to Him and to your fellows. Clear away the wreckage of your past. Give freely of what you find and join us. We shall be

with you in the Fellowship of the Spirit, and you will surely meet some of us as you trudge the road to happy Destiny.

May God bless you and keep you until then.

ACKNOWLEDGMENTS

God for everything.

Bill Wilson and Bob Smith for the greatest of gifts.

The men and women of Alcoholics Anonymous all over the world.

George Carlin for steering me in the right direction.

Norma R for consistently hearing everything.

Michelle T for guiding me out of the desert.

Anita W for sharing the boat.

Trevor W for being a great friend.

Alex L for teaching me how to make hard decisions.

Bill N for the lessons on club selection.

Ed S, Brad B, God bless you guys.

Everybody at Shamrock.

Everybody at Elmslie.

John Perkins for the courage to shine a light and to tell his truth.

Peg Booth at Booth Media.

Susan Piver for teaching me to be still.

Erin G for being amazing.

Paul L for the floggings!

Bus Crash, You guys rock!

Ann K for your insight.

Anne A, tell 'em what you're going to tell 'em. Tell 'em.

Tell 'em what you told 'em.

Mark W, I miss you my friend, and it is great being me.

Synopsis

In 2008 Barrak Obama was elected President of the United States by the largest majority in history. His campaign slogan, "Change You Can Believe In," was embraced by the American people. But the change Americans had hoped for didn't happen. Perhaps one of the reasons it didn't happen is because one man, even if he is the President, can't possibly create the kind of change the world needs. Perhaps change on that level can only materialize if the majority of the people themselves are ready to embrace that change.

Amy Goodman from Democracy Now recently stated, "The only thing that is powerful enough to change our world is the will of the people." And I concur. For generations people from politicians to rock stars have encouraged peace and, despite knowing that violence isn't the answer, these same generations have observed an escalation in violence. Telling people to stop killing each other has been as effective as telling a raging alcoholic to stop drinking. Alcoholics needed more. They needed a recipe for change and that recipe came in the form of the 12 Steps. And while some have clamored for peace the fact is the 12 Steps is the only program I am aware of which is capable of including every single human being on the planet regardless of race, wealth, or religious affiliation. All that is required is a commitment to live in peace.

For the past few months I have been asking people, "Can our society continue in the same direction we have been going in for the past several years? Is this working?" The response has been an almost unanimous, resounding, "NO!" People want change. And, not only do I believe change of this magnitude to be possible, I have seen it happen. Millions of people are now living in peace after having their desperate and chaotic lives miraculously transformed by simply choosing the manner of living described by the 12 Steps in Alcoholics Anonymous.

As I began writing *Peace Anonymous – The 12 Steps to Peace* I began to see the spiritual malady of our society. How many of us, in the depths of our souls, really want to inflict pain on other human beings? How many of us want to see children suffer and die? How many of us have become numb to the pain and suffering around us? Why do we accept the killing of thousands in war and other acts of violence? Are we spiritually bankrupt? Have we become, as Pink Floyd put it, "Comfortably Numb?"

The spiritual malady regarding peace was first revealed to me during my first trip to the Middle-East in 2005. It had been a grueling flight and I thought the knot in my stomach was a direct result of the trip. However, after 3 weeks I was still feeling a great deal of anxiety and I started to ask myself, "Why?" The answer came in one word: Fear! What I then discovered was following 9/11 and the Iraq invasion I had heard the media consistently telling me about the threat in the Middle East. I had come to believe all of the people there wanted to kill all westerners. However, as I looked at the impoverished people of Yemen I could see no threat. As we pumped the oil out of the ground in their country many of their children went without education or shoes. How could they be a threat? Our armies went to Iraq to "liberate" their people. And as we pumped the oil out of their country none of the Iraqis I talked to during my time there felt liberated. They were angry which strikes me as being a very reasonable response considering what has happened to their country and their lives.

Since 2005 I have worked and travelled extensively. What I have discovered in Yemen, Iraq, Afghanistan, Libya, Columbia, Uruguay, Thailand, Cambodia, and more is the desire for peace among the people of the world. I believe the vast majority of the people around the world, including North America and Europe, want peace. This begs the question: If a resounding majority wants peace why do we not have it? And the 12 Steps invite and encourage you to search for those answers. But please bear in mind my anxiety was fostered by the media of television. By all means watch the news but you will only obtain a balanced perspective by subscribing to news websites online and I also suggest reading a lot of books on world economics and politics. The truth will also reveal itself to you if you follow one basic rule: If a situation doesn't seem to make any sense, follow the money!

Many of us feel helpless. The dissatisfaction in our culture is widespread and has fuelled such movements such as Occupy Wall Street which has brought a great deal of attention to the issues of corporate greed and corruption in our financial sector. Changing our society is a daunting task.

But it begins with the simple understanding that the thought precedes the action. An alcoholic thinks about picking up the drink before he actually picks it up, and the 12 Steps of Alcoholics Anonymous have taught millions of people to change how they think about picking up a drink. Can we not use the same recipe in an effort to learn to change the way we think about picking up a gun? Or to fix the environment? Or to change the financial system? Or to simply do the next right thing for no other reason than it is the right thing to do?

Spiritual lifestyles are surging to the forefront in our society. More and more people are looking inside themselves for the answers to the world's problems. Yoga, meditation, and 12 Step programs have all added a spiritual dimension in the lives of individuals. However, in a democracy we must also accept the responsibility for the direction our country is heading. We must become aware of the truth in our world and engage in the political process in order to solve the problems we now face. I am grateful to live in a democracy, but democracy also means responsibility. I must be responsible in making sure my voice is heard and to advocate for change when change is required.

We are at the end of our rope. The challenges of peace, the environment and social justice threaten our very existence. Like an alcoholic hitting bottom, we are discovering we have nowhere to turn. We must accept our problem and assume responsibility for the solutions, as daunting as the task may be. We realize that if we keep doing the same thing we will keep getting the same results. It is time for change and we can build the society many dream of. But we cannot do it alone. It is only by working together towards common goals according to spiritual principles, such as honesty and mutual respect, will we even have a world for the generations to come.

You do have a choice.

CPSIA information can be obtained at www.ICGtesting.com
Printed in the USA
BVOW030259091112

305067BV00003B/1/P